READING CHINESE TRANSNATIONALISMS
Society, Literature, Film

Edited by

Maria N. Ng and Philip Holden

T0345750

香港大學出版社
HONG KONG UNIVERSITY PRESS

Hong Kong University Press
14/F Hing Wai Centre
7 Tin Wan Praya Road
Aberdeen
Hong Kong

© Hong Kong University Press 2006

Chapter 12: Chow, Rey. Sentimental Returns: On the Uses of the Everyday in the
Recent Films of Zhang Yimou and Wong Kar-wai. New Literary History 33:4 (2002),
639–653. © New Literary History, University of Virginia. Reprinted with the
permission of The Johns Hopkins University Press.

Hardback	ISBN-13: 978-962-209-796-4
	ISBN-10: 962-209-796-0
Paperback	ISBN-13: 978-962-209-797-1
	ISBN-10: 962-209-797-9

British Library Cataloguing-in-Publication Data
A catalogue record for this book is available from the British Library.

Secure On-line Ordering
http://www.hkupress.org

Printed and bound by Pre-Press Ltd., Hong Kong, China.

Hong Kong University Press is honoured that Xu Bing, whose art
explores the complex themes of language across cultures, has written
the Press's name in his Square Word Calligraphy. This
signals our commitment to cross-cultural thinking and the distinctive
nature of our English-language books published in China.

"At first glance, Square Word Calligraphy appears to be nothing more
unusual than Chinese characters, but in fact it is a new way of rendering
English words in the format of a square so they resemble Chinese
characters. Chinese viewers expect to be able to read Square Word
Calligraphy but cannot. Western viewers, however are surprised to find
they can read it. Delight erupts when meaning is unexpectedly
revealed."

— Britta Erickson, *The Art of Xu Bing*

READING CHINESE TRANSNATIONALISMS

Hong Kong University Press thanks Xu Bing for writing the Press's name in his Square Word Calligraphy for the covers of its books. For further information, see p. iv.

Contents

Contributors

Mark Betz is a Lecturer in Film Studies at King's College, University of London. His articles on European cinema and archival practice have appeared in *Camera Obscura* and *The Moving Image*, and his book *Remapping European Art Cinema* is forthcoming from the University of Minnesota Press. He has recently contributed book chapters on art/exploitation cinema marketing and on the academicization of film studies via book publishing. He is currently working on a study of art film distribution in America.

Lily Cho is an Assistant Professor in the Department of English at the University of Western Ontario in London, Ontario. Her essays on the Chinese head tax in Canada, diaspora studies, and the poetry of Fred Wah appear in *Essays on Canadian Writing*, the *Canadian Review of American Studies* (forthcoming), and *Culture, Identity, Commodity* (Hong Kong University Press, 2005). In collaboration with David Chariandy, she is presently working on a book-length manuscript on diaspora theory.

Rey Chow is Andrew W. Mellon Professor of the Humanities at Brown University where she teaches in the Departments of Comparative Literature, and Modern Culture and Media. She is the author of numerous titles, including *Woman and Chinese Modernity* (1991), *Writing Diaspora* (1993), *Primitive Passions* (1995), *Ethics after Idealism* (1998), and *The Protestant Ethnic and the Spirit of Capitalism* (2002). Her writings in English have been widely anthologized and translated into various Asian and European languages. A collection of essays, translated into Italian, was published under the title *Il sogno di Butterfly: costellazioni postcoloniali* in 2004. Her latest book, *The Age of the World Target: Self-Referentiality in War, Theory, and Comparative Work*, was published by Duke University Press in Spring, 2006.

Petra Fachinger is an Associate Professor in the German Department at Queen's University. She holds a Ph.D. in Comparative Literature from the University of British Columbia (thesis title: "Counter-Discursive Strategies in First-World Migrant Writing"). Fachinger is the author of *Rewriting Germany from the Margins: "Other" German Literature of the 1980s and 1990s* (McGill-Queen's University Press, 2002) as well as several articles on ethnic-minority writing in English and in German. Among her primary research interests are German Jewish, Turkish German, Jewish American as well as Asian American literature. She is presently working on a comparative/contrastive study of German Jewish and Jewish American literature.

Philip Holden is an Associate Professor in the Department of English Language and Literature, National University of Singapore. He is the author of books on Hugh Clifford and Somerset Maugham (*Modern Subjects, Colonial Texts* [2000] and *Orienting Masculinity, Orienting Nation* [1996]) and co-edited the recent *Imperial Desire: Dissident Sexualities and Colonial Literature* (2004) with Richard Ruppel. His essays, largely on Singapore literature and culture, life-writing and (post)colonial modernity, have appeared in journals such as *English Studies in Canada, Ariel, Communal/Plural, Biography, Journal of Commonwealth Literature* and *Victorian Literature and Culture*. He is at present working on a project on nationalism, decolonization, and autobiography.

Kristjana Gunnars is Professor Emeritus of English and Creative Writing at the University of Alberta. She is the author of several books of fiction, poetry and non-fiction, and her essays and creative works have appeared in numerous journals and anthologies in Canada, Europe, and the United States, including *Silence of the Country* and *Night Train to Nykoping*. She has received various provincial awards for her books (McNally Robinson Award, the George Bugnett Award, and the Stephan G. Stephansson Prize), and her book *Zero Hour* was nominated for the Governor General's Award. Her recent titles are a collection of stories, *Any Day But This* (Red Deer Press) and a book of essays on writing, *Stranger at the Door* (Wilfrid Laurier University Press), both published in the fall of 2004. Professor Gunnars has also edited collections of academic essays on Margaret Laurence and Mavis Gallant.

Jennifer W. Jay is Professor of History and Classics at the University of Alberta, Canada. Her main publishing activity is in Chinese historiography, as in *A Change in Dynasties: Loyalism in Thirteenth Century China* (Bellingham, WA: Center for Asian Studies, Western Washington University, 1991). Current projects include Chinese Canadian literature and the social history of eunuchs in imperial China.

Laifong Leung is Professor of Chinese Language and Literature at the Department of East Asian Studies, University of Alberta. She received her Ph.D. from the University of British Columbia. Her books include *Morning Sun: Interviews with Chinese Writers of the Lost Generation* (1994), *A Study of Liu Yong (985?–1053?) and His Lyrics* (1985), *Early Spring in February: A Study Guide to the Film* (1998). In 1987, she initiated and co-founded the Chinese Canadian Writers Association (CCWA) in Vancouver. Since the 1990s she has helped the CCWA organize several symposiums on the literature of the Chinese Diaspora. She does research on contemporary Chinese literature.

January Lim is a graduate student in the Department of English and Film Studies at the University of Alberta. Her research interests and critical practice are feminist materialist, and her work has focused on definitions of race and racial identities in African and Asian American writing and media narratives. Her Ph.D. project explores the ways in which fashion, bodies, and desires are complexly inter-imbricated in Asian American texts by Jessica Hagedorn, Mavis Hara, Lydia Minatoya, David Henry Hwang, and Chay Yew.

Maria N. Ng is an Associate Professor in the Department of English at the University of Lethbridge, Canada. She has taught at the University of British Columbia and was the Chiang Ching-kuo Foundation Assistant Professor in Comparative Literature, Religious Studies and Film/Media Studies at the University of Alberta. Ng wrote her Ph.D. dissertation on travel writing and is the author of *Three Exotic Views of Southeast Asia: The Travel Narratives of Isabella Bird, Max Dauthendey, and Ai Wu 1850–1930* (New York: East Bridge, 2002) as well as essays on Chinese Canadian culture and writing. Her research areas are transnationalism and literature, immigrant cultures, popular culture, and gender representations. She is currently working on a book on colonial Hong Kong in the 1960s and 1970s.

Edgar Wickberg is Professor Emeritus of History at the University of British Columbia. He is the author of the classic *The Chinese in Philippine Life, 1850–*

1898 (Yale 1965; republished Ateneo de Manila Press, 2000) and co-author and editor of *From China to Canada: A History of the Chinese Communities in Canada* (1982). His research interests focus on the global Chinese, their history, organizations, and ethnicity. He has also helped organize the new Chinese Canadian Historical Society of British Columbia.

Jane Parish Yang received her Ph.D. from the University of Wisconsin-Madison and at present is an Associate Professor of Chinese in the Department of Chinese and Japanese at Lawrence University, Appleton, Wisconsin. She was instrumental in restructuring the East Asian Languages and Cultures Department into the newly created East Asian Studies program. She served on the executive board of the Chinese Language Teachers Association, 1999–2001, and has presented papers at MLA, AAS and ACTFL/CLTA conferences. Yang translated Nieh Hualing's postmodern novel *Mulberry and Peach*, which won an American Book Award in 1990.

1

Introduction

Maria N. Ng and Philip Holden[1]

Transnationalism, and particularly Chinese transnationalism, is very much the concept of the moment in anthropology, literary, and cultural studies. Gayatri Spivak's 1999 declaration in *A Critique of Postcolonial Reason* that she had made a transition "from colonial discourse studies to transnational cultural studies" (x) is now paradigmatic for a generation of intellectuals. While postcolonial studies still has resolute and, in our opinion, thoroughly justified defenders, transnationalism as an area of inquiry has certain advantages for contemporary scholarship.[2] First, it dispenses with both the "colonial" and the "post" to which "postcolonial" is always, if uneasily, tied.[3] Transnational studies are neither bound to return to the question of the colonial nor tied to a progressive historical narrative of cause and effect in which elements of colonialism must be shown to persist or to have been left behind. Second, the transnational, and its associated terminology — diaspora, migrancy — have provided a way of talking about ethnicized communities without the essentializing terminology of race.[4] Third, transnationalism enables us to look not only outside but before the nation, to see continuities in the flow of people, cultures, and capital in a *longue durée* without the epistemic break of "liberation" that postcolonialism inevitably, albeit with increasing trepidation, posits.

Initially, transnational studies celebrated the emancipatory possibilities of leaving the nation behind, the emergence of "imagined communities of modernity" as "national spaces/identities of political allegiance and economic regulation are being undone" (Wilson and Dissanayake 6), or a "new global cultural economy [...] understood as a complex, overlapping, disjunctive order, which cannot any longer be understood in terms of existing center-periphery models" (Appadurai 296). In the late 1990s, however, this came increasingly to be seen as a metropolitan perspective: if the transnational might, in Europe and North America, be seen as post-national, nationalisms in the South had a long history of living with, accommodating, and even productively using, transnationalism. Given developments in the years after the attacks on the United States, on September 11, 2001, we might further question the notion that the nation-state is eroding. Many countries, especially the United States, have taken precautions guarding their borders. Since September 11, people of certain visible ethnic origins, even if they are holders of Western passports, are first and foremost indexed as possible terrorists. The Canadian writer Rohinton Mistry, experiencing repeated border harassments, told the audience at Toronto's International Festival of Authors, 2002, that he had decided not to go to America on promotional tours: "The way you look, where you were born, these things are what will determine how you will be treated at certain airports" (Freeze "Mistry Suffers"). In the spring of 2003, people of East Asian ethnicity had to defend themselves internationally against a generic suspicion as carriers of Severe Acute Respiratory Syndrome. One example was the banning of representatives from Taiwan and Hong Kong at the Far Eastern Film Festival held in Udine, Italy ("Chinese Guests"). Another effect of linking SARS with Chinese was the boycotting of Chinatowns, both in North America and in Europe ("Chinatown's Virus Fears"). Yet the spectacle of Asian American US troops assisting in the toppling of Saddam Hussein's statue in Baghdad in May 2003 indicates the ways in which the nation does not merely reject but makes use of the transnational — in Partha Chatterjee's words, transnationalism, to look beyond the nation, we might first look within.[5]

In this situation, Aihwa Ong's work on transnationalism gains increasing currency. Writing against what she sees as an "innocent concept of the essential diasporan subject" in North American transnational cultural studies, one that celebrates hybridity, "cultural" border crossing, and the production of difference" (*Flexible Citizenship* 13), Ong has argued that transnationalism cannot be studied without reference to capital and to the manner in which capital flows are embedded in the nation-state. In her discussion of the area, Ong has used the specific experience of Chinese transnationalism as powerful touchstone for a discussion of transnationalism in general. Her collection *Ungrounded Empires*, co-edited with Donald Nonini, has a broad historical sweep reaching before the formation of modern nation-states. Chinese transnationalism, Ong and Nonini note, can be seen as a "third culture," or as an alternative modernity, one of a number of "cultural forms that are organically produced in relation to other regional forces in the polycentric world of late capitalism" (15). In her later monograph *Flexible Citizenship*, Ong continues her inquiry into Chinese transnationalism, again emphasizing that transnational identities and collectivities are not automatically emancipatory (20–1) — indeed, the word "transnational" was first used in the 1970s by global companies rethinking developmental strategies (21) — nor post-national, having been actively employed in the national imaginaries of nation-states such as Singapore. Attempting to negotiate between "political-economic" approaches to transnational studies and those which "focus almost exclusively on the cultural, imaginative, and subjective aspects of modern travel and interconnections" (15), Ong calls for an "anthropology of transnationalism" (240–4) which views the transnational process as a number of "situated cultural practices" (17).

This collection responds to Ong's work and yet takes the study of Chinese transnationalism in a new direction. Like Ong, we take Chinese transnationalism as our central focus — if Chinese transnationalism is not paradigmatic, it is at least the most widely publicized and studied transnationalism. Like Ong, we also emphasize historicity and lived cultural experience; hence, our inclusion of historical work such as Edgar Wickberg's account of transnational connections between Fujian and the Philippines. However, while agreeing with Ong on the importance of culture as a primary object of analysis, we have extended the meaning of the cultural to encompass not only anthropological "cultural practices" but also cultural artifacts which intervene in conversations and debates concerning the transnational: restaurant menus, cultural campaigns, and then, with closer focus, literature and film.

Our intention here is not to accede to a mode of analysis that Ong criticizes, "an anemic approach that takes as its object culture-as-text or that reduces cultural analysis to a North-American angst-driven self-reflexivity" (*Flexible Citizenship* 242) but rather to transform the terms of the debate. If transnational cultural studies has celebrated nomadic, migrant inquiry, it has also mourned the loss of the possibility which nationalism and its associated world order promised, an international public sphere, a place of Habermasian "self-supporting higher-level intersubjectivities" where autonomous parties might meet (364). "Contemporary publics in Asia," Ong and Nonini note, "are not apolitical arenas but thoroughly infused with the cultural politics of transnational capitalism" (330). In this light, we might turn to the writings of another transnational subject, Singaporean playwright Kuo Pao Kun. In an essay published only two years before his untimely death, Kuo meditated on the absence of civil society — the institutions which might occupy the public sphere so dear to Habermas — in Singapore. Such institutions might not, Kuo noted, be found through the "rational," through "radical changes in the mode of production," but rather through the "opening up of the space for personal and community free play" (216). That space of "play as serious business" (217), Kuo noted, was the arts.

Both editors of this collection also have personal and cultural experiences of living and thinking transnationally in which "Chineseness" has been a continued presence and problematic. Though it would be impossible to pinpoint an exact time frame when transnationalism became an intellectual currency, for Ng it began with Ien Ang's "On Not Speaking Chinese" (1994), now extended into a collection of essays of the same title (2001). Warning against "the formalist, postmodernist tendency to overgeneralize the global currency of so-called nomadic, fragmented and deterritorialized subjectivity," Ang instead stresses "the importance of paying attention to the particular historical conditions and the specific trajectories through which actual social subjects become incommensurably different and similar" (4–5).[6]

As a Chinese academic and cultural critic in Canada, Ng has ample opportunities to experience and observe the conflictual meaning of looking ethnic, thinking international, and being legislatively Canadian. She has also witnessed the changes within Chinese Canadian culture since arriving as an immigrant from Hong Kong in the 1970s. Ng's initial response to being an immigrant was twofold. Like the postwar Chinese immigrants described in historian Ng Wing Chung's *The Chinese in Vancouver 1945–80*, she saw the so-called Chinese culture evident in Canada as inauthentic, consisting of run-down Chinatowns and hybrid restaurants serving chop-suey variety of dishes. In a way, Ng would have been one of the Chinese-speaking Chinese who held it against overseas Chinese people for their lack of cultural knowledge or language or both (Ang 16). And, she was aware that to be accepted and to get ahead, one needed to acculturate, and thus could sympathize with the local-born Chinese, the *tusheng*, whose knowledge of Chinese culture was very much superseded by that of Canada, and who saw themselves as "cultural brokers" who could "bring the Chinese minority ever closer to mainstream Canada" (Ng Wing Chung 52).

At the time of Ang's essay, changes have been taking place in the demographics of Chinese Canadian culture, especially in the big Canadian cities with a large immigrant population, such as Vancouver and Toronto. In a 2001 census, twenty-six percent of the residents in Vancouver claimed to speak Chinese as their mother tongue (Ward A1). In the 1980s and 1990s, the profiles of Chinese immigrants to Canada were diverse and reflected the political situations globally. Because of the reformist era under Deng Xiaoping, some mainland Chinese students were allowed to stay overseas, including

Canada. Canada also received an influx of Hong Kong Chinese who were worried about the return of the colony to China in 1997. And while China and Taiwan exchanged hard words over autonomy and repatriation of the island nation, Chinese from Taiwan were also immigrating to Canada in large numbers. The immigrants from Hong Kong and Taiwan came with capital and often kept two households, one in Canada and one back home. This well-off immigrant culture gives rise to new terms such as "monster house" and "astronauts." These Chinese Canadians are full participants in what Aihwa Ong calls "The Pacific Shuttle" in *Flexible Citizenship*.

Implicit in the rhetoric of the monster house that has been the focus of much debate about cityscape in Vancouver and other Canadian cities, writes geographer Katharyn Mitchell in "In Whose Interest? Transnational Capital and the Production of Multiculturalism in Canada," is "a perceived threat to an established way of life, a way of life predicated on the symbols, values, and distinction of a white, Anglo tradition" (231). No longer would these immigrants from the 1980s and 1990s claim, as did Kew Dock Yip, the Vancouver-born Chinese lawyer who helped repeal the *Chinese Exclusion Act*: "I am not Chinese — I am Canadian" ("Kew"). The result of this diversity in Chinese immigrants is that in Canada today we are encountering a microcosm of Chinese people as they can be found around the world and not just Chinese as short-order cook or Chinese planning to take over Vancouver real estate. In Canada are Chinese speaking different and mutually incomprehensible dialects and writing in two different scripts, and Chinese with diverse ancestral histories. Their professions, class status, and political affiliations cut across the board in Canadian society.

Under such rapid and "existence"-related changes, the subject-position of a Chinese Canadian has to be revised.[7] A Chinese Canadian who immigrated in the 1960s and 1970s might find herself developing new affiliations with the Canadian-born Chinese; like them, this particular group could not fit in comfortably with the affluent influx who exemplifies the transnational capital flow so well analyzed in Ong's *Flexible Citizenship*. Often economically independent and secure, recent immigrants from Hong Kong or Taiwan feel less urgency in adapting to the Canadian mainstream culture. They could shop in neighbourhoods that are predominantly Chinese, and their critical mass means that they could establish networks without having to reach out to the non-Chinese communities.[8] Their process of acculturation is considerably slower. This intra-ethnic diversity and potential divisiveness also means that cultural critics have to reconsider what it meant and means to be a Chinese Canadian in the twenty-first century, when changing patterns in immigration and mobility could affect identity construction and politics within a single decade instead of through half a century or even longer. Although it might be hyperbolic to claim that "the West itself is slowly becoming, to all intents and purposes, 'Asianized'" (Ang 8),[9] Vancouver and other cities like it are.

Thus we begin to think of Chinese Canadian *identities,* instead of *identity,* within transnational discourse. In another decade or two, the Chinese who immigrated to Canada in the 1990s would have developed a different relationship with Canadian culture, especially when their children begin to join the professional ranks, establish local familial ties and friendships, and form Canadian allegiances. As this collection illustrates, Chinese have been on the move and settling down since the nineteenth century and before. Their Chinese identities depend on where and when these transnational Chinese establish their homes and their businesses. Recent works such as Pál Nyíri's *New Chinese Migrants in Europe: the Case of the Chinese Community in Hungary* (1999) and Benton and Pieke's *The Chinese in Europe* (1998) show that Chinese communities the world over are different and similar. To understand twenty-first-century transnational Chineseness then, one needs both historical and spatial contextual references, bearing in mind that these references need to be updated continually. This contextualization augments Homi Bhabha's interventionist "Third Space," which rejects historical identity of culture as a "homogenizing, unifying force, authenticated by the originary Past, kept alive in the national tradition of the People" (37).

Philip Holden's own experience of Chinese transnationalism is in many ways the reverse of Ng's. Holden first went to China in 1986 as a *waiguo zhuanjia,* a foreign expert teaching English and American literature at Hunan Normal University in Changsha. Located in south central China a few miles from Mao Zedong's birthplace, Changsha, in a China emerging from the traumatic introspection of the Cultural Revolution and its aftermath, might have seemed the epitome of nationalist insularity. And yet even here there were traces of the transnational. There were ongoing connections between Yale University and one of the medical colleges it had founded early in the twentieth century as a means of spending money from reparations from the so-called Boxer Rebellion. In the *zhuanjialou,* the foreign experts building, were two young women casually referred to as the "Singapore girls": they were the daughters of Eu Chooi Yip (Yu Zhu Ya), former secretary of the Malayan Democratic Union, Singapore's first political party, and later a leading cadre in the Malayan Communist Party. Eu's daughters were connected to a network of MCP exiles in Changsha, now quietly making a living after Deng Xiaoping's growing rapprochement with ASEAN had shunted them onto sidings of history while the through train of capitalism went by.

In Canada as a graduate student, as a non-Chinese auditing Chinese language classes, Holden experienced from a different angle many of the contradictions of Canadian multiculturalism that Ng describes. Yet his own experience of transnationalism has been profoundly shaped by an academic career spent in Singapore, where Chineseness is again configured differently within a national space that makes use of the transnational. If, in Canada, state discourses of multiculturalism stress difference within sameness (how to be, variously, Chinese Canadian), Singaporean state discourses of multiracialism encourage sameness through difference: Singaporean citizens in the 1980s and 1990s increasingly addressed the state as racialized individuals, with ascribed cultural pasts and "mother tongues." Within this multiracial order, Chineseness is remolded, shorn of much of its historical radicalism and cultural complexity in Southeast Asia. A vision of Chinese culture as intrinsically amenable to capitalism has animated Singapore's development from the 1980s onwards, and this vision in turn frequently dovetails neatly with notions of a "cultural China" and Confucian capitalism. Lived Chinese ethnicity in Singapore, however, frequently contradicts the parameters within which the state might wish to contain it.

Our own personal and academic histories suggest, then, that transnational Chinese identities cannot be analyzed in discrete parts that claim them as only immigrant, ethnic, diasporic, or local-born. This volume tries to present intellectual connections between Chinese who left China in the nineteenth century and Chinese who are still on the move today; between Chinese who produce culture in China and those who produce in Hollywood. We have intentionally resisted a homogeneous approach in reading Chinese transnationalisms; thus, contributors are encouraged to take various disciplinary methodologies. *Reading Chinese Transnationalisms* also includes two other chapters in which extensive reference to other transnationalisms is made. They are reminders that it is not only Chinese who claim transnationality in the twenty-first century and, indeed, indicative of the possibilities that other transnationalisms have to interrogate Chinese transnationalism. *Reading Chinese Transnationalisms* also draws upon different disciplines — history, film study, and literature — to illustrate the necessarily multidisciplinarity of "doing" transnationalism. Beginning with the historical splintering of China into several Chinese-influenced economical/geopolitical sites, this volume follows Chinese identity-forming and -articulation across oceans and time, and looks towards the coming decades.

The essays in this volume make connections between and across each other. We have included three essays that address relationships between mainland Chinese and international Chinese cultures (Chow, Jay, and Leung).

There are also essays analyzing Chinese identities constructed within Southeast Asian history and society (Wickberg, Holden, and Lim). Essays by Gunnars and Fachinger juxtapose Chinese writing with literature from other East Asian cultures (Korea, Japan) as well as North American culture. Both Yang and Cho focus on Chinese in North America; Yang examines it as a literary critic, whereas Cho provides the social and historical context. And lastly, Betz discusses ethnic articulation within the context of European cultural production. Broadly speaking, these essays themselves represent a transnational body of criticism, and they illustrate a variety of critical approaches that illuminate the question of Chinese transnationalism from a variety of perspectives. The essays examine film, literature, and history from explicitly — and at times implicitly — transnational perspectives. Overall, these essays propose that to approach a subject — history, film, and/or writing — transnationally through a variety of critical filters is perhaps the most fruitful way in ethnicized cultural criticism.

The volume is structured into three sections. The first section centers on issues of nation-ethnic identity construction. Edgar Wickberg looks at the history of Chinese migrant movements between southern Fujian counties and the Philippines in "Hokkien-Philippines Familial Transnationalism, 1949–1975." Although a body of scholarship already exists that investigates southern Chinese migration, these studies "focus either on the period before the Cold War, or the period after China opened up to freer movement of persons and investments" (Wickberg 19). To redress this oversight, Wickberg chooses the period 1949–78 as his temporal framework, seeing that this period is "when the Philippines had no formal relations with the People's Republic of China" (19). This essay reminds the reader that study of overseas Chinese cultures requires attention to particular historical context, as witness Wickberg's claim that "the Chinese of the Philippines enjoyed a pre-eminent position in the economy of their country of residence — quite unlike the situation of the Western Hemisphere Chinese" (19). Thus, in his essay, Wickberg shows "how a Chinese transnational migration system of intense bipolar interaction became [...] multipolar" and suggests that "[e]thnicity should be studied at several levels: national, regional, and local; and across time: as historically changing, rather than as a given or fixed entity" (31).

In "On Eating Chinese: Diasporic Agency and the Chinese Canadian Restaurant Menu," the second essay in the section focussing on history and society, Lily Cho wants to "turn to the possibility of considering [...] a seemingly anachronistic Chineseness [...] as a site of diasporic resistance and agency" (37). To Cho, an important part of Chinese Canadian history has been overshadowed by critical attention that has concentrated chiefly on

Chinese culture in urban centers such as Vancouver. Thus, "On Eating Chinese" is an important reminder of the long history of Chinese immigrant culture in small towns in Canada. Engaging the writings of critics such as Bhabha and Ong, Cho suggests that instead of relying on a spatial dynamics that privileges the metropole, diasporic studies should attend to the temporal and "look at the challenges which Chinese diasporic communities in Canada pose [...] against the dominant European Enlightenment march of progress" (43).

Equally grounded in history is Philip Holden's "Putting the Nation Back into the Transnational: Chinese Self-Fashioning and Discipline in Singapore," the last essay in the first section of *Reading Chinese Transnationalisms*. Using Lee Kuan Yew's historical announcement of Singapore's independence from the Malaysian Federation in 1965 as his starting point, Holden sees Lee's emotional breakdown to "have a powerful heuristic function in examining the embedding of transnational notions of Chineseness within the Singaporean national imaginary" (63). As a result of Singapore's transformation into modern nation-state, ethnicity itself becomes a "technology of the self" (65) and "citizens engage the state not simply as citizens but through racial communities and racialized selves" (66). Holden's analysis highlights the intersection of ethnicity as a function of statehood and as an integral part of the flows of capital and concludes that the "'transnational desire' of much contemporary cultural commentary and theory is often a result of the particular national location of a migrant subject" (74).

The second section, on literature, offers the most diverse ethnic intersections in this volume of essays and illustrates the variety of critical approaches that characterizes the volume. Kristjana Gunnars's "Trans-East Asian Literature: Language and Displacement in Hong Ying, Hikaru Okuizumi, and Yi Mun-yol" exemplifies the focus in this section. The essay uses three works of fiction by mainland Chinese, Japanese, and Korean writers to support her argument that "when people migrate, there is inevitably a canvas of pain involved," and a concomitant loss of linguistic production. But once narrative can be reassembled in a new life, "every story [...] [becomes] a triumph against the dissembling effect of pain" (77). Gunnars works not only with a specific type of migratory movement but with various forms of displacements. Thus, characters in Hong Ying's *Summer of Betrayal* are subsumed by historical moments beyond their control, whereas Hikaru Okuizumi's *The Stones Cry Out* explores one man's attempt to overcome the trauma left by history. In *The Poet,* by Yi Mun-yol, a man whose life is his language, is forced to wander while he attempts to keep his language alive in spite of emotional and psychological pain. What Gunnars wants to show in her essay is the experience of "physical injury that leads to the loss of language and the disintegration of personality, which in turn leads to the serious struggle to re-acquire these" (79). She sees this as analogous to the disintegrating effects migration could have on people. Written from a comparative literature perspective, Gunnars's essay thus approaches the question of transnationalism inductively, through the medium of the texts she reads: in her concentration on displacement, she excavates and explores an issue central to transnational studies from a radically different perspective.

A companion piece to Gunnars's exploration is Petra Fachinger's "Cultural and Culinary Ambivalence in Sara Chin, Evelina Galang, and Yoko Tawada." Whereas the characters in Gunnars's essay are still located in their home countries, though buffeted by transnational historical events, those examined in Fachinger's essay are their overseas counterparts: they bear the marker of "Asian" ethnicity in the Western world, as Chinese or Filipina American, or as a Japanese in Germany. Fachinger finds that the protagonists in these stories share a profound skepticism about textual authority, and their "split" relationship with their work, which exposes them to "mediated language from which they feel alienated," is reflected in their metaphorical and real relationship to food (90). These women, in their search for identity within the capitalist flow of transnationalism, consume and are at times consumed by their ethnic marker. In their struggle, the protagonists "reveal how identity is a negotiation of terms and meanings, in which 'authenticity,' heritage, and culture are produced and re-articulated" (102).

The next essay in this section on writing and transnational subjectivity continues to make connections to the other essays in the volume, through examining writing within an adapted homeland. Jane Parish Yang's " 'The Tao is Up'— Intertextuality and Cultural Dialogue in *Tripmaster Monkey*" ranges widely in geography. At first glance, Yang's essay deals with one work by one author, Maxine Hong Kingston. But to Yang, Kingston's work is an "interplay of voices" that "revolves around what Chinese, American, and Chinese American means" (104). Thus, Yang reads *Tripmaster Monkey* through the allegorical novel *Journey to the West* from the late Ming Dynasty as well as the American seminal text *Moby Dick*. To Kingston, Chinese American subjectivity travels back and forth as a "constant dialogue or inner war" between competing identities (104).

This section closes with Laifong Leung's essay exploring the relationship between mainland Chinese and overseas Chinese literary production and criticism: "Overseas Chinese Literature: A Proposal for Clarification." If Leung's essay may initially seem to belong to the realm of Chinese literary studies rather than transnational studies, it is germane for us to remember that transnational cultural production is not simply a dialogue between Europe and North America on the one hand, and the rest of the world on the other. Leung repositions Chinese literature as always already containing, and yet struggling to confront, the question of transnationalism. As Leung writes, having observed that mainland China generally resisted overseas Chinese writing, "I wanted to know if there had been any change in the attitude towards literature written not in Chinese by overseas Chinese" (119). The answer is that, in 2002, overseas Chinese writing was still considered foreign. Thus, even though Chinese in mainland China and overseas are interested in similar issues, such as "identity, alienation, national consciousness, and nostalgia," (119), mainland Chinese academic culture desires to maintain hegemony over what can be considered "authentically" Chinese. To Leung, it seems a "narrow-minded attitude" that needs to be challenged (119). This essay contextualizes the conflictual grounds that transnational writing must traverse; it also provides the cultural and historical background against which the issues in *Reading Chinese Transnationalisms* are discussed.

The third section consists of four essays, each looking at cinematic culture. The film industry provides the most familiar examples of transnational cultural production, one of the reasons being the collaborative nature of filmmaking. In the film industry itself, the director Ang Lee has been central in refashioning notions of transnational, and specifically trans-Pacific, cultural production. Lee is also unusual among Chinese directors in that he has been recognized by Hollywood as one of their own by making films such as *The Ice Storm* (1997) and *Hulk* (2003), and he has been awarded Best Director for the acclaimed *Brokeback Mountain* (2005) at the 78th Annual Academy Awards®. Two of our essays thus focus on his works. Jennifer Jay's "*Crouching Tiger Hidden Dragon*: (Re)packaging Chinas and Selling the Hybridized Culture in an Age of Transnationalism" provides a perfect illustration of the collaborative nature of such transnational cultural production. In her essay, Jay looks at "how Ang Lee rounded up the talent among the Chinese diaspora and China to construct a transnational China" and then marketed it as "the conglomerate Chinese culture" (131) made palatable for Western consumption. Jay meticulously traces the many ethnic strands that have gone into the final product: the differences among the dialects spoken by the actors as well as the technicians on the set, the literature that inspires the cinematic genre of kung-fu movies, as well as the religions/ideologies limning the narrative of *Crouching Tiger Hidden Dragon*. The end result, as Jay writes, is a China "not plagued by domestic or international politics" but a "transnational China with fantasized superhuman strength [...] and martial skills" (134).

Jay finds that the transnational nature of Ang Lee's *Crouching Tiger Hidden*

Dragon provides a space for feminist discourse: "Women dominate the film with their presence and strong personalities" (140). Such is not the case in *The Wedding Banquet,* another Taiwan-American co-production from Ang Lee. January Lim argues in "Father Knows Best: Reading Sexuality in Ang Lee's *The Wedding Banquet* and Chay Yew's *Porcelain*" that this film, as well as Chay Yew's play, *Porcelain*, reaffirms "the lies, silences, and denials" that dominate the patriarchal family in diaspora (144). Grounding her argument on the metaphor of the closet, Lim writes that *The Wedding Banquet* legitimizes the closet, resists homosexual union while affirms hetero-normative ones.[10] The concept of the closet thus "satisfies the father's excess privilege and desire to perpetuate both family lineage and ethnic identity in the diaspora" (150). A father's excessive power in the film is contrasted by a son's sexual excess in the play. In *Porcelain*, Lim sees the main character's excess "as an attempt to reinvent new narrative strategies emerging in the early 1990s [...] in order to address the concerns of Asians living in the diaspora" (152). Sexual transgression in *Porcelain* also emphasizes that "the paternal figure," one of authority in traditional Chinese culture, is "just a nostalgic romantic illusion" in diaspora (159).

If diasporic modernity is destructive of familial and normative values in *Porcelain*, it is the force that informs the works of Taiwanese director Tsai Ming-liang. In "The Cinema of Tsai Ming-liang: A Modernist Genealogy," Mark Betz recognizes in Tsai a "contemporary, East Asian filmmaker working explicitly within, and in many ways extending, the modernist project of postwar European cinema's various new waves" (161). In his examination of Tsai, dubbed ironically "the First Modernist," Betz conjoins two main influences whose combination makes Tsai a unique auteur among other contemporary Taiwanese directors. The first is Tsai's aesthetics, "[I]n casting and approach to character, theme and tonal quality, formalist rigor and visual style, and reflexivity with respect [...] to the medium itself," all pointing to an affiliation with European art cinema of the 1960s and 1970s (162). This claim is supported by an overall examination of Tsai's works at the time of writing, including, in the postscript, the 2003 *Goodbye Dragon Inn*.

Although Taiwan's New Cinema is generally "concerned with its country's unresolved and complex national identity," Betz finds Tsai's "personal circumstances add a further dimension to the torsion of Taiwanese national identity" (165). Born in Malaysia and having moved to Taiwan at the age of 20, Tsai experiences diaspora in Taiwan, and this explains "the confluence of human and spatial emptiness where there should be fullness in Tsai's films, set not just in Taiwan but more specifically Taipei" (165). Objecting to viewing Taiwanese, or Asian cinema generally, as relational always to the production of "the First World," Betz reminds the reader that "historical time is palimpsestic and dispersive in all cultures" and aesthetic forms translate "across cultures in multiple circuits of exchange and appropriation" (169).

In "Sentimental Returns: On the Uses of the Everyday in the Recent Films of Zhang Yimou and Wong Kar-wai," Rey Chow turns the focus on two of the most important Chinese filmmakers today from China and Hong Kong, the other centers of Chinese film culture. In this essay, Chow uses Zhang's *The Road Home* and Wong's *In the Mood for Love* as examples to "consider specific uses of the everyday in representational practices" (173). Chow refers to Pier Paolo Pasolini's theorization of cinematic signification in order to understand contemporary Chinese cinema's specialization in "the sentimentalism of nostalgia," which Chow explains as "a mode of filmmaking that often invokes specific eras of the past as its collective imaginary" (175). In juxtaposing the two films, Chow affirms the difference between Zhang's and Wong's representations of Chineseness: "Chineseness in Zhang is a residual structure of feeling that results from the specifics of a country's political history" (186), whereas for Wong, "ethnicity is at once more local and more fluid," and his film prefigures a more "casual, tenuous relation to Chineseness as a geopolitical or national issue" (186–7). This difference, so superficially elusive and yet germane to Chinese cultural discourses, is what this volume is about.

Society

2

Hokkien–Philippines Familial Transnationalism, 1949–1975

Edgar Wickberg

Introduction

One way to think broadly about transnationalism is to define it as the regular movement across national boundaries of persons, money, goods, and ideas. The literature on Chinese transnationalism that fits this definition has often described transnational networks of diasporic Chinese business or other organizations which link groups of Chinese to each other or to China. In recent years, much of this literature has been specifically about Chinese business networks that facilitate the investments of globalized Chinese in the modern development of their "home," or ancestral localities in south China. In such studies, the ultimate research interest is economic. Culture — usually taken as an unchanging "given" — plays a role as a linking device that facilitates economic and social action.[1]

A less commonly studied form of Chinese transnationalism has been its familial features. Familial transnationalism speaks of regular family interactions across transnational space. It often, as in this paper, is concerned with family strategies of personal migration, income earning, and remittances (and sometimes public works donations) to the family's basic site. Research on Chinese familial transnationalism takes the family as the central unit of study — at least initially — and, drawing upon the usages of immigration history and cultural analysis, examines the system of migration of which the family is part, and the cultural outcomes for its members. That, in a general way, is the method used here.

Until recently, research on Chinese familial or migrant transnationalism has been concerned with contemporary or recent developments or expressions — either in the form of contemporary networks or contemporary cultural expressions.[2] Though it is generally recognized that this kind of transnationalism also has a history, there has been little writing in that vein. Now, two recent works have started us down that path. Madeline Hsu's book, *Dreaming of Gold, Dreaming of Home* (2000), studies Cantonese families in Taishan [Cantonese: Toisan] county in southwestern Guangdong Province and their relationships with family members living in California. The Taishan-California migration system that developed over sixty years (1882–1943) is examined, as well as the interactions between the two family fragments and the consequences at each end of this system. During this period, family members regularly migrated to the United States, sought income, remitted parts of it to members remaining in China, and dreamed of returning to the ancestral village, though they often did not do so.

A more recent book by Adam McKeown, *Chinese Migrant Networks and Cultural Change* (2001), looks comparatively at three sites of Chinese overseas settlement: Chicago, Lima (Peru), and Hawaii, covering roughly the same period as Hsu's book. Unlike Hsu, who focuses on family interactions, McKeown's treatment is more general. Moreover, his is a study of comparative cultural adaptation, on the part of three different groups of Overseas Chinese, all harboring what Hsu describes as dreams of gold and of home. McKeown sees the Chinese of these three sites as poised between a generalized culture of south China, from which they came, and the local culture found in each of the three overseas localities. How each group adapted is the subject of his work. In another piece, McKeown has addressed the transnational problem of migrant flows of Chinese women into the United States in the early twentieth century.[3]

In this essay, I draw upon the work of Hsu and McKeown but pursue a different course. Like Hsu, the point of origin here is very local. In this case, it is a dozen or so county-level areas in southern Fujian Province. The core of these, in relation to the migration system I discuss, is the area known broadly as Jinjiang [Hokkien: Chinkang]. This area includes the administrative units of Jinjiang, Quanzhou [Hokkien: Tsoanchiu], and Shishi [Seksai]. The other end of the bipolar migration system under discussion is the Philippines. But rather than call this a Jinjiang-Philippines system, I will speak of it as a Hokkien-Philippines system. The reason is that Jinjiang is the core part but by no means the total emigrant catchment area dealt with. The people of southern Fujian that inhabit this area call themselves Hokkien — the local dialect version of "Fujian." Hence, I call this the Hokkien-Philippines migration system in order to emphasize both the area of origin and the language and cultural specifics of these emigrants.

The migration system discussed was originally a simple bipolar one, similar to that Hsu discusses. But this one is much older, and during the period discussed, it became more complex. Both migration systems had a basic pattern of sojourning males, who usually left families behind in China, supported them with remittances, and planned an eventual return to China. The period here differs from that studied by both Hsu and McKeown. Their period, essentially the first forty years of the twentieth century, is one in which there were restraints on the ability of Chinese to go to the United States; but the access of those Chinese to ancestral localities in China was unimpaired. The period I am considering (1949–78) has rarely been studied in relation to Chinese outside China and their migration and cultural flows and consequences.[4] It is a period during the Cold War, when China was blockaded by an American-led alliance, applying a strategy of containment against China's presumed expansionist ambitions. This Cold War situation made it difficult to maintain the existing migration systems, both in the Philippines and in other countries. It is of interest that recent studies of connections between Overseas Chinese and China focus either on the period before the Cold War or the period after China opened up to freer movement of persons and investments (1978–).[5] The period in between, 1949–78, is seen as merely a kind of deviation, or interruption, and the effects of this period of interruption on migration systems and Overseas Chinese cultural life are rarely examined. These are the tasks of this paper. The dates I have chosen are those when the Philippines had no formal relations with the People's Republic of China (1949–75). The latter date is only three years prior to the beginning of China's "opening up" policies.

Three other points: (1) Unlike McKeown, I try, in this and future works, to focus more narrowly by area and cultural life on the Hokkien region of south Fujian rather than on a "south China" culture area as he has done. (2) It needs to be remembered that the proximity of the Philippines to China makes for a very different situation from that experienced by the Chinese of the Western hemisphere about whom Hsu and McKeown write. For many people in the Philippines, China was an all too near and sometimes frightening presence. Its very nearness had made for an intense exchange of persons, back and forth — especially by the 1930s — something Western hemisphere Chinese could not experience until the development of jet air travel in the 1960s. (3) As elsewhere in Southeast Asia, the Chinese of the Philippines enjoyed a preeminent position in the economy of their country of residence — quite unlike the situation of Western hemisphere Chinese.

New Realities, 1949–1966

By 1949, the relations between southern Fujian counties and Philippine sites had enjoyed eighty years of almost uninterrupted intensification. Only the Japanese occupation of Fujian and the Philippines had briefly suspended the connection during the Pacific War of 1941–45. The intensification referred to had begun in the 1870s. At that time, steam travel in Asian waters reduced Fujian-Philippines voyages from one week's duration to that of two and one-half days.[6] Travel back and forth thus became much more frequent than before, and many Hokkien males were founding and sustaining dual families — one in Fujian and the other (with a Filipina or Chinese mestiza as spouse) in the Philippines. The male head of the two families shuttled between them — an early astronaut. The Chinese population of the Philippines greatly increased. By the 1960 census, the best official figures we have for our period, there were 181,000 Chinese in a Philippine population of 27,000,000. Eighty percent were from Fujian, and half of those were from Jinjiang.[7]

Although Jinjiang families also sent family members to Singapore, Indonesia, Malaya, and elsewhere in Southeast Asia, the Philippines was the most popular destination of familial migration. It was geographically closest, travel between it and Jinjiang was easy and hence more frequent, and remittances from the Philippines during the 1930s had become larger than those from elsewhere in Southeast Asia. Not only ancestral rural districts but the city of Xiamen as well benefited from this migration system. Philippine Hokkiens invested in real estate, and built houses in Xiamen. And eventually, if they could afford it, they were buried in Gulangyu, across the harbor from Xiamen.[8]

Despite high levels of intermarriage, the relations between ethnic Chinese and Filipinos were full of ambiguities and ambivalences. Historically, ethnic Chinese and Filipinos had often struggled together against colonial rule but just as often might be on opposite sides. Ethnic Chinese were generally accepted as essential to the Philippine economy, but their leading role in so many sectors of it was widely resented. For their part, Chinese tended to regard Filipinos as barbarians. The Hokkien term *huan-a* (barbarian) was countered by the Filipino term *intsik* (roughly, "chink").[9]

After 380 years of colonial rule by the Spaniards, Americans, and Japanese, the Philippines finally achieved independence in 1946. Filipino nationalists, keen to reduce the role of Chinese in economic life, put into effect, in the 1950s, the nationalization of retail trade, of the rice and corn business, and (observing the increasing numbers of local Chinese attending Philippine universities) the professions. These new laws set a premium on citizenship, and Philippine law and practice made achievement of that difficult for ethnic Chinese. Both Philippine law and Chinese law of that era considered anyone born of a father who held Chinese citizenship to be a Chinese national, even if born in the Philippines.[10] Thus, Philippine-born children of a Chinese father were Chinese citizens; and naturalization was expensive and difficult.

Meanwhile, since the early twentieth century, the governments of China had tried to draw the Philippine Hokkiens closer to China and its national objectives. Chinese schools in the Philippines were increasingly supported by China's national governments, which increasingly, by the 1930s, promoted a patriotic focus upon China. Remittances were seen as a patriotic way to balance China's trade deficit, and "Overseas Chinese" fund-raising to support China's defense against Japan's territorial encroachments became common. These blandishments from China encouraged the anxieties of Philippine governments, even before independence, about the political loyalties of the local "Chinese." In the Asian context, China was a large and nearby force about which the Philippines, one of the closest countries to it, had constantly to be aware.

But while both the Philippines and China treated the Philippine Hokkiens as Chinese — in a national framework — the Hokkiens also pursued their own interests, often of a non-national sort. By the 1920s, a vigorous generation of Philippine Hokkien business leaders was investing money in the modernization of the Hokkien city of Xiamen and participating in the local government, one of them even becoming mayor of the city in 1933 under the short-lived breakaway Fujian government.[11] Later in that decade, Japan's invasion of China caused many family members in Fujian to relocate to the Philippines. But family ties in Fujian were retained, including lineage ties, and that included intervention by Philippine Hokkiens in lineage disputes in Fujian. By the 1930s, as more than one scholar has noted, affairs in the ancestral districts had become part of the daily life of Philippine Hokkiens.[12]

Meanwhile, the American colonial government of the early 1900s had applied the *Chinese Exclusion Law* then in force in the US. In the Philippines, that policy had allowed some new immigration, but mostly by Chinese who had relatives already established in business there.[13] The result was formally to limit the immigration to the same counties in south Fujian and the same families that had maintained the transnational link with the Philippines. Remittances, apparently interrupted by the Japanese occupation, surged once the war ended. In Quanzhou prefecture — part of the Jinjiang region — during the period 1945–49, some sixty percent of total remittances to that prefecture from all Southeast Asian Hokkiens were from the Philippines, despite the existence of larger Quanzhou settlements in places like Singapore and Indonesia. Philippine Hokkien investments in Fujian's small industries, communications, hotels, and real estate resumed their pre-war importance. Aid to schools and other public facilities was also substantial.[14]

But it was not a simple matter of China's national pulls versus a Hokkien local focus on Fujian. The Philippine Hokkiens also had interests in the Philippines and versions of Filipinized Chinese culture maintained there. Thus, though China's governments tried to reduce it to a simple effort needed to overcome the tensions of provincial versus national interest, with slogans like "*ai guo ai xiang*" (love both nation and locality), the reality was a complex set of priorities and rankings involving family interests in the Philippines and Fujian as well as attraction to the national interests of China and the Philippines.

The new realities of 1949 were these: a new Communist government in China (The People's Republic, or PRC), an émigré survivor government in Taiwan (The Republic of China, or ROC), and a newly independent Philippines with leaders bent on reducing ethnic Chinese economic influence in the country. Internationally, the Cold War put the Philippine Hokkiens unavoidably in the hands of Taiwan. Ideological and geopolitical interests of both the ROC and Philippine governments encouraged closeness, and the subsequent creation of the American containment policy made them allies. Both governments depended for survival on the United States. Given these conditions, the political and cultural involvement of Taiwan became greater in the Philippines than anywhere else in Asia.

The Cold War brought into being new structures of organization and control in Philippine Hokkien society. The overwhelming majority of local Hokkiens were necessarily citizens of the ROC, which was now next door in Taiwan, not — as before 1949 — in distant Nanjing. The pre-war Manila Chinese Chamber of Commerce, whose leaders included some who had been deeply involved in Fujian affairs, was replaced as the "umbrella organization" for ethnic Chinese by the new Federation of Chinese Chambers of Commerce and Industry (popularly called "The Federation"), whose pro-Taiwan leaders now possessed, through their more efficient organization, more power over the ethnic Chinese population than the old chamber had ever had. Now, the political leadership of Chinatown (and thereby its cultural definers) was made up of three groups in balance: the Federation, the ROC Embassy, and the Taiwan-based Guomindang (KMT) political party.[15] With the encouragement and active involvement of the embassy, five new pyramids of organization and control appeared, created for ethnic Chinese business, education, home-district and same-surname mutual aid associations, anti-Communist organizations, and KMT party branches.[16]

The formal unity of the ethnic Chinese thus achieved helped insure that anti-Communist orthodoxy and the idea of Taiwan as the home of true Chinese culture could be maintained. Taiwan now became the proposed cultural substitute for southern Fujian and for China as a whole. The ROC Embassy supervised the schools, the Taiwan Overseas Chinese Affairs Commission provided curriculum and texts, and teachers came from Taiwan.[17] One might think that this would have helped retain some aspects of Hokkien culture in the Philippines, given that the population of Taiwan is made up largely of people whose ancestors came from the same parts of Fujian as the Philippine Chinese. But the specifically national-level objectives of the ROC government ruled out any educational compromise, at this point, with local Taiwanese culture. The version of Chinese culture taught was Chinese national culture as promoted by the ROC government. Students were encouraged to take Taiwan as not only a cultural and political substitute for ancestral localities but a career substitute as well. Learning Mandarin well so one could go to Taiwan was a common exhortation of Chinese school-teachers.[18]

This is not to say that Hokkien popular culture was completely suppressed in the Philippines. As in Taiwan, Hokkien popular religion flourished. More temples appeared, and in the 1960s, perhaps in anticipation of the Cultural Revolution, the images of several local cult deities in Fujian were brought to Manila and housed in temples built with materials that frequently came from Taiwan.[19] Families taught what they knew of Hokkien versions of Chinese culture, and Hokkien language continued as the familial language, and the Chinatown lingua franca.

But much would depend upon whether links to Fujian could be maintained somehow. It is widely believed that the immigration tap was turned off completely. In fact, a dribble of immigrants continued to arrive. In the early 1950s, Philippine policy essentially cut off even the fifty Chinese per year officially allowed into the country.[20] That led to immigration on other bases, beginning in the late 1950s. The conduit for this was Hong Kong. By the mid-1950s, a Hokkien colony in the North Point neighborhood of Hong Kong had reached a considerable size. Now, would-be migrants from Fujian could get Chinese government permission to visit their Hong Kong relatives. Once in Hong Kong, they overstayed and established themselves. Some members of this group with relatives in the Philippines then obtained Philippine visas as temporary visitors and, once in Manila, they overstayed, thereby adding to the local population, especially in Manila, where most remained.[21] I know of no statistics on the size of this group. Most have since been legalized through amnesties. Many speak fondly of their educational experience: elementary school in Fujian, middle school in Hong Kong, high school in Manila.[22]

Remittances also did not end in 1949, although the Philippine government attempted to severely limit them. At the other end in Fujian, Philippine remittances continued to arrive even in years when Overseas Chinese dependents were supposed to be deprived of their material privileges in an otherwise socialist society.[23] In the early 1950s, Philippine remittances continued the upswing of the late 1940s, going directly to Fujian. By the late 1950s, as the North Point colony became well established, two-thirds of Philippine remittances went to it. Just how much remained with family members there and how much was forwarded to south Fujian is not entirely clear. We do know that of RMB63 million (PRC currency) in remittances to the Quanzhou area of Fujian in 1954, sixty-nine percent came from the Philippines. Philippine remittances continued to account for over half of those received in Quanzhou until the late 1960s In 1969, of RMB44 million received there, forty-six percent was from the Philippines. But twenty-six percent was from Hong Kong, some of which must have been ultimately from the Philippines. Business investments and infrastructure donation funds also continued to come from the Philippines.[24]

The North Point colony and the Philippine-Taiwan connection thus created an apparently unique Hokkien Quadrangle (that is, Fujian, Hong Kong, the Philippines, and Taiwan), whose activities have yet to be investigated. Between Fujian and Taiwan, direct movement of persons, money, goods, and culture was not possible. But the other links were in place, and the three sites were in touch with each other. Remittances and investments went north to Fujian from Manila and Hong Kong. Culture went south from Fujian, Hong Kong, and Taiwan to the Philippines. Persons moved in both directions. But the critical points were these: the number of family members who could make it from Fujian to Manila was small, and the number of Philippine Hokkiens who could make it to Fujian very small indeed. Of most importance, for the younger generation growing up in the Philippines, regular contact with newcomers was slight, personal contact with Hong Kong occasional, and direct contact with Fujian almost impossible.

Meanwhile, members of this generation who went to university were coming into contact with other Filipino students. And middle-class Hokkien parents who now moved out of Chinatowns brought their children thereby into more contact with members of the growing Filipino middle class. In short, there was plenty of "Chinese" culture available to the youth but little in the way of specifically Hokkien cultural refreshment. They continued to speak the Hokkien language at home and in business, but their cultural environment otherwise was increasingly Filipinized beyond that of the two previous generations.[25]

Politically, the pro-Taiwan organizations in Philippine Chinatowns had become the dominant or mainstream group. Dissenters clustered, as non-mainstreamers, around some older organizations and some new ones that now proliferated, particularly in Manila. What they sought was not so much political power as autonomy in relation to the mainstream group.[26] Despite the five organizational pyramids, the mainstream's control was incomplete. Among the new organizations were brotherhoods (made up mostly of younger men who were not doing well), and new small-district (or *xiang*) mutual aid associations, which provided more social support than the large surname associations were now prepared to give. In fact, Hokkien society was becoming polarized between the successful, who had somehow overcome the limitations of discriminatory economic policies, and the rest, who had not.[27] But while these new organizations reflected this social polarization, the *xiang* organizations among them may also, from what we now know of the continuing connections with Fujian, have had more specific links to ancestral localities in mind.[28] We know that one motivation for creating these *xiang* organizations was to teach "Chinese" culture (that is, *qiaoxiang* — or ancestral district — culture) to the younger generation. Another had to do with supporting schools in the ancestral localities.[29]

Meanwhile, the ROC continued to try to be a substitute for mainland China — and not only for the Philippine Hokkiens. There were encouragements to "Overseas Chinese" around the world to invest in the development of Taiwan, "loyalty" delegations were sponsored for annual visits to Taiwan on the ROC's national holiday, and various other activities were promoted. But, as a cultural substitute, Taiwan was incomplete. Traditionally, for Philippine Hokkiens, there had been a connection among culture, economic interest, political interest, and family ties. These, for the Philippine Hokkiens, had always been together in Fujian. After 1949, it was very difficult for that to be maintained. Taiwan could substitute for some connections. But familial ties to ancestral districts and the veneration of ancestors could not easily be replaced. To be sure, there were same-district associations established in Taiwan relating to Fujian. But these were for Taiwanese whose ancestors had long since settled on the Island. In the 1950s and 1960s, authorities in Taiwan encouraged the establishment of family, or surname, associations on an international basis, and large genealogic volumes were published to promote them.

These associations, in relation to any substitute family feeling, may have been a "hard sell" to the Philippine Hokkiens. In the Philippine case, there were many peculiarities. Migration to the Philippines came from a narrowly focused ancestral zone. Ancestral locality and surname overlapped. Many villages were single lineage units; hence, everyone from there bearing the same surname was actually related. Some of the migrants, once in the Philippines, had formed home-locality (*xiang*) associations and, because of the concentration of surnames, these might be actual kin groups. Alternatively, surname associations, in the course of time, would become segmented. Instead of membership that included all those of common surname, newer organizations were formed whose members were only those of common surname who had lived in a certain ancestral district and hence, in many cases, were actually related to each other. So, unlike many other Overseas Chinese sites, where surname association membership did not necessarily imply actual kinship, in the Philippines, surname associations focused on a given ancestral district often were similar to local branches of a lineage in Fujian.[30]

But, kinship aside, there were other reasons to join surname associations. The Taiwan surname associations were often not directly related to any specific locality in China. Some of the major surname associations in the Philippines were also that way. These associations were often powerful in the Philippine context and, when they were linked to associations of the same surname in Taiwan, there was no doubt of the political and business networking advantages of such bodies. Even without Taiwan links, large surname associations were powerful — their influence only exceeded by the Federation and the Guomindang. It was said that the ROC Embassy would only work through them and the Federation. Members of small district associations could not get the embassy's attention.[31] Therefore, it seems likely that Philippine Chinese who joined super-sized surname associations did so for business, political, and personal prestige reasons.

Some Philippine Hokkiens went on "loyalty" delegations, invested in Taiwan, and moved there — especially in the 1960s, most conspicuously, the entrepreneur Tan Yu.[32] But the ancestral district and — usually — the ancestral tablets, remained in Fujian.

Crisis and Transition, 1966–75: A Newer Reality

The years 1966–72 were a time of crisis in all four points of what I have called the "Hokkien Quadrangle": Fujian, Hong Kong, the Philippines, and Taiwan. For the PRC, including Fujian, it was the high tide of the Cultural Revolution. In Hong Kong, the Cultural Revolution spilled over, stimulating radical political action by some, but for others — well-established persons

— creating anxieties about local stability and an urge to migrate elsewhere: to Canada, the US, Australia, or New Zealand. In the Philippines, amid a general breakdown of centralized order keeping, radical university student groups demanded an end to the domestic status quo of increased polarization of wealth and power and the blackout on information about mainland China and Maoism. Many radical students were Chinese, members of a 1960s age cohort unlike any of its predecessors. A substantial number of university students were now of Chinese background and they had begun to mix with their non-Chinese peers.[33] This phenomenon caused alarm among cultural conservatives in Chinatown. They feared that this generation was losing the proper Chineseness its members had been taught in the Chinese schools, and in danger of becoming assimilated into Filipino society — worst of all, to that sector of Filipinos that was attracted to Maoism. There was much public discussion about assimilation (*tongwa*) or integration (*yonghap*) as alternatives. But the older Chinese educators wrote essays about cultural retention and against both integration and assimilation.[34] To them, it seemed that the right kind of Chineseness — what they had taught — was now about to be swept aside by this generation in favor of the wrong kind of Chineseness and excessive doses of Filipinoness. To deal with the attractions of radicalism — including the Cultural Revolution — some Philippine Chinese schools now introduced discussion of the Cultural Revival Movement in Taiwan, which was one of the ways in which the ROC government had tried to counter the Cultural Revolution's possible attractiveness in Taiwan itself.[35]

Some ethnic Chinese leaders in the Philippines now began to join those middle-class Filipinos who sought refuge overseas, including one of the leaders of the Federation, who parked his family in Vancouver for a time. Other Chinese entrepreneurs, annoyed by continuing restraints on Chinese business in the Philippines and the deteriorating law-and-order situation there, now moved their investments abroad, including to Taiwan.

The deteriorating security situation in the Philippines worried local ethnic Chinese leaders, who counted on the ROC Embassy, the Federation, and the KMT to maintain stability and unity. One leader spoke repeatedly of the need for "Grand Unity" (*da tongyi*).[36] But the authority of the Embassy was being eroded as Cold War arrangements began to crumble. In 1970, Canada and Italy had recognized the PRC, and in 1972, Nixon had gone to the Mainland. Even in 1966, the ROC ambassador had remarked to me that "a small number" of Philippine Chinese were now "sneaking in" to Fujian via Hong Kong, but "we know who they are."[37] Ironically — and amazingly — the same ambassador could not avoid being involved in two cases concerning direct intervention by Philippine Hokkiens in local disputes in

Fujian.[38] In its turn, the Federation tried to strengthen and unify the Chinese "community" by reaching out to the major dissident organizations in the non-mainstream. For a time, the Manila Chinese Chamber of Commerce, the titular, or symbolic leader of the non-mainstream, was talked into becoming an organization under the Federation's umbrella.[39]

But it was the Guomindang, the third component of mainstream leadership, that took the most assertive action. Allegedly working with US intelligence units in the Philippines, and with the knowledge of President Ferdinand Marcos, the KMT arranged for the deportation of two independent local Chinese newspapermen, the Yuyitung brothers. The Yuyitungs — born in the Philippines — were doing two things that threatened the status quo under the mainstream leadership. They attempted to collect and publish news and information about affairs in the PRC. And, in the early and middle 1960s, both of the brothers had spoken out in favor of the assimilation or integration of ethnic Chinese into Philippine society. It is hard to say which offended the mainstream group more: the possible availability of news direct from mainland China in a local Chinese language newspaper, or the possibility of the local ethnic Chinese population's becoming legally part of Philippine society and hence beyond the reach of ROC control. Now, the result of the KMT's efforts was a bizarre midnight kidnapping, in which the Yuyitung brothers were taken to Taiwan to stand trial for sedition against the ROC.[40] At this point, the International Press Institute and Amnesty International intervened, the sentences pronounced on the brothers were reduced, and they were sent into exile — one of them to San Francisco and the other to Toronto. Without them, their newspaper suspended publication, resuming only in the mid-1980s, after the fall of Marcos.

In 1972, Marcos dissolved Congress and declared martial law. Shortly thereafter, he issued a constitution that extended citizenship to children of Filipino mothers with alien (that is, Chinese) husbands — to be effective from that date on. For various reasons, Marcos now began to move the Philippines in the direction of rapprochement with mainland China. To prepare for this domestically, he took major steps to Filipinize the Chinese schools. From this date, all school administrators had to be citizens of the Philippines. The ROC flag and pictures of ROC leaders were no longer to be displayed, nor were causes related to Taiwan to be presented. Curricular materials were to be prepared in the Philippines. A second provision dealt with languages and subjects of instruction. Now, the study of Chinese language was to be limited to roughly one and one-half hours per day.[41] The previous arrangement had been for school instruction to be half-time in English and half-time in Chinese (Mandarin). The Chinese courses had included language study and China-related courses.

The long-term effect of the new provision would be to progressively reduce the ability of younger Chinese to read and write in that language. Having dealt with the schools, Marcos, in further preparation for establishing relations with the PRC and having a PRC embassy in Manila, provided for mass naturalization of most of the Chinese population of the Philippines. Overnight, what had been a majority of citizens of the Republic of China became a majority of citizens of the Philippines.[42] Marcos then established relations with the PRC in early 1975, causing a formal break with the ROC, though informal ties through non-official representative offices remained.[43]

All these changes had far-reaching significance for the Philippine Hokkiens. First, they now, as Philippine citizens, would no longer be under any Chinese embassy. Second, as the law restricting certain occupations and opportunities in the Philippines to citizens was still in place, the Hokkiens could now qualify for those occupations. Retail trade and grain dealing were open once more, and university studies could be pursued in the knowledge that one need not go abroad after graduation in order to practice a profession. The right to vote, of course, was also there. Of perhaps most interest to us, Philippine Hokkiens could visit their families in Fujian — but now as Philippine citizens (*huaren*, or ethnic Chinese of non-China citizenship).

Three years after the establishment of Philippine-PRC relations, the new "open policies" in China came into being. These various events brought an end to the familial transnational system as it had existed. Now, both Philippine Hokkiens and Fujian Hokkiens had many more opportunities than ever before. Families in Fujian had less need for remittances, now that they had greater economic opportunities where they were, and greater opportunities to travel elsewhere in China seeking economic betterment. The remittances that had continued to come from the Philippines plummeted after 1978,[44] presumably because of this, and because so much of the Fujian group had already migrated to Hong Kong. Philippine investments in ancestral localities continued but now were often merely parts of portfolios that might include Shanghai and other, more lucrative investment sites. Some Philippine Hokkiens returned to Fujian, but only a few older persons decided to retire there. Younger Hokkiens, in search of their own roots, and with usable skills, worked for a time in Fujian, sometimes as teachers of English. Under certain circumstances, elderly Hokkiens who wished to rejoin their relatives by retiring to Manila could be admitted to the Philippines. Some Fujian entrepreneurs might also have opportunities there. In the other direction, Philippine donations to Fujian for private school creation and support, the reconstruction of ancestral lineage halls and the erection of ceremonial gates were common.[45]

The dual family system came to an end. As some have argued, in the 1930s the Fujian family had been more important to the Hokkien migrant than the Philippine family. But the long-term lack of direct contact with members of the Fujian family and the opening up of new opportunities and a new and secure status for Chinese in the Philippines put the balance on the side of the Philippine family.[46]

In short, what was supposed to be a community of mostly sojourners in aid of a family in China had become a colony of settlers with more important local commitments than transnational ones. One now hears stories of Fujian wives of Philippine Hokkiens who have been left without remittances and totally ignored.

In the Philippines, the Chinese schools struggled on through the 1970s and 1980s with declining interest in things Chinese on the part of their students. The majority of ethnic Chinese students now sought university entrance. The prerequisite academic preparation for that now took up increasing amounts of their secondary school time, leaving little time for Chinese language or China-related subjects. Non-Chinese might now attend the Chinese schools, avoiding the language courses if they wished. This last provision meant still more opportunities for interaction between ethnic Chinese and non-Chinese. The same thing was occurring as more Chinese entered the professions and worked with non-Chinese, or entered businesses that had nothing to do with Chinatown or Chinese matters.[47] In the 1990s, the Chinese schools began to be revived. In Manila, a new Chinese Education Center sought information from everywhere on how to teach Chinese as a second language. Teachers and students traveled to both mainland China and Taiwan for short-term courses. The two leading Chinese high schools of Manila, formerly separated by political stances ("Pro-Mainland" versus "Pro-Taiwan"), now collaborate in these programs.[48]

By the 1980s, a group of middle-class Chinese who had graduated from university in the late 1960s and early 1970s was creating an integrationist organization, the Kaisa para sa Kaunlaran. Its objectives were to be a bridge between the older generation, whose members were seen as "more Chinese," and the new, younger generation of the 1980s, said to be "not very Chinese," as well as a bridge between ethnic Chinese in the Philippines and the Philippine population at large. This organization promotes publications in Chinese, Filipino, and English. It also has created a Chinese Heritage Center in Manila, which includes a museum of the history and achievements of Chinese in the Philippines. Kaisa has assumed the role of a spokesperson organization for Chinese Filipinos who favor integration. It consistently takes a public stand on issues directly affecting ethnic Chinese, and those of a broader nature as well. Kaisa also speaks about the Chinese in relation to "other minorities" in the Philippines. It has not used the term *multiculturalism*, but its policies and statements seem to imply future advocacy in that direction.

Some General Considerations

This essay has described how a Chinese transnational migration system of intense bipolar interaction became, in a time of impairment, multipolar, and the effects of this period of change upon Philippine Hokkien Chinese ethnicity. In this concluding section, I wish to make four points. (1) The period 1949–78 should not be seen as necessarily an interruption of all contact between ancestral localities and Chinese abroad. Contact could be and was maintained with Chinese in some countries via Hong Kong. The period should be studied in that light. (2) The international political and cultural role of Taiwan in this period is important and worth researching. (3) Migration systems are not necessarily bipolar. (4) Ethnicity should be studied at several levels: national, regional, and local; and across time: as historically changing rather than as a given or fixed entity.

Some writings on Overseas Chinese that cover the period of mainland China's separation from much of the overseas world, 1949–78, present a picture of nearly complete lack of communication by Chinese abroad with ancestral localities.[49] Whatever might have been the case elsewhere, that was not so for the Philippines. Some writings also cite the change in the Overseas Chinese policy of the PRC in the mid-1950s, in which Overseas Chinese were encouraged to seek local citizenship, as an important factor in ethnicity change among Chinese outside China. (Cut off from China and cut loose by China.)[50] That would have been less the case for Chinese in the Philippines, where the presence of Taiwan and its dominating role in Philippine Chinatowns made this kind of PRC policy change less relevant, at least in the 1950s and 1960s. What mattered there was Taiwan's Overseas Chinese policies, which were to claim Chinese outside China as citizens of the ROC and to campaign for their political and cultural loyalties. Indeed, from a Taiwan perspective, the 1950s and 1960s were a time of ROC-PRC competition for the world's Chinese.

The substitute role of Taiwan for "China" in those countries whose policies made it impossible to allow local ethnic Chinese to have direct contact with mainland China has yet to receive sustained academic study. Besides the Southeast Asian countries so affected — the Philippines, South Vietnam, and Thailand — there were major countries outside the region, most conspicuously, the United States and Canada. Taiwan (the Republic of China/ROC) was clearly dominant in the Chinatowns of North America during this period. Its influence was both political and cultural, as it was in the Philippines, though hardly to the same degree. Studies of North American Chinatowns acknowledge this but rarely give much attention to the educational and cultural dimension. Like the Philippine Chinese, America's Chinese, as Madeline Hsu has noted, could not prevent international changes over which they had no control. Among those, from my point of view, were the Cold War and the dominance of Taiwan in many local Chinatowns. The Philippine Chinese could adapt, by bringing in not only Taiwan but also Hong Kong. For them, ancestral localities might have been mostly unavailable, but frequent visits to sources of Chineseness close to those localities were still possible. The same, on a less frequent basis, was probably true for American Chinese.

In his study of three Chinese societies of the pre-1940 era, Adam McKeown outlines some of the discourses of self-presentation of Chinese, especially from the 1920s onward.[51] In this essay, I have not attempted a description of Philippine Chinese cultural characteristics or self-expressions. But it seems reasonable to me that discourses that claim modernity for themselves, as used by McKeown's Chinese, would also have been part of the rhetoric of Philippine Chinese leaders of the 1950s and 1960s.

So would, given the environment of the time, discourses of anti-communism. The Taiwan culture as presented in Philippine Chinese schools of that era attempted to contrast ROC culture, as genuine Chinese culture, with what was being promoted on the Mainland. In contrast to PRC Communism, there was familism. Indeed, the Grand Family Association of the Philippines, a federation of surname associations, was created in Manila by the ROC Embassy at least partly as a propaganda vehicle for anti-communism.[52] The general norms of courses on Chinese culture in Philippine Chinese schools emphasized what were presented as traditional Chinese values. Among the salient features of these, besides general familism, were paternalism, self-restraint, the importance of education, and a general respect for tradition. These values had been part of the pre-1949 Philippine Chinese school system, which even then was heavily influenced by ROC-supported values. At that time, cultural conservatism, seen as a preservation of traditional values, was balanced by encouragement of various forms of modernity. The post-1949 difference was that once the ROC was removed to Taiwan and the "two Chinas" propaganda emerged, the conservatism of the ROC-promoted culture became more pronounced and emphatic, as a call for a return to traditional norms. Parenthetically, given this educational environment, Amyot, writing in the late 1950s, was surprised at the degree of individualism shown by the Philippine Chinese students he observed.[53] Besides these "Chinese" influences, we would expect norms derived from the Filipino environment, and some from Hong Kong as well, to be part of the mix of influences shaping Philippine Hokkiens' senses of themselves. That is an obvious topic for further research.

In the foregoing, I have presented Chinese national culture and Hokkien culture as if almost antithetical to one another. In fact, they go together and are part of the heritage of any Hokkien. I separated them and opposed them here because I wished to bring out the often conflicting interests that surface when Chinese governments — whether on the Mainland or Taiwan — have insisted upon enforcing "Overseas Chinese" promotion and loyalty to national culture (however delineated), thereby creating conflicts for ordinary Chinese who have also their own local interests, memories, and commitments that may clash with those of the national entity. Hence, part of the process of defining and redefining identities is an effort that must include and adjust both local and national conceptions of Chineseness. The literature on the Hokkiens in the Philippines — both from the Philippines and from China and Taiwan — deals with them as Chinese, and the Filipinos as Filipinos, that is, at a national level. It seems important in considering ethnicities and identities that we take everything into account, not assuming any uniform, uncomplicated "Chinese" beliefs or behaviors. What nations think they mean by loyalty and citizenship is not so clear-cut a matter to ordinary persons who must deal with the complex of influences — some of them finely grained — that make up their sense of self. What we have here is a group of Southeast Asian persons of Hokkien Chinese background and familial links and a context of varied meanings of "Chinese" in which they had to maintain a sense of self.

Those — principally Kaisa representatives — who have popularized the "Chinese Filipino" or "*tsinoy*" identity demand further discussion. What caused the emergence of these younger people with this vision of self from 1970 onward? Some writers, explaining the greater Filipinization of post-1970 Philippine Chinese and the feelings of distance they now have about China, usually explain the latter as chiefly due to the isolation of these people from mainland China, implying that lacking ancestral community experience they must feel somehow less Chinese and more Filipino than previous generations.[54] Yet, as we have seen, Chineseness, of various kinds, was available to them. It seems to me possible to argue that it was not so much the impairment of the transnational system that was critical in alienating young Philippine Hokkiens from China. It was more the growing prosperity of many

Philippine Hokkien families and the availability to them of higher education in the Philippines that made the difference.

In an earlier study, I spoke of the Philippine Chinese and the Filipinos of the early decades of the twentieth century as being on different learning courses: the Chinese seeing themselves bound for a future of national modernity as defined by China, and the Filipinos headed also for national modernity but defined in American and Filipino ways.[55] After 1949, the Chinese schools in the Philippines continued to teach Chinese national modernity as the framework in which their students' lives would unfold. But the better off among those students also went to university, where the norms of American higher education, in its Filipino versions, prevailed. Exposure to both of these educational streams gave those youth a sense of possibility: of their being simultaneously both Chinese and Filipino — at least Filipino in the ways that Filipinos are Americanized. By the time academics began studying Philippine Chinese university students, in the early 1970s, they had become very different from what students were in 1949, even though their professional opportunities in the Philippines were still limited.[56] Then, in 1975, the citizenship change opened up professional opportunities to them as well, and opportunities of all kinds to local Chinese of all social levels. Finally, in 1978, greater freedom and opportunity opened up to their relatives in Fujian. All of this caused new ways of thinking and feeling about Hokkienness, Chineseness, and familial obligations. The impairment and modification of the transnational migration system did have an influence in creating *tsinoys* — persons of Hokkien Chinese background, who distinguished between culture and home place. But its greatest influence was probably on the Chineseness component of their ethnicity. I think, in other words, that even if there had been no impairment of access to Fujian, the *tsinoys* would have emerged as they did by 1970. But without the impairment and the modification of the migration system, their sense of Chineseness would have been different.[57]

The Kaisa organization, as speaker for the *tsinoys*, and as inventor of this and other expressions of ethnicity, deserves further attention. Kaisa's names for itself, for example, are interesting and revealing. Addressing Filipinos, the name is Kaisa para sa Kaunlaran, a Tagalog language statement of "alliance for progress." The accompanying logo shows two hands joined in a handshake, along with a heart symbol. Nothing is said about who the hand-shaking alliance partners are or about the goal of the "progress" referred to. In view of Kaisa's literature, it is obvious that the hands are those of ethnic Chinese Filipinos and ethnic Malay Filipinos joined in affection to pursue the cause of integration. Addressing English speakers, there is no organizational name used other than the Tagalog one. But addressing Chinese readers, the name is not Kaisa but a Chinese language non-equivalent, *Huayi Qingnian Lianhe Hui* (Mandarin), or Federation of Overseas-Chinese-Descended Youth. Here the term used (*huayi*, or Chinese descendent) is one commonly used by international and national Chinese. It stresses the Chinese heritage — a kind of reclaiming of generations born overseas, as seen from the perspective of someone in China and Taiwan. It is as if their Chinese descent is the most important thing about them, and their youth the next. Nothing is said about relations with Filipinos or indeed any of the goals of Kaisa.

The terms Kaisa uses to characterize the groups they represent, "Chinese Filipino" and "*tsinoy*," are also revealing. "Chinese Filipino" privileges the "Filipino." It says that the Chinese Filipino is a Filipino first and last, loyal to the Philippines. He or she just happens to be of Chinese background — quite a contrast to *huayi* above. This usage addresses the common supposition among many Filipinos that Chinese cannot be trusted to be loyal to the Philippines. "Chinese Filipino" is a personal political statement of loyalty to the Philippines but with a cultural background that includes things Chinese. The term "*tsinoy*" is made up of "*tsi*" (pronounced "chee") for "Chinese" and "noy" for Filipino. It is an adaptation of the Filipino slang term for themselves, "*pinoy*." The term "*tsinoy*" may suggest someone who is half Chinese and half Filipino — a cultural hybrid. There may be a sense of equal parts about it. But it could instead be taken as a compound of an adjective (*tsî*) modifying a noun (*noy*) and thus be like "Chinese Filipino." Whichever the case, it also has an informality that suggests a desire for more intimacy between Chinese and Filipinos. These terms are now widely used in the Philippine media in English and Filipino. Some earlier terms survive in *tsinoy* usage. "Sino," a pejorative term in earlier English-language writings about ethnic Chinese, is now used in *tsinoy* publications to refer to non-Philippine Chinese. "*Intsik*," besides its continued usage by Filipinos, also appears at times among *tsinoys*, as in "a genuine *intsik*," referring to a Philippine Chinese less acculturated than the *tsinoy* who is speaking.

Finally, a word about the Quadrangle. Despite the sense of arms-length distance that is now felt between the Philippines and both mainland China and Taiwan, Hokkiens still travel between and work within each of the four elements of the Quadrangle. Taiwan entrepreneurs invest in Fujian and in the Philippines. Philippine Hokkiens go to work for Taiwanese entrepreneurs in Taiwan or teach school in Fujian. Hong Kong Hokkien migrants keep alive Fujian's business connections to the outside world. Taiwanese students study at Philippine universities. Where Philippine Chinese investment in Fujian is concerned, family members living in Fujian are often the local partners rather than dependents as in the past. As partners, they may provide labor recruitment, local political and business connections and arrangements, and local management — a formula that is often called, after the popular locality name, the "Jinjiang Model."[58]

The research agenda implicit in this essay has many dimensions. In relation to the transnational system, we have studied its effects only upon the Philippine Hokkiens' cultural life. The experience of non-Hokkiens — the fifteen to twenty percent of Philippine Chinese who are Cantonese — is an obvious topic. The various aspects of transnationally influenced life in Hong Kong, Taiwan, and Fujian during this period is another. A second question during this period: does the family's home base shift from rural China to the overseas residential site (in this case, Hong Kong or the Philippines) — now to be seen as the base of family operations and hence perhaps the new site of ancestral tablets? If so, when? Was this happening before the post-1975 era of globalization that is now being written about?[59]

And last, regarding Overseas Chinese comparisons, there is the topic of China-substitutes, specifically Taiwan in this period. We should compare the experiences of Philippine Chinese with those of the ethnic Chinese of South Vietnam and Thailand, the two other Southeast Asian countries that had official relations with Taiwan during the 1950s and 1960s Comparison with the experiences of the Chinese in North America should also be attempted.

3

On Eating Chinese: Diasporic Agency and the Chinese Canadian Restaurant Menu

Lily Cho

Almost nobody does it anymore. If you take the slower road south down the middle of Alberta from Edmonton to Calgary, following the old rail line, you will cut across Main Street, Olds, Alberta, where you might stop for lunch at the A & J Family Restaurant (see Figure 3.1). In 1915, you would have stepped across the railway platform (the railway stopped running a long time ago but the station is still there, empty and abandoned) and ordered a hot lunch at what was then known simply as the Public Lunch Counter (see Figure 3.2). There is a long history to the small-town Chinese Canadian restaurant. Work on Chinese diaspora communities in Canada has tended to focus on representations of Chinese immigrants in large urban centres such as Vancouver and Toronto. Although locations such as Vancouver's Chinatown continue to be crucial sites for exploring Chineseness in Canada, relatively little attention has been paid to the more disparate but nonetheless persistently present communities of Chinese people in small towns across Canada. Recently, critics such as Ien Ang and Aihwa Ong have explored the important ways in which postmodern ethnicities and flexible citizenships intervene in a hegemonic idea of China as a centre of identification. And yet, in the speed of the shifts that critical discussions of Chinese diaspora culture have adopted, I want to turn to the possibility of considering slowness, of a seemingly anachronistic Chineseness — for example, that of the small-town Chinese Canadian restaurant — as a site of diasporic resistance and agency. Chinese immigration changed the restaurant industry in Canada. According to the 1931 Canadian census, Chinese made up less than one percent of the Canadian

Figure 3.1 A & J Family Restaurant

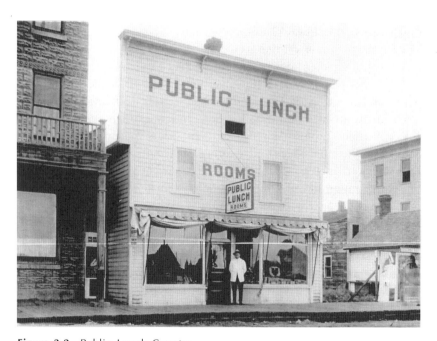

Figure 3.2 Public Lunch Counter

population, and yet one out of every five restaurant-, café-, or tavern-keepers was of Chinese origin. More than one out of every three male cooks was Chinese (Reiter 30). It is no exaggeration to say that there are very few small towns in Canada without Chinese restaurants. This essay explores the small-town Chinese Canadian restaurant and traces the possibilities of Chinese diasporic agency in the text of menus taken from three time periods: the Exclusion era of the 1920s; the 1950s; and the contemporary period, late-twentieth and early-twenty-first centuries. Taking a slower path, along the abandoned rail lines which carry in them the echo of a history of indentured Chinese labour,[1] and stopping in at the restaurants which are inevitably located near now empty train stations, I hope to recover the bond between slowness and memory, one location of Chinese diasporic agency, in the time of the menu.

Non-Urban Diasporas and the Problem of Agency

One of the strongest arguments for diasporic agency lies in reading them as challenges to hegemonic nation-state formations. Diasporas have been read as social formations that contest the integrity of the European nation-state. As Khachig Tölölyan notes, just as the nation-state has begun to encounter limits to its hegemonic desires, diasporas have emerged in intellectual discourses as exemplary communities of this particular transnational moment (4). For Tölölyan, the "*nation's* aspiration to normative homogeneity is challenged by various forms of cultural practices and knowledge production, *especially in major urban centers* and in the arts and humanities departments of many North American and Australian universities" (4, latter emphasis mine). I agree with Tölölyan's subsequent observations in the article around the need for rigorous attention to the ways in which diasporic critical practice may in fact collude with the very forms of hegemonic power that these critical practices see diasporas as challenging.[2] However, I want to take issue with Tölölyan's emphasis on the metropolitan diaspora. Tölölyan's discussion gestures to a wider tendency in current diaspora studies which naturalizes and emphasizes the diasporic as a distinctly urban formation. In the discussion of diaspora's challenge to the nation-state in particular, critics have relegated the disruptive potential of diasporas solely within the realm the metropolitan migrant.

Building on his work in *The Black Atlantic*, in *Against Race*, Paul Gilroy argues that "[c]onsciousness of diaspora affiliation stands opposed to the distinctively modern structures and modes of power orchestrated by the institutional complexity of nation-states. Diaspora identification exists outside of and sometimes in opposition to the political forms and codes of modern citizenship" (124). For Gilroy, diasporas allow for the emergence of complex subjectivities which work against forms of nationalism: "… valuing diaspora more highly than the coercive unanimity of the nation, the concept [of diaspora] becomes explicitly antinational. This shift is connected with transforming the familiar unidirectional nature of diaspora as a form of catastrophic but simple dispersal that enjoys an identifiable and reversible originary moment — the site of trauma — into something far more complex" (128). Similarly, Leela Gandhi sees diasporas as locations of post-national culture. Although she criticizes overly romanticized conceptions of diasporic exile, she follows Gilroy in viewing diasporas as locations of transnational and post-national cultural formations. Noting that "[s]ubsequent waves of voluntary and unwanted migrations continue to challenge the cultural and demographic stability of the Western world," Gandhi sees diasporas as "troubling [the] reciprocity between the metropolitan center and the colonial periphery" so that "the metropolis is not safe from the cultural contagion of its own 'peripheral practices'" (134). Gandhi's reading of diaspora's potential as a contagious force returning to infect the culture of the metropolitan centre echoes Homi Bhabha's argument for diasporic agency within the context of nationalism.

In "DissemiNation," Bhabha reads in the figure of the diasporic migrant the potential for a disruption of the integrity of the colonial national through the haunting return of the post-colonial migrant. Productively intervening in Benedict Anderson's use of Walter Benjamin's idea of "homogenous empty time,"[3] Bhabha highlights the profound ambivalence in Benjamin's concept of homogenous empty time that is overlooked in Anderson's use. Bhabha suggests that the time of the nation is actually split into a performative and a pedagogical time: "In the production of nation as narration there is a split between the continuist, accumulative temporality of the pedagogical, and the repetitious, recursive strategy of the performative. It is through this process of splitting that the conceptual ambivalence of modern society becomes the site of *writing the nation*" (Bhabha 145–6). In diasporic subjects, Bhabha locates a disruptive potential in which cultural difference frustrates the desire for repetitious similarity in the articulation of the nation:

> The aim of cultural difference is to rearticulate the sum of knowledge from the perspective of the signifying position of the minority that resists totalization — the repetition that will not return as the same, the minus-in-origin that results in political and discursive strategies where adding to does not add up but serves to disturb the calculation of power and knowledge, producing other spaces of subaltern signification. (Bhabha 162)

In this idea of a culturally different migrant who disturbs the enunciation of the Western nation, Bhabha sees the beginnings of diasporic agency. The principal agency of the diasporic subject in "DissemiNation" is that of the haunting return of the avenging angel of the post-colonial subject migrating to the colonial metropole. Writing of Salman Rushdie's archangel Gibreel Farishta in *The Satanic Verses*, Bhabha suggests "Gibreel's returning gaze crosses out the synchronous history of England, the essentialist memories of William the Conqueror and the Battle of Hastings" (168). In this configuration of diasporic agency, "through Gibreel, the avenging migrant, we learn the ambivalence of cultural difference: it is the articulation *through* incommensurability that structures all narratives of identification, and all acts of cultural translation" (Bhabha 169).

While this reading of agency illuminates the way in which difference disturbs the unifying time of nationhood, it also poses some substantial conceptual problems for thinking about diasporic agency. What does it mean for diasporic agency to lie solely in the act of a ghostly haunting? This reading risks reducing diasporic agency to something that happens only in the mind of the colonizer. Although there are a number of issues within this reading, let me focus on two major limitations with Bhabha's conception of the agential, avenging diasporic angel.

The first lies in the forgetting of historical diasporas. Although Bhabha gestures to the diasporas produced by slavery, indenture, and dispossession,[4] their inclusion in a list does not translate into a full recognition of their particularities. The historical "old" diasporas of indenture,[5] such as those of the West Indian plantation workers or Chinese railway workers, do not have a place in the diasporic agency of "DissemiNation." As I outline later in this essay, their agency does not necessarily lie in their return to metropole, their haunting of metropolitan consciousness. Rather, we might read the agency of old diasporas precisely in their non-metropolitan persistence.

The second limit lies in the unrelenting urbanity of Bhabha's avenging diasporic subject. Closing the essay with a meditation on the English weather, "DissemiNation" begins with the scattering of peoples and ends with "their gathering in the city. The return of the diasporic; the postcolonial" (169). He argues that the city is the primary site of this diasporic agency:

> ... it is to the city that the migrants, the minorities, the diasporic come to change the history of the nation. If I have suggested that the people emerge in the finitude of the nation, marking the liminality of cultural identity, producing the double-edged discourse of social territories and temporalities, then in the West, and increasingly elsewhere, it is the city which provides the space in which emergent identifications and new

social movements of the people are played out. It is there that, in our time, the perplexity of living is most acutely experienced. (Bhabha 170)

Bhabha's diasporic agent is relentlessly metropolitan. And yet, in the case of indentured railway workers or sugar plantation workers, we have diasporic subjects who do not need to engage in any kind of haunting return to the metropolitan centres of subjugation. They were there before the nation became a nation. Chinese migrant labourers arrived in Canada in 1858, nearly ten years before Canada would become Canada.

In many ways, much of the discussion that follows can be viewed as a dialogue with Bhabha's "DissemiNation." The influence of the essay as an enormously useful intervention in our thinking on Anderson's imagined communities and the idea of the nation makes a critique of its notion of agency even more crucial. While the essay never declared itself to be a meditation on diasporic agency, the closing discussion of Rushdie's archangel Gibreel is one of the few places in critical discussions where the agency of diasporic subjects is discussed explicitly in their challenge to the European nation-state. And yet, the overwhelming emphasis on the urban location, on the city as the site of agential return, has led to a series of omissions. As I examine later in this essay, in discussions of the Chinese diaspora, work such as Aihwa Ong's *Flexible Citizenship*, the discussion of diasporic and transnational agency in Chinese communities has come at the expense of a different kind of flexible citizen — that of the non-metropolitan migrant who has slowly and persistently asserted a particular and subversive script of nationhood.

Sometimes abandoned where rail line contracts ended,[6] sometimes voluntarily seeking out locations for new work, a significant number of early Chinese migrants settled in non-urban locations, in small towns and villages throughout Canada. These migrants have no place in Bhabha's metropolitan migrancy. They do not perform a return to the centre. Rather, they engage in a form of emplacement. Through texts such as the menus of small-town Chinese restaurants, we can trace some of the ways in which they participate in the scripting of their incorporation into the body politic of Canada.

As I noted earlier, Chinese immigrants dominated the early restaurant industry in Canada. Following a variety of paths, Chinese immigrants operated more restaurants than did any other single immigrant group in Canada. As Wickberg's work on the 1921 census of Canada shows, Chinese immigrants operated forty percent of the restaurant industry in Alberta, fifty percent of the restaurant industry in Saskatchewan, and about a third of the restaurants in Manitoba and Ontario (Wickberg, Table 12). The history of Chinese who had worked as cooks on railway and lumber camps as well as domestic servants in Vancouver and Victoria suggests that there would have been a substantial number of Chinese immigrants who had already been trained in cooking for non-Chinese tastes. What is so interesting, then, is the way in which Chinese immigrants in Canada have taken positions of servility and unwanted labour and used them to embed within a text such as the restaurant menu their own definitions of Canadian or Western.

In the menus of small-town Chinese restaurant menus, Chinese cooks and restaurateurs create and then contain the particular text of nationhood that emerges on the menu. They execute precisely the split of nation time that Bhabha outlines in "DissemiNation." However, in the time of the menu, Chinese diasporic subjects emerge as manipulators of this split enunciation of nation time. The homogenous empty time of the Chinese restaurant menu emerges from the hands of Chinese restaurateurs as a subversive text that defines and delineates the idea of Canada for Canadians. In this sense, I locate the agency of Chinese diasporic subjects in Canada not in an impossible return to metropole but in the engineering of a mechanics of incorporation. The naturalization of the Chinese restaurant in the landscape of small-town Canada speaks to the way in which Chinese migrants have embedded particular forms of knowledge and practices, disseminating a vision of what "Canadian" and "Chinese" mean through the text of the restaurant menu and asserting a different time of experience. Rather than reading for agency in spatial terms, in the haunting presence of an avenging diasporic angel, in the discreetly demarcated spaces of urban Chinatowns, I want to look at the challenges which Chinese diasporic communities in Canada pose temporally. That is, against the dominant European Enlightenment march of progress, the small-town Chinese Canadian restaurant menu suggests an alternative temporality.

In his book of poetry about his father's restaurant in Nelson, British Columbia, *Diamond Grill*, Wah writes that "[m]aps don't have beginnings, just edges. Some frayed and hazy margin of possibility, absence, gap"(1). Reading the menu as a map to an alternative discourse, this essay explores three margins, three spaces of possibility, which work together to produce the agency of Chinese migrants — an agency which emerges not in a haunting of the metropolitan centre but in the persistence of the pedestrian, the slow embeddedness of everyday life.

Canadian or Western food: Inventing Canadian food

Nowhere else is Canadian food more consistently defined than on the menus of small-town Chinese Canadian restaurants (see Figure 3.3). Although dishes

PARKVIEW

CHINESE CUISINE
& WESTERN FOOD *Restaurant*

☎ 398-3650

114 - 6 Ave., THORHILD, ALBERTA

NAME _____ PHONE NO. _____ DATE _____

ADDRESS _____ SUB TOTAL FORWARD $ _____

QTY.		PRICE	QTY.		PRICE
	APPETIZERS			**SEAFOOD**	
	01. Egg Roll (each)	1.70		45. Deep Fried Shrimp in Batter	8.25
	02. Fried Chicken Wings	5.75		46. Curry Shrimp //	9.75
	03. Dry Garlic Pork Spareribs	6.25		47. Pan Fried Shrimp //	9.75
	04. Deep Fried Wonton	4.50		*fresh prawns with shell overloaded in a spiced seasoning*	
				48. Shrimp with Black Bean Sauce	9.75
	SOUP			*fresh shell off prawns sauteed with a black bean sauce*	
	05. Wonton Soup	3.00		49. Shrimp with Mixed Vegetables	9.75
	06. Chinese Chicken Noodle Soup	3.95		*fresh shell off prawns sauteed with vegetables*	
	07. War Wonton Soup (for two)	7.75		50. Shrimp with Tomato Sauce	9.75
	CANTONESE STYLE CHOW MEIN			**COMBINATIONS**	
	(Vegetable with Noodle)				
	Your Choice of			No. 1	6.50
	08. Beef, Pork or Chicken Chow Mein	6.95		Sweet & Sour Pork Spareribs	
	09. Shrimp Chow Mein	9.75		Deep Fried Shrimp in Batter	
	10. Special Chow Mein	7.50		Chicken Fried Rice	
	FRIED RICE			No. 2	6.50
	Your Choice of			Chicken Chop Suey	
	11. Beef, Chicken, or B.B.Q. Pork Fried Rice	5.25		Sweet & Sour Boneless Pork	
	12. Mushroom Fried Rice	5.25		Chicken Fried Rice	
	13. Shrimp Fried Rice	5.95			
	14. Special Fried Rice	6.25		No. 3	6.50
	15. Plain Fried Rice	4.50		Sweet & Sour Chicken Balls	
	16. Steamed Rice	1.00		Beef with Mixed Vegetables	
				Chicken Fried Rice	
	PORK & SPARERIBS				
	17. Sweet & Sour Pork Spareribs	6.50		No. 4	7.25
	18. Sweet & Sour Boneless Pork	7.25		Sweet & Sour Chicken Balls	
	19. Honey & Garlic Pork Spareribs	6.75		Beef with Mixed Vegetables	
				Chicken Fried Rice	
	CHOP SUEY (Bean Sprout)			Dry Garlic Pork Spareribs	
	Your Choice of				
	20. Beef, Chicken or B.B.Q. Pork	5.50		**SUGGESTIONS FOR GROUPS**	
	21. Shrimp Chop Suey	5.95			
	22. Special Chop Suey	6.25		Dinner For 2	16.95
				Egg Roll (2)	
	CHOW MEIN			Deep Fried Shrimp	
	(Bean Sprout with Dry Noodle)			Sweet & Sour Boneless Pork	
	Your Choice of			Beef with Mixed Vegetables	
	23. Beef, Chicken or B.B.Q. Pork	5.95		Chicken Fried Rice	
	24. Shrimp Meat Chow Mein	6.25			
	25. Special Chow Mein	6.50		Dinner For 4	34.95
	26. Shanghai Chow Mein w/ Bean Sprout	6.50		Egg Roll (4)	
	27. Hong Kong Style Chow Mein			Deep Fried Shrimp	
	with Bean Sprout	6.50		Sweet & Sour Chicken Balls	
				Beef with Mixed Vegetables	
	EGG FOO YONG			Chicken Fried Rice	
	Your choice of				
	28. Chicken, B.B.Q. Pork or Mushroom	6.50		Dinner For 6	57.95
	29. Shrimp Meat Egg Foo Yong	6.95		Egg Roll (6)	
				Shrimp with Mixed Vegetables	
	BEEF			Honey Garlic Pork Spareribs	
	30. Tender Beef with Broccoli	7.25		Sweet & Sour Boneless Pork	
	31. Beef & Vegetables	7.25		Sweet & Sour Chicken Balls	
	sliced tender beef cooked with assorted greens			Szechuan Beef • Special Fried Rice	
	32. Beef with Black Bean Sauce	7.75			
	tender beef sauteed with vegetables & a black bean sauce				
	33. Beef with Green Onions	7.75		**Western Fast Food - Burger**	
	sliced tender beef sauteed with green onions			50. Hamburger with Fries	3.20
	34. Curry Beef //	7.75		51. Cheese Burger with Fries	3.50
	35. Szechuan Beef ///	8.50		52. Cheese Burger Deluxe	4.25
	crispy beef sauteed in ginger & hot sauce			53. Super Burger with Fries	4.75
				54. Gravy	0.25
	CHICKEN			55. Sweet & Sour Sauce	0.25
	36. Sweet & Sour Chicken Balls	6.95			
	37. Chicken with Mixed Vegetables	7.25		**Special Orders**	
	38. Hung Yun Soo Guy	7.25			
	deep fried chicken breast with almonds				
	39. Lemon Chicken	7.25			
	40. Almond Chicken (Guy Ding)	7.50			
	tender sliced chicken sauteed w/ diced veg. & almonds				
	41. Cashew Chicken	7.50			
	tender sliced chicken sauteed w/ diced veg. & cashew nuts				
	42. Mushroom Chicken Balls	7.50			
	43. Chicken with Black Bean Sauce	7.75			
	sliced chicken sauteed w/ veg. & a black bean sauce				
	44. Curry Chicken //	7.75			

Prices Subject to Change without Notice   */ Slightly Hot   // Hot   /// Very Hot*   *Prices Do Not Include G.S.T.*

Figure 33.(a) Parkview Restaurant menu

WESTERN FAVORITES
(Below Items Come with French Fries)

Cheese Burger	4.50
Bacon Cheese Burger	5.50
Chicken Burger	4.50
Fish Burger	5.50
Club House Sandwich	5.50
Chicken Nuggets	4.95
Fried Chicken	6.95
Fish and Chips	5.50
Steak Sandwich N.Y. Strip with Garlic Toast	8.50
Hamburger Steak	5.95
Beef Liver & Onion	5.95
Hot Hamburger Sandwich	5.95
Hot Turkey Sandwich	5.95
Hot Beef Sandwich	5.95
**********	
Spaghetti with Meat Sauce & Garlic Toast	4.95

Chinese & Western Smorg
Includes Salad Bar and Dessert

Hours
Everyday 11:30 a.m. - 2:00 p.m.
Every Night 5:00 p.m. - 8:00 p.m.

**Special Price For Kids
Discount For Seniors**

Suggestions For Chinese Dinner

(A) Dinner For 1
Pineapple Chicken Balls
Or, Sweet & Sour Shrimps
With Chicken Fried Rice
6.00

(B) Dinner For 1
Sweet & Sour Ribs Or,
Breaded Dry Ribs with
Chicken Fried Rice
6.00

(C) Dinner For 1
Egg Roll
Sweet & Sour Ribs
Chicken Chow Mein
Chicken Fried Rice
7.50

(D) Dinner For 1
Egg Roll
Sweet & Sour
Chicken Ball
Fried Beef With Broccoli
Chicken Fried Rice
7.50

(E) Dinner For 1
Sweet & Sour Shrimp
Fried Beef with Chinese
Greens
Chicken Fried Rice
7.50

(F) Dinner For 1
Ginger Beef
Sweet & Sour
Chicken Balls
Fried Beef with
Chinese Greens
Chicken Fried Rice 9.50

(G) Dinner For 2
Egg Rolls (2)
Chicken Mushroom
Chow Mein
Sweet & Sour Ribs
Pineapple Chicken Balls
Chicken Fried Rice
18.00

(H) Dinner for 3
Egg Rolls (3)
Deep Fried Shrimp
In Batter
Sweet & Sour Ribs
Fried Beef with
Chinese Greens
Chicken Fried Rice 28.00

(I) Dinner For 4
Egg Rolls (4)
Deep Fried Shrimp
In Batter
Fried Beef with
Chinese Greens
Chicken Fried Rice
Pineapple Chicken Balls
Or, Sweet & Sour
Boneless Pork 38.00

(J) Dinner For 5
Egg Rolls (5)
Deep Fried Shrimp
In Batter
Pineapple Chicken
Balls
Club Special Chop Suey
Ginger Beef
Club Special Fried Rice
46.00

(Additional Person For G to J - $9.90)

Printed by CITY PRINTS LTD. (403) 271-8999

Club Café

MAIN STREET, INNISFAIL
FULLY LICENSED
SPECIALIZING IN CHINESE FOOD

**OPEN 7 DAYS A WEEK
TAKE-OUT MENU**

PLEASE PHONE

227☎3179

FREE DELIVERY SERVICE WITH
MINIMUM FOOD ORDER OF $15.00
WITHIN TOWN LIMITS.

PICK-UP ORDER OVER $15.00
10% OFF WHEN PAID BY CASH.

5% OFF ON CREDIT CARD.

Prices Subject To Change Without Notice

Appetizers
Spring Rolls (each)	1.50
Crisp Egg Roll (each)	1.50
Deep Fried Wonton	5.50
Grilled Pork Dumplings (10)	5.95
Deep Fried Chicken Wings	5.95
Hot Spice Chicken Wings	5.95
Honey Garlic Chicken Wings	6.50

Soup & Noodles
1.	Hot and Sour Soup	4.95
2.	Chicken Noodle	3.95
3.	Beef or Pork Noodle	3.95
4.	Wonton Soup	3.95
5.	Wor Wonton Chinese Style	8.95
	(for 2 to 3 person servings)	

Chow Mein
6.	Chicken Chow Mein	6.25
7.	Chicken Mushroom Chow Mein	6.50
8.	Mushroom Chow Mein	6.25
9.	Shrimp Chow Mein	6.25
10.	Beef Chow Mein	6.25
11.	Pork Chow Mein	6.25
12.	Chow Mein Cantonese Style	8.95
	(shrimp, chicken, beef and pork)	
13.	Shanghai Fried Noodle	6.95

Chop Suey
14.	Chicken Chop Suey	5.95
15.	Chicken Mushroom Chop Suey	6.25
16.	Mushroom Chop Suey	5.95
17.	Shrimp Chop Suey	6.95
18.	Beef Chop Suey	5.95
19.	Pork Chop Suey	5.95

20.	Club Special Chop Suey	8.95
	(shrimp, chicken, beef and pork)	
21.	Stir Fried Mixed Vegetable	6.50

Rice
22.	Vegetable Fried Rice	4.95
23.	Chicken Fried Rice	5.65
24.	Shrimp Fried Rice	6.50
25.	Beef Fried Rice	5.65
26.	Pork Fried Rice	5.65
27.	Mushroom Fried Rice	5.65
28.	Curried Beef Fried Rice	5.65
29.	Club Special Fried Rice	6.95
30.	Steamed Rice	1.25

Dainty Eggs
31.	Vegetable Egg Foo-Yong	5.95
32.	Chicken Egg Foo-Yong	6.50
33.	Shrimp Egg Foo-Yong	6.85
34.	Mushroom Egg Foo-Yong	6.50
35.	Beef Egg Foo-Yong	6.50
36.	Pork Egg Foo-Yong	6.50

Seafoods
37.	Deep Fried Shrimp in Batter	8.25
38.	Deep Fried Shrimp with Fresh Tomatoes	8.25
39.	Sweet and Sour Shrimps	8.25
40.	Pineapple Shrimps	8.50
41.	Chow Har Lock with Vegetables	9.95
42.	Curried Shrimp with Vegetables	9.95
43.	Palace Shrimp (Hot Dish)	9.95
44.	Dried Salt & Pepper Shrimp (Shell)	13.95
45.	Dried Salt & Pepper Squid	8.95

Chicken
46.	Sweet & Sour Chicken Balls	6.95
47.	Pineapple Chicken Balls	7.25
48.	Chicken Balls with Fresh Tomatoes	7.25
49.	Mushrooms & Vegetables Chicken Balls	7.25
50.	Palace Chicken (Hot Dish)	9.95
51.	Curried Chicken With Vegetables	7.95
52.	Diced Almond Chicken (Guy Ding)	7.85
53.	Breaded Almond Chicken Soo Guy (with bean sprouts)	7.85
54.	Chicken with Black Bean Sauce	7.85
55.	Moo Goo Guy Pan (Chicken)	7.85
56.	Breaded Chicken with Lemon Sauce	7.85
57.	Dried Salt & Pepper Chicken	8.95

Beef
58.	Fried Beef with Broccoli	6.95
59.	Fried Beef with Green Peppers	7.25
60.	Fried Beef with Chinese Greens	7.25
61.	Fried Beef with Tomatoes	7.95
62.	Curried Beef with Vegetables	7.95
63.	Ginger Beef (Hot Dish)	8.25

Spareribs
64.	Sweet & Sour Ribs	6.95
65.	Pineapple Ribs	7.25
66.	Breaded Garlic Dry Ribs	7.25
67.	Honey Garlic Ribs	7.25
68.	Spareribs with Black Bean Sauce	7.95
69.	Sweet and Sour Boneless Pork	7.50

Figure 3.3(b)   Club Café menu

such as tortière, Atlantic seafood chowder, or beaver tails are arguably more "Canadian" than the hamburgers and french fries that are typical of the "Canadian" portion of the Chinese Canadian restaurant menu, the Chinese Canadian restaurant menu specifically names a series of dishes as Canadian or Western. More than that, "Canadian" is often used interchangeably with "Western." I want to suggest that one margin of possibility for locating Chinese diasporic agency in Canada lies in the way in which Chinese cooks and restaurateurs name and define Canadian and Western for Canadians. The question is not so much what exactly is Canadian about hamburgers and fries, but what it means for this version of Canadianness to circulate with such persistence through the Chinese restaurant. After all, what does it mean that the Chinese restaurant has become the defining locus of Canadian?

In his essay "Steak and Chips" in *Mythologies*, Roland Barthes gestures towards a way of reading the semiotics of food and national culture. For Barthes, an "item of food sums up and transmits a situation; it constitutes an information; it signifies" ("Psychosociology" 21). Reviewing the story of General de Castries's first meal after the armistice in what is now Vietnam, Barthes associates chips, *les frites*, with Frenchness:

> [C]hips are nostalgic and patriotic like steak. *Match* told us that after the armistice in Indo-China '*General de Castries, for his first meal, asked for chips*'… the General's request was certainly not a vulgar materialistic reflex, but an episode in the ritual of appropriating the regained French community. The General understood well our national symbolism; he knew that *la frite*, chips, are the alimentary sign of Frenchness. (63–4)

Barthes's description of the Frenchness of *frites* links the alimentary sign not only to French culture but also to a moment of French colonialism and nationalism. Chips function in this story to signify and consolidate French power on foreign and colonized soil. Even in Indo-China, the general will have his steak and chips. And yet a few decades after the French general's meal in Indochina, on the contemporary Chinese Canadian restaurant menu, *les frites*, french fries, have somehow becomes an integral part of what is understood as Canadian.

In placing the french fry, what had been a symbol of French colonial power, under the category of Canadian, the contemporary Chinese restaurant menu does more than simply gesture towards an increasingly homogenized fast-food culture. The french fry's migration from French national symbol to that of a staple of what is labelled Canadian on the menu gestures towards one way in which we can read the interchangeability of "Canadian" and

"Western" on the menu. The collusion between Canadian and Western situates the idea of Canada within the terrain of Westernness, something that stands in stark opposition to the plural and multicultural visions of Canadian nationalism that have been such a significant part of post-1970s Canada. Of course, the idea of Western is a relative one. But on menus, it is very clear that Canadian or Western is defined over and against Chinese. The text of the menu suggests that Canadian is a specifically Western, in the sense of Western European, construction. By understanding restaurant workers and operators as writers, as producers of the text of the menu, we can read the menus as scripting a notion of Canadian that explicitly excludes Chinese, even though Chineseness frames this scripting of the idea of Canadian.

Through the form of the menu, Chinese diasporic subjects recode Canadian settler colonial discourse. Along with Benedict Anderson's linking of the novel and the newspaper, the menu can be thought of as a textual form that helped to consolidate a particular idea of national culture. Like the novel and the newspaper, the menu benefited from the rise of print capitalism in the eighteenth century. Rebecca Sprang's work in *The Invention of the Restaurant* suggests a close connection between conceptions of French culture and the French restaurant menu in the eyes of others. Drawing on the doubled meaning *la carte* — the map and the menu — Sprang notes that the menu provided a tangible, bound, iconic space in which to imagine the space of the nation (192–3). "French 'national character' revealed itself to foreign tourists in the dining rooms of Paris restaurants. 'Tell me what you eat, and I will tell you who you are,' wrote Brillat-Savarin in 1826 …" (197). The *carte*, the map, the menu, remains with us as one of the primary means by which food is represented, textualized.

The form of the menu gestures to the way in which Chinese restaurateurs have seized a specifically European, French in this case, restaurant convention and used it as a means of reproducing and disseminating Chineseness while defining the idea of Canada for Canadians. The menu as we now know it — a printed object, often folded in quarto or as a small booklet, with a list of the restaurant's offerings and the prices next to them — is intimately related to the history of European literary innovation. Exploring the development of the restaurant through print culture, Sprang traces the changes in the eighteenth- and nineteenth-century French menu with the innovations in French literary production.

> The shape and appearance of menus changed considerably during the nineteenth century, but each new format was shared by every place that was 'a restaurant.' The menu's layout consistently mimicked the century's

typographic innovations: first a single large folio, packed with columns of closely printed type; then a small booklet, leather-covered and bound with silken cord; then again a single sheet, hand-decorated with languid goddesses and stylized flowers. Thus, while the early menus looked like the newspapers of the Consulate and the first Empire, mid-nineteenth century menus resembled fat realist novels, and those of the Belle Époque, poster art. The menu kept pace with the era's literary production because it was itself a sort of literary product, the restaurant's most marked — and marking — generic innovation. (Sprang 188–9)

The development of the menu follows the trajectory of the rise of other major eighteenth-century literary forms — the novel and the newspaper. In the imaginary community of a dining public, the production of the menu as a text whose typography and form adopted an increasingly stable structure helped to stabilize the restaurant as a distinct industry. As Sprang notes, the menu differentiated the restaurant as a restaurant from all other public eating institutions. The introduction of a printed menu marked one of the most significant moments in the invention of the Western restaurant. In eighteenth-century France, the printed menu distinguished the restaurant from other public eating establishments such as inns or cafés, and standardized what would become an industry. "Before restaurants could be distinguished from one another, they first had to be separated from all other eateries, and the highly standardized menu structure did just that, making a number of businesses into a specific sort of cultural institution"(Sprang 189). Although the eighteenth-century French restaurants of Sprang's study are far removed from the Chinese restaurants of this discussion, both institutions share a name, and through the idiosyncrasies of naming, a genealogy. The menu, like the novel, reflected the changes in European typographic traditions.

Sprang's connection between the menu and the novel brings us back to some of the earliest work in post-colonial studies in which the empire wrote back to the centre by seizing imperial tools.[7] The post-colonial novel wrote back and rewrote the novel, the generic literary form that consolidated an entire European literary tradition in the eighteenth and nineteenth centuries. The diasporic Chinese menu functions also as a seizure of a form of cultural representation.

However, the standardization of burgers and fries as typical offerings on the Canadian side of the Chinese Canadian restaurant menu is a relatively recent occurrence. I would like to turn now to a menu from the 1950s, the menu of the Diamond Grill, a restaurant made famous by Fred Wah's book. A diner walking into the Diamond Grill would be given a menu in which the hamburgers and french fried potatoes are a very small part of a multitude of non-Chinese food offerings. Unlike contemporary menus, which mark the categories of Chinese and Canadian or Western explicitly, the Diamond Grill menu of the 1950s does not name its non-Chinese dishes as Canadian or Western. The non-Chinese food offerings are plentiful and diverse, going far beyond hamburgers to include seemingly more sophisticated dishes such as "Lyonnaise Potatoes," "Fresh Cracked Crab en Mayonnaise," "Lobster a la Newburg," and "Waldorf Salad." In contrast, the Chinese food offerings almost seem like an afterthought, tacked on at the end of the menu, after the listing of the beverages and just before the fountain menu. Small-town restaurants operated by Chinese people did not always serve Chinese food. In the 1920s, when New Dayton was a thriving small town that had not yet been swallowed up by Lethbridge, Charlie Chew's New Dayton Café did not serve any Chinese food at all[8] (see Figure 3.4). Even though the New Dayton Café was clearly a restaurant operated by a Chinese migrant, like the Diamond Grill, it does not declare itself to be a Chinese restaurant, much less a Chinese and Canadian one. Moreover, there is almost no consistency among the 1923 menu of the New Dayton, the 1950s menu of the Diamond Grill, and that of contemporary restaurants such as the Golden Wheel or the Parkview. The Westernness of the menu constantly shifts, reinventing itself throughout the period of this sample.

In this shifting Westernness of the menu items, the pedagogical time of Canadianness emerges on the menu. Like a novel progressing through the empty national time of Canadian nationhood, the Canadian menu grows into itself. In the clocked, calendrical time of Canada's emergence into nationhood, the story of national emergence can be read in the simultaneity of the its progressive shifts from the simple short order and fountain menu of the New Dayton, to the full and impressive selection at the Diamond, and then to its streamlined modernity at the Club Cafe.

Chinese Food: Reproducing Chineseness

Unlike the Western dishes on the menus, the Chinese dishes have changed relatively little since their first appearance on the 1950s Chinese Canadian restaurant menu. The offerings of Chinese food on the contemporary menu may be more numerous than those at the Diamond Grill, but they read as merely variations on the same reliable basics as the Diamond Grill offered. Turning to the back of the menu to the "Diamond Grill Special Chinese Dishes," a diner would encounter chicken chop suey and rice first on the list. At the Diamond, you could get one kind of chop suey. At the Club Cafe,

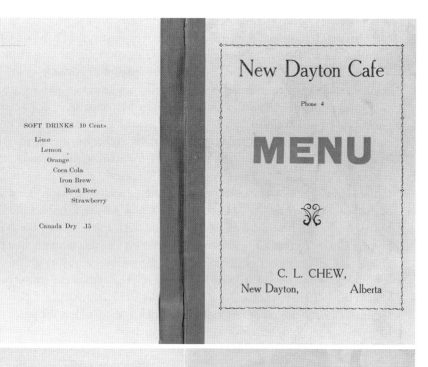

SOFT DRINKS 10 Cents

Lime
Lemon
Orange
Coca Cola
Iron Brew
Root Beer
Strawberry

Canada Dry .15

New Dayton Cafe

Phone 4

MENU

C. L. CHEW,

New Dayton,   Alberta

Short Order Bill of Fare

BREAKFAST

Bran Flakes with Milk	.15
Corn Flakes	.15
Shredded Wheat	.15
Hot Cakes and Syrup	.25
Toast and Tea or Coffee	.15
French Toast with Jelly	.45
Hot Milk Toast	.25
Cream Toast	.35

Canned Soup .... .30

Eggs and Omelettes .50

Ham and Eggs............

Poached,   Fried,   Boiled

Steak and Chops........ .50

Steak,   Pork Chops,   Rib Steak,   Hamburger Steak

Fried Fish   Sausage

Canned Pork and Beans   Canned Salmon
Canned Sardines   Tamales
                               Chili Con Carne

Extra with Steak, Fried Onions............ .10

SHORT ORDERS

T-Bone Steak	.75
Sirloin Steak	.65
Pork Chops Breaded	.60
Canned Crab Meat	.65
Canned Veal Loaf	.55
Canned Spaghetti	.55
Canned Oysters	.60
Canned Shrimp	.60

Bacon and Eggs ....

PASTRY

Apple Pie	.10
Raisin Pie	.10
Mince Pie	.10
Cream Pie	.10
Sauce Fruit	.10

BEVERAGES

Coffee, per cup	.10
Tea, per pot	.10
Glass of Milk	.10
Cream, per glass	.20

SANDWICHES

Combination	.30
Ham and Egg	.25
Cold Ham	.15
Cheese	.15
Fried Ham	.20
Sausage	.20
Hamburger	.25
Egg	.15
Denver	.30
Sardines	.25

ICE CREAM AND SOFT DRINKS

Plain Ice Cream	.15
Marsh Mallow	.20
Strawberry	.20
Pineapple	.20
Butter	.20
Chocolate	.20
Maple Walnut	.25
Whole Cherry	.25
Orange-Grape	.25
Banana	.25

SPECIALS

David Harum	.35
Merry Widow	.55
Banana Split	.40

ICE CREAM SODA

Lemon	.15
Cherry	.15
Pineapple	.15
Strawberry	.15
Chocolate	.15

SODA SPECIALS

Egg Nog	.15
Cold Lemonade	.15
Hot Lemonade	.15

Toast with Sandwiches is Extra

Coffee or Tea is Extra with all Sandwiches.

Figure 3.4 New Dayton Café menu

there are eight to choose from including: vegetable, BBQ pork, chicken, beef, and shrimp. Different, and yet basically the same. In the Chinese portion of the menu, the performative time of Canadian nationhood emerges through the menu's mechanical reproduction of a particular stereotype of Chineseness.

Although chop suey is a dish that has become iconic of inauthentic Chinese food, let me take seriously the Chineseness of chop suey and consider it as a sign of Chineseness under negotiation through reproduction. The Diamond Grill menu explicitly names chop suey as Chinese. In that naming, the menu textualizes Chineseness, providing a medium through which Chineseness can be reproduced and disseminated. As Sprang notes, menus develop in dialogue with one another — one restaurant will copy another's. In this process of pilfering and printing, a standardized restaurant cuisine emerges.

> As restaurateurs (and café-keepers) copied and reused menus, they disseminated a specialized terminology to a wider and wider audience. Insofar as very similar texts, if not exactly the same dishes, were available in a wide variety of eateries, names could spread semi-independently of that to which they had once referred ... The menu, by fixing names and titles, both addressed the fantasy and further created the expectation of identity and uniformity. Eaters were not meant to be uniform, but the eaten was, and if it was not, then differences ought to be understood and apparent, capable of being erected into a taxonomy. (191–2)

The print menu has helped to standardize what we have come to know as Chinese food. The menu develops dialogically, one copying another, one menu echoing the offerings of another one in an entirely new location. The menu is not only a record of displacement but also one of emplacement — it puts into place a kind of Chineseness that persists through the dissemination of the menu.

The standardization of Chinese dishes produces a soothing sameness in the representation of Chineseness on the menu. Just as you can walk into any small town in Canada and expect to find a Chinese restaurant, you can sit down at any one of these restaurants, open the menu, and find chop suey. Chop suey's representation of Chineseness produces a fixity and stability in the Chineseness in Canada. As Homi Bhabha notes in "The Other Question," one of the hallmarks of racial stereotypes is that of a fixity of representation:

> The stereotype is not a simplification because it is a false representation of a given reality. It is a simplification because it is an arrested, fixated form of representation that, in denying the play of difference ...

constitutes a problem for the representation of the subject in significations of psychic and social relations. (75)

The Chineseness represented on the Chinese restaurant menu functions within a persistent kind of stereotypicality. In the glowing artificiality of the red sauce for sweet and sour pork, there is a phantasmatic fixity to the representation of Chineseness on the menu. While the egg foo yong or the chow mein might be different from one restaurant to another, they use the same names for their dishes. Walking into the Parkview Restaurant in Thorhild, Alberta, a diner could reasonably expect to eat the same lemon chicken as he or she would eat at the Golden Wheel in Ponoka, Alberta. The expectation of a kind of sameness, a regularity to the experience of the menu, speaks not only to the rise of the Chinese restaurant as an institution but also to the institutionalization of a kind of standardized Chineseness disseminated through the menus of Chinese restaurants across the landscape of western Canada. Looking at the menus across a span of geographical space, they *are* remarkably similar. They are organized the same way; they have the same categories of food items (appetizers, soup, chop suey, chow mein, egg foo yong, and so on). They are structured along the lines of similar culinary expectations.

However, unlike colonial texts, the menus are texts in which the fixing occurs through those who are stereotyped. The Diamond Grill menu, for example, fixes and names the category of Chinese. In this sense, the menus function as a counter-text, institutionalizing the category of Chinese through items such as chop suey and chicken chow mein. This standardized sameness creates a language of Chineseness which functions as a different textualization circulating within Canadian culture. At once at the margins of culture, disparately spread out over vast geographies and away from urban centres, the consistency of the menus nonetheless asserts a pervasive Chineseness that departs from the definitions of Chinese perpetuated in Canadian law.[9]

As Bhabha usefully argues, a critique cannot be located at the level of whether or not good or bad stereotypes are being perpetuated; rather, it needs to be centered on the process of subjectification itself (75). In that sense, it would not be enough simply to say that an apparatus such as the restaurants produces counter-stereotypes that challenge the "negative" ones of a Euro-Canadian regime. And yet, in the case of the stereotypical Chineseness produced by Chinese restaurateurs on the menus, Chinese diaspora subjects are producing and perpetuating Chinese stereotypes. These are not necessarily "positive" stereotypes that have been put into circulation. In fact, the images in circulation eerily echo the projections of dominant culture. In that sense, they are actually serving back to power precisely its own projection. The unsettling moment happens not in the production of a stereotypical trope (fake Chinese food, the Chinese cook) but in the reproduction of the eerily familiar coming from the other.

In the Chineseness on the Chinese restaurant menu, there is an excessiveness to the representation. It is so simple, so uncomplicated, so palatable in that it is exactly what whiteness might expect of Chineseness. This diasporic staging of difference contests the ambivalence of colonial power because it exploits that ambivalence. And so the sameness.

> The process by which the metaphoric 'masking is inscribed on a lack which must then be concealed gives the stereotype both its fixity and its phantasmatic quality — the *same old* stories of the Negro animality, the Coolie's inscrutability, or the stupidity of the Irish *must* be told (compulsively) again and afresh, and are differently gratifying and terrifying each time. (Bhabha 77)

Yet, it is the Chinese diasporic subject who retells the same old story. It is the subject of settler colonial dominance who facilitates, through the space of the restaurant and the text of the restaurant menu, the compulsive return to the stereotype. It is so comforting because it anticipates projected desires. It is exactly what you ordered, what you wanted, given back to you. It fulfills the colonial hunger for itself; they consume their own projection. As I have discussed in the previous essay in the context of sweet and sour pork and the violence of identification, Chinese restaurateurs serve back to Europe-in-Canada their own Europeanness.

The menu stabilizes a kind of Chineseness that offers the consumer the possibility of a reassuring uniformity not only in the Chinese food on the menu but also in the Chineseness which Chinese food signifies. Chinese restaurant menus present a comforting, palatable Chineseness that can be reproduced and disseminated through the institution of the restaurant. The Diamond Grill menu presents eight unassuming "Special Chinese Dishes": items such as chicken chop suey and rice, chicken noodle, Chinese style, egg foo yong, and sweet and sour pork spare ribs and rice. The Chinese portion of the menu is very small compared to the restaurant's offerings of more than twenty-five different egg dishes, thirty different sandwiches, and thirty-two sundae options. The Chinese food on the menu does not challenge Western food for representational space on the menu, nor does it challenge the non-Chinese diner in content. The Chinese food items on the Diamond Grill menu have become standard fare at Chinese restaurants across the Prairies. Although the contemporary menus have more options, all of the dishes that the Diamond

Grill offered are still there. The uniformity of Chinese food on the menus suggests the creation of a uniform Chineseness that could be reproduced, disseminated and identified.

At the same time as the menu names and makes knowable a palatable Chineseness, it also troubles the possibility of fixing an authentic ethnicity. Inherent in the notion of reproduction is the problem of the original. While the menu allows for a mediated form of cultural contact, it also complicates the idea of an authentic or original Chineseness. The apparatus of mechanical reproduction in the printing of the restaurant menu mocks attempts at authenticity. Walter Benjamin argues in "The Work of Art in the Age of Mechanical Reproduction" that mechanical reproduction challenges the idea of authenticity: "From a photographic negative, for example, one can make any number of prints; to ask for the 'authentic' print makes no sense" (224). It makes no sense to ask for authentic chop suey. We already know that it is a copy of something that is outside the margins of the menu. Any number of chop suey dishes can be produced, but no one is more authentic than another. The reproducibility of Chineseness embodied in the restaurant menu frustrates the construction of a knowable authentic Chinese subject at the same time as it offers up a palatable Chineseness that gives the impression of knowability. As Benjamin observes, reproducibility endangers the authority of the object.

> The authenticity of a thing is the essence of all that is transmissible from its beginning, ranging from its substantive duration to its testimony to the history which it has experienced. Since the historical testimony rests on the authenticity, the former, too, is jeopardized by reproduction when substantive duration ceases to matter. And what is really jeopardized when the historical testimony is affected is the authority of the object. (221)

The reproduction of Chineseness on the menu jeopardizes the authority of the Chinese food on the menu to stand in for Chinese — it puts into question the possibility of knowing Chinese authoritatively through the Chinese food on the menu. In naming Chineseness for the Euro-Canadian community, Chinese food on the restaurant menu brings to the surface the uneasiness of attempts at knowing and identifying otherness. In an essay exploring the implications of mechanical reproducibility on the construction of the native subject in the academy, Rey Chow writes of the possibility of the native's gaze reflecting back on the colonizer in the colonial gaze:

> Contrary to the model of Western hegemony in which the colonizer is seen as a primary, active "gaze" subjugating the native as passive "object,"

I want to suggest that it is actually the colonizer who feels looked at by the native's gaze. This gaze, which is neither a threat nor a retaliation, makes the colonizer "conscious" of himself, leading him to his need to turn his gaze around and look at himself, hence-forth "reflected" in the native-object. (51)

The menu functions on this order, delivering or serving up a palatable Chineseness at the same time as it jeopardizes its own authority as a text of Chineseness. Chinese food on the menu betrays the version of Chineseness that white communities can consume, revealing more about whiteness than about Chineseness. More than that, Chineseness on the menu tells us about how Chinese diaspora subjects negotiate the reproduction and dissemination of Chineseness.

The menu attests to a self-conscious and utterly aware production of fictive ethnicity. It functions as a reminder that the racialized other herself might also produce an inauthentic and imperfect Chineseness as a strategy of resistance. The legacy of the menu suggests that Chinese diaspora subjects exploit the capacity of the menu for the reproduction of a cultural space in order to produce an ethnicity that can be made palatable and frustrates the desire for an authentic Chineseness.

The mechanical reproduction of Chineseness renders the issue of authenticity at once irrelevant and disturbingly pertinent in that it reintroduces the problem of authenticity with every repetition. The problem of authentic Chinese is not so much about fake Chinese food, or even Chinese food for non-Chinese consumers, but Chineseness disseminated through food culture, which responds to the pressures of racism by producing and mechanically reproducing through the menu a familiar and comfortable racial otherness. Chinese food on the restaurant menu naturalizes what is in actuality an unnatural situation of racial isolation.

Slowness and Alternative Temporalities

Unlike many of the non-Chinese items on the Diamond Grill menu, chop suey retains its place on contemporary Chinese Canadian restaurant menus. The white or Western items feel antiquated and anachronistic. We know what chicken chop suey or sweet and sour pork spare ribs might be. However, a Love Me Special fancy sundae or a Manhattan Sandwich feel foreign, as though they belong to another time or space. This stability of the Chineseness of the menus across time stages the disjuncture between the historical shifts in whiteness and that of Chineseness.

The progressivist reading of this disjuncture would be that of the dominant one of European progress — whiteness changes, advances, and develops more rapidly than that of Chineseness. And yet, the Chineseness of the restaurants is not just outdated, but it is *out of time*. In his discussion of the problem of the writing of minority histories, Dipesh Chakrabarty challenges Fredric Jameson's injunction to "always historicize": "historicizing is not the problematic part of the injunction, the troubling term is 'always.' For the assumption of a continuous, homogeneous, infinitely stretched out time that makes possible the imagination of a 'always' is put to question by subaltern pasts that makes the present, as Derrida says, 'out of joint'" (111). The heterogeneity of the time of the Chinese restaurant menus challenges the continuous empty one of European history. The very outdatedness of the restaurants can be read as a form of diasporic resistance.

The first lines of the menu read: "Diamond Grill, Nelson's Newest and Most Modern Restaurant." From the perspective of the twenty-first century reader, the Diamond Grill's claim to be modern seems quaint and yet antiquated. And yet, contemporary small-town Chinese restaurants are also seen as being quaint and outdated. The Diamond Grill's antiquity relates to the antiquity of contemporary restaurants such as the Club Café in Innisfail or the A & J in Olds (see Figure 3.5 and Figure 3.1). They are old, relics. There is a sense that very little has changed. On contemporary menus such as those of the Club or Golden Wheel, the Chinese food offerings are largely elaborations of the Chinese dishes at the Diamond: different kinds of chop suey, chow mein, egg foo yong, and so on.

Compared to the cosmopolitan bustle of twenty-first-century Chinatowns of Vancouver and Toronto, these restaurants do seem old-fashioned and out of step with the changing pace of new immigration patterns and new immigrant identities. This quality of being out of step correlates with Homi Bhabha's theory of the time lag or belatedness of racialized subjects. From the perspective of history, this belatedness would be what Chakrabarty has called the time knot of subaltern history; that is, the idea of a plurality of times existing together or the disjuncture of the present with itself (109). Whether we read the discordant time of the restaurants as belated or disjunctive, they contain an alternate or different temporality, which challenges the desire of late modern capitalist formations to write them out of the present. This is more than just the story of survival. The menus assert a slowness in the construction of Chineseness which poses a challenge to the speed of a supposedly new global order that insists on its own newness.

In analyses that call for a move beyond a perceived idea of an outdated Chineseness, the desire for a certain freedom from the past is part of a larger

Figure 3.5 Club Café

goal towards a more agential understanding of the Chinese diaspora subject in North America. In her 1998 article, "Can One Say No to Chineseness?" Ien Ang argues that one of the central problems for Chinese diaspora studies is around that of modernizing Chinese and, at the same time, creating a modernity that is Chinese:

> Central to the intellectual problematic of cultural China is what one sees as the urgent need to reconcile Chineseness and modernity as the twentieth century draws to a close. There are two interrelated sides to this challenge. On the one hand, the question is how to modernize Chineseness itself in a way that will correct and overcome the arguably abject course taken by the existing political regime in China, a course almost universally perceived as wrong ... On the other hand, there is also the question of how to sinicize modernity — how, that is, to create a modern world that is truly Chinese and not simply an imitation of the West. (229–30)

Ang's call for modernizing Chineseness belies an investment in an idea of the march of historical progress in which Chineseness needs to catch up to European modernity. Similarly, Aihwa Ong's discussion of flexible citizenship also invests in a sense of urgency around the need to separate old and new diaspora subjects. Ong argues for an agential view of modern Chinese transnationalists who "subvert the ethnic absolutism born of nationalism and the processes of cultural othering that have intensified with transnationality" (24). This appeal for a consideration of a new migrant subjectivity divorced from the old one of indentured and migrant labour movements hopes to fend off contemporary racism by arguing against archaic representations of Chineseness that are not representative of contemporary Chinese diasporic populations.

And yet, the desire to make the past past risks relegating what might be considered old diaspora subjectivities into the dustbin of Chinese diaspora history rather than thinking through the ways in which these identities not only haunt modern diaspora subjectivity but are constitutive of it. Recognizing the constitutive role of the past, Chakrabarty suggests that "difference is always the name of a relationship, for it separates just as much as it connects ... one could argue that alongside the present or the modern the medieval must linger as well, if only as that which exists as the limit or the border to the practices that define the modern" (110). In differentiating the new diaspora from the old, the history of coolie labour migration lingers on the border of the cosmopolitan transnationalist entrepreneur. In her consideration of diaspora culture, Spivak warns against too easy distinctions between the old diasporas and the new. She asks, "What were the old diasporas, before the world was thoroughly consolidated as transnational? They were the results of religious oppression and war, of slavery and indenturing, trade and conquest ... [A]re the new diasporas quite new? Every rupture is also a repetition" (245, 248). Similarly, Vijay Mishra proposes the idea of a "diasporic imaginary" as a way of thinking about the way in which old and new diasporas work together in the construction of diasporic subjectivity. He also warns of a too easy celebration of transnationality and deterritorialization. Cautioning against reading diasporas as "*the* ideal social condition," Mishra suggests that essentialist narratives of homeland and exile will continue to haunt them so long as the spectre of racist culture persists (426). Mishra's identification of the perseverance of racist culture is important for thinking about why attempts by new diaspora subjects, savvy and educated flexible citizens, cannot break through in a cultural space that will continue to question their right to full citizenship in the first place.

I do not want to glorify the old-fashioned or the outdated. Nor do I want to claim the Chinese cook or restaurateur as the ideal Chinese diasporic subject. However, I am doubtful of claims to the new, to something that too easily divorces itself from an ugly past of state-sanctioned labour exploitation and legalized racism. In her discussion of the problem of developing a materialist feminist historiography, Rosemary Hennessy argues that newness can function as a particular kind of conservatism:

> The conservative face of the new appears in its function as a mechanism whereby oppositional modes of thinking are sutured into the prevailing regimes of truth in order to maintain a symbolic order. The discourse of the new can serve to anchor emergent modes of thinking in traditional categories that help support rather than disrupt the prevailing social order ... In its conservative manifestation, the appeal to new-ness serves as the guarantor of repetition, an articulating instrument whereby the *preconstructed* categories that comprise the symbolic infrastructure of the social imaginary are sustained through moments of historical crisis by their dissimulation in the guise of the new. (103–4)

Similarly, declarations of a new diaspora risk re-entrenching the conventions of the old. In the anachronism invested in small-town Chinese restaurants, there is a sense that they are not only not representative of contemporary Chinese Canadian subjectivities but also that they are moving towards extinction. Part of this is tied to a pervasive narrative of increasing urbanization. In this narrative, we will all eventually live in major cities, our food will come from mega-agricultural operations, and the small town will eventually die. I find this narrative suspicious. The air of inevitability has the imprint of one of European modernity's favourite narratives — progress, the march of time towards some sort of developmental utopia, one in which, in this case, we will all be transnational cosmopolitans identifying more with our mega-cities than with our national boundaries. The declaration of newness carries in it the desire for a divorce from what has been declared uncomfortably old and old-fashioned. Chinese Canadian restaurants are old. But they are not extinct. Chinese immigrants still work as cooks. I am not suggesting that the small-town Chinese Canadian restaurant is only ever a relic of the past, that there are no new restaurants operated by new immigrants, but that the restaurants have been and continue to be understood as antiquated and anachronistic. I want to pause on this anachronism. Analyses such as Ong's and Ang's leave no space reading the challenges posed by spaces such as the non-metropolitan formations.

Even though the Chineseness of Chinese Canadian restaurants doesn't seem to fit with the new image of savvy and educated Chinese immigrants, I want to hang on to the politics of their unsuitability. Rather than jettisoning their Chineseness as unrepresentative, I have tried to think through the way in which their lack of fit with what might be called new Chinese diaspora subjectivity reveals the repetition in the rupture of new diaspora subjectivity. It is not that Chineseness should be stable or that it is doomed to a cycle of being tied to coolie labour trajectories, but that the restaurants suggest an alternate and simultaneous temporality that is out of step, which challenges the European narrative of linear progress.

Citing G. E. Lessing's observation about the newly freed subject of Enlightenment progress, Reinhart Koselleck observes an acceleration of the future that is intimately tied to the concept of European historical progress:

> The bearer of the modern philosophy of historical process was the citizen emancipated from absolutist subjection and the tutelage of the Church: the *prophète philosophe*, as he was once strikingly characterized in the eighteenth century … Lessing has described this type for us: he often "takes well-judged prospects of the future," but he nonetheless resembles the visionary, "for he cannot wait for the future. He wants this future to come more quickly, and he himself wants to accelerate it … for what has he to gain if that which he recognizes as the better is actually not to be realized as the better within his lifetime?" (17–8)

When the Church lost its grip on the future, when the End of the World continued to be prorogued, the liberated Enlightenment subject rushed faster and faster towards a future steeped in the brightness of unfulfilled possibility.

"This self-accelerating temporality robs the present of the possibility of being experienced as the present, and escapes into a future within which the currently unapprehendable present has be captured by the historical philosophy" (Koselleck 18). Against the velocity of a modernizing futurity, we can read in the Chinese restaurant menu a slowness that captures the present in its possibility. More than the time lag of Bhabha's prescient coinage,[10] slowness opens up the present to that which Enlightenment progress has suppressed. Rather than using the past as a means of developing a prognosis for the future, we might understand the way in which the past reveals the possibilities of the present.

In the assertion of a new Chinese diaspora, we risk not hearing the resistance of the old and instead re-articulating the racist history that confined it. The answer is not, of course, to cling to the past. But perhaps we might be able to read through texts such as the menu the way in which the past inhabits the present. As Chakrabarty suggests, "because we already have experience of that which makes the present noncontemporaneous with itself that we can actually historicize. Thus what allows historians to historicize the medieval or the ancient is the very fact that these worlds are never completely lost. We inhabit their fragments even when we classify ourselves as modern and secular" (112). In reading against the grain of a history that wants to progress into a future of increasing liberalized tolerance with racism as an unfortunate spectre of its past, I am not suggesting that we cling stubbornly to the racism of the past. Instead, I am hoping to make way for a reading of resistance that recognizes the kinds of strategies and negotiations that might be at work in negotiating the racism of the everyday.

I recognize that it is not only the desires of middle-class ascendancy which might cause us to want to keep the past in the past, to be swept up in the giddy momentum of a triumphancy in which we have, through the sacrifices of sweat and blood, achieved the small signs of gaining a toehold in a ruthless world of socialized racism: a house in a good neighbourhood, children with university degrees, a front lawn which does not have to do double duty as an extra vegetable patch. It is very tempting to fight to "arrive" and then to turn and say, *I am not one of them. Don't confuse me with them.* These are not easy pasts. But declaring them to be in the past, rather than recognizing that the "new" Chinese immigrant is just as likely to be a dishwasher at a Chinese restaurant or a garment worker as she is to be a member of the transnational élite, works precisely within a racist regime in which the linear march of time and progress wants to situate the dispossessed simply as an unfortunate feature of the non-modern. The precariousness of migrancy means that the ugly head of racism will always threaten to emerge. The words "go home" will continue to resonate. It is for this reason that we need to find a way to move in slowness and embrace the constant intrusion of the past in the present. The secret bond between slowness and memory lies in finding a way to make peace with pasts that harbour pain and humiliation.

In considering the Chinese Canadian restaurant menu across space and time, I have been arguing for a way of reading the menu as a text which bears witness to the agency of Chinese Canadian diaspora subjects in their scripting of "Canadian" for Canadians and their production of a Chineseness. These representations challenge the notion of authentic Chinese at the same time as they serve up a comforting and fixed Chineseness. They also challenge the progressive and linear time of European history. In being out of time, they stage the constructedness of European time. Against the speed of an insistently globalized world order that denies the constitutive role of the past, the diasporic agency of slowness emerges in the time of the menu.

Acknowledgements

I would like to thank the Glenbow Museum and the Provincial Archives of Alberta for granting permission to reproduce the following illustrations in this chapter:

p. 38, Figure 3.2, Public Lunch Counter, Glenbow Museum, NA-1926-1

p. 50, Figure 3.4, New Dayton Cafe Menu, Provincial Museum of Alberta, Accession no. PR1994.0119

4

Putting the Nation Back into the Transnational: Chinese Self-Fashioning and Discipline in Singapore

Philip Holden

It is a short, rather grainy black and white video, a series of flickering images that most Singaporeans of my age or older are very familiar with. The scene is a press conference on August 7, 1965, hastily called by then Prime Minister Lee Kuan Yew to announce Singapore's independence from the Malaysian Federation, which it had entered only two years previously. Lee sits at a coffee table, surrounded by other members of his government, and the camera alternates fitfully between a long shot and an almost overly intimate close-up. When Lee speaks, he is barely audible, and his voice lacks its usual surety and confidence. "For me it is a moment of anguish because the whole of my adult life," he says, "I have believed in Malaysia, merger, and the unity of these two territories." He pauses, in a heavy silence hissing with static, and then seems to begin again. "You know ... its people connected by geography, economics, and ties of kinship." Another pause, and then Lee's voice breaks, and he dissolves into tears: "Do you mind if we stop for a while?"[1]

Lee's tears, of course, illustrate Singapore's exceptionality as a postcolonial nation. What other leader of a newly independent nation in the twentieth century has broken down and noted that the formation of the nation represents the destruction of a life's work? Yet Lee's breakdown may serve as an image that may have a powerful heuristic function in examining the embedding of transnational notions of Chineseness within the Singaporean national imaginary in thefour decades since independence. It is not only a national spectacle, but it is one that focuses, through the lens of the nation, other factors — ethnicity, discipline, masculinity, the body and the body's integrity —

which will all form key components of the imagining of citizenship in the new Singaporean nation to which Lee's regretful words give birth.

The signification of Lee's breakdown can initially be explored through representations given by biographers and commentators, reading Lee himself, as he would wish to be read, as a metonym for the city-state. Writing in the early years after independence, two sympathetic expatriates, Dennis Bloodworth and Alex Josey, Lee's early biographer and press secretary, made similar moves in their portrayal of Lee's tears. Bloodworth adopts the more Orientalist explanation:

> Lee Kuan Yew ... broke down and wept so bitterly that proceedings had to be suspended for some twenty minutes. Lee's grief was sincere enough. Human defense mechanisms are traitors, however, and he was in danger of facing the press with a quite deceptive and unbecoming composure if he failed to give way. It was meet that he should weep ... . Chinese crying by numbers is like Christian church-going: laudable on the prescribed ritual occasion, if otherwise suspect. (*Chinese Looking Glass* 257)

Alex Josey, quoting Bloodworth, adds that Lee wept for "the Chinese left behind in Malaysia" on Singapore's claiming independence (608).[2] While giving different explanations, both of these comments on Lee's grief use his tears as a means of re-ethinicization, of reclaiming ethnicity, in parallel with Lee's own painful public metamorphosis from affluent middle-class Anglophone Harry Lee to Hokkien- and Mandarin-speaking Lee Kuan Yew.

In Lee's own memoirs, *The Singapore Story*, published much later in 1998, however, the incident is interpreted very differently. Lee notes that the press conference was filmed during the daytime, but it was not shown on Radio & Television Singapore until the evening, and he thus had the opportunity to cut out the incident of the breakdown. He decided not to do so because of the urgings of P. S. Raman, director of RTS Singapore, "a Tamil Brahmin born in Madras and a loyal Singaporean" (16).

> Among Chinese, it is unbecoming to exhibit such a lack of manliness. But I could not help myself. It was some consolation that many viewers in Britain, Australia and New Zealand sympathized with me in Singapore. (16)

Here Lee indulges in a performance under Western eyes, a spectacular sacrifice of ethnicity — "Among Chinese, it is unbecoming to exhibit such a lack of manliness" — for the benefit of the nation. Yet in this retrospective telling of the story there is also hope for a future in which Singapore will be purged of weakness, re-gendered and re-ethnicized after colonialism's degeneration passes: there will indeed be a time when Singapore can "help itself," when ethnicity and nationalism are not in conflict but work for each other.

The change in the manner that the incident is ethnicized may give us important clues to the transformation of the Singaporean national imaginary over the last thirty years. Singapore as a colonial entrepôt and as nation-state profoundly dependent on trade has always been caught up in the global economic flows that form part of what Immanuel Wallerstein has described as a "world-system."[3] Yet it has also been part of a parallel "global cultural economy" (Appadurai 32) which has gained in force, and the nation has, rather than being opposed to transnational constructions of ethnicity, often provided a space in which these become embedded in the local.[4] From a vision of modernity in which ethnicity vanishes, then, Singapore has evolved a vision of modernity in which ethnicity matters — in which "Chineseness" as a majoritarian ethnic identity becomes central to the manner in which the body of the citizen becomes caught in transnational capital flows.[5] Ethnicity here becomes a "technology of the self" in a Foucauldian sense, a means by which "individuals ... effect by their own means or with the help of others a certain number of operations on their own bodies and souls, thoughts, conduct, and way of being, so as to transform themselves in order to attain a certain sense of happiness, purity, wisdom, perfection, or immortality" (Foucault 18).

Before exploring the mechanisms by which such disciplinary practices have been instituted, we need to register Singapore's exceptionality as a postcolonial nation-state. Despite a precolonial history as a trading centre, Singapore's current polity is very much a child of an earlier form of transnationalism, colonialism. Its population is largely immigrant — predominantly Chinese, with Malay, Indian and Eurasian/Other minorities, drawn to the city-state through its function as a colonial entrepôt. There can thus be no imaginative connection with a magnificent precolonial past, in the manner of Ghana or Zimbabwe: Singapore's nearest approach to a founding national myth is the tawdry Merlion which graces the Singapore River and is replicated, in a larger form, in the Merlion tower on the tourist island of Sentosa. Nor does Singapore have a history of anti-colonial struggle, in contrast to Vietnam or the city-state's close neighbor, Indonesia. As Lee's tears show, Singapore's independence was an accident, an unlooked-for conclusion to an anti-colonial narrative that should have ended with the founding of Malaysia.

Singapore is exceptional, however, in more than just absences. Unlike the vast majority of former colonies, its per capita GDP now equals that of its colonial power, the United Kingdom. Singapore is a wired and networked city, perhaps here less an exceptional space than a precursor for other late modern cities. In a sense this may be a return to a former role. Colonial port cities were transnational before transnationalism, postmodern before postmodernity, globalized before globalization. In the next millennium these cities — Shanghai, Hong Kong, Singapore, Mumbai — may begin to emerge from the nation's shadow as generative areas of a certain kind of modernity. When Lee himself went to London in the late 1940s, he listened in awe to members of the British left, such as Harold Laski, who were committed to ending colonialism and the founding of the welfare state. In January 1996, Tony Blair's first major announcement of his vision for a new Britain was made not in Britain itself but on a visit to Singapore in January 1996, which included a meeting with Lee. Singapore's success as a "stakeholder society," — "supply-side" socialism as then Minister for the Arts George Yeo called it (quoted in Chua, "'Asian Values' ..." 587) — managing the worst effects of capitalism, Blair noted "very much reflects my own political philosophy" (quoted in Cumming-Bruce 1).[6] Ethnicity is also a part of this modernity. Singapore has a Chinese majority population, but citizens of Chinese descent and Chinese culture have no explicit constitutional or legal privilege in the city-state, in contrast to Malaysia's promotion of the *bumiputera*. In one sense, Singapore's modern polity is clearly "above" ethnicity. Singaporean children at school daily pledge to build "a democratic society" "regardless of race, language and religion," and multiracialism is seen as a core value of Singaporean society. At the same time, the state achieves a certain legitimacy through "technologies of ethnicity"[7] in which the boundaries of racial communities are artificially solidified; citizens engage the state not simply as citizens but through racial communities and racialized selves. In some ways, this again represents a partial return to the "plural society" of colonialism, in which members of distinct communities meet as individuals only through the marketplace but address the state as communities (Furnivall 304). In this process, Chineseness is dominant. Lee himself has famously compared the "hard" races of East Asia to the "soft" ones of South and Southeast Asia, and Singapore's economic success in the late twentieth century has been attributed to Confucian capitalism.[8] Chineseness is increasingly seen as a kind of discipline which is a motor for capitalist modernity, to such an extent that it is difficult for young Chinese people in Singapore today to think what being Nanyang Chinese in 1950s Singapore might have been: revolutionary, nationalist, committed to social transformation.

It is possible to speak of three levels of Chineseness or identification with Chinese ethnicity that are important in Singapore. The first is a series of everyday lived Chinese subjectivities experienced by individuals within overlapping communities in Singapore. Here, Chineseness is rich and varied. For an older Chinese-speaking Singaporean, there may be a strong identification with a non-Mandarin language and a local homeland identity; a younger citizen might well identify with a transnational Mandarin-speaking community marked not just by Taiwanese popular music but by Japanese and Korean TV serials dubbed into Mandarin. Some younger Singaporeans of Peranakan heritage resist Mandarin as linguistic colonization; others, as members of a large racial majority, may have little sense of Chineseness in a society which increasingly looks beyond the region to the United States until, often on excursions within the region or further afield, they are confronted with their identity in the eyes of others. This lived Chinese identity intersects troublingly with the Chinese identity expressed in Lee's memoirs, a second level of Chineseness as a key component of a hegemonic national identity based upon multiracialism, in which ethnicity is managed through disciplinary practices as part of national culture. This "national ethnicity" of Singaporeans sits more comfortably within both discursive and material practices which foreground the presence of Chineseness and Confucian capitalism within global capital flows, beyond the nation's boundaries.

In this chapter, discussion focuses primarily on the interplay between the second and third levels of Chineseness in Singapore discussed above. These two levels are not as distinct or as directly opposed to each other as they might at first sight appear. The nation in Southeast Asia is very much caught in transnational flows of capital; and such flows may not necessarily erode it but rather deposit new sediments. In Singapore, the nation-state has perhaps provided a crucible in which ethnicity and capitalism may be brought together and made to work for each other. The revolutionary discipline of Chinese modernity of the 1950s was put to work for multinational corporations in the 1970s: by the 1990s, entrepreneurs such as Creative Technologies' founder, Sim Wong Hoo, had replaced Lei Feng. More starkly, Lee's own body, and ethnicized, particularly Chinese male bodies, became representative of social transformation: the "beer swilling, bourgeois" (Lee, *Singapore Story* 233) golf-playing Harry Lee metamorphosed into the cool rationality of Lee Kuan Yew, the Confucian *junzi*.

The place of Chinese ethnicity as discipline within Singaporean modernity can, I think, be divided into two distinct phases. The first, from 1959 to the late 1970s, was largely concerned with the construction of model Malayan, Malaysian, and then finally Singaporean citizens for whom race was given a place but subordinated to the demands of capital. From the late 1970s onwards, however, there has been a re-ethnicization of disciplinary practices, marked by initiatives such as the bilingual education policy, ethnic self-help groups, and by the People's Action Party's embrace of Confucian capitalism within the ambit of shared values or Asian values.[9] Such ethnicization has produced a discourse of Chineseness which is increasingly divorced from the life worlds of individual citizens: in a sense, it is Chineseness without Chinese.

Lee's concern with cultural revitalization had begun in the 1950s in his own self-confessed encounter with the "the completely different world of" Chinese-speaking leftists, who were "well-organised, disciplined and cohesive" (Lee 168), in contrast to the "ill informed and naïve" English-educated élite. Such energy, Lee felt, might be harnessed in the production of a national culture which might be embedded in capitalism, the "new nationalism" of devotion to work whose praises were sung by Singapore's first minister for culture, S. Rajaratnam ("The Modernising Nationalism" 1). In a speech to the University of Malaya Society on July 25, 1959, just after the first People's Action Party government took power, Lee rebuked the class he now saw himself as now having left. "If, as you say, in between bouts of swallowing beer and whiskey, we can develop culture, let us never forget that all those who belong to our generation are here because of an accident of history" (Speech at a Dinner given at the University of Malaya Society, July 25, 1959, 2). This accident, Lee noted in a speech given a month or so later, had produced a people who "are devitalised, almost emasculated, as a result of deculturalisation. ... [T]here is a certain loss of confidence in themselves. When you see the Chinese-educated products from the Chinese schools, particularly when they speak on public platforms, you will understand what I mean" (Address at the Singapore Union of Journalists Lunch, August 16, 1959, 2). Chinese Singaporeans should contribute to the production of a Malayan culture, a "historical process of Asians who first became Western-educated and ceased to be Asians giving way to Asians who have learned Western languages and are proud to be Asians" (5).

While Lee's hopes for a cultural renaissance based on a return to cultural roots were the staple of the national imaginary of many new countries emerging from colonialism, Singapore was perhaps unique in its ability to put such cultural reconstruction into effect, and the manner in which such reconstruction might be embedded in a multiracial and capitalist modernity. Events such as popular "cultural shows" attempted to build Malayan culture through touring performances which had, as separate items, traditional Chinese opera, Indian and Malay dance. National day parades from independence in 1965 onwards, while now emphasizing Singaporean, not Malayan/Malaysian identity, combined calisthenics and military displays with cultural performances — again no hybridity here, but each race performing its ethnicity within an overall disciplinary framework. A further crucible for the production of this new national subject for whom race was subsidiary, yet always present, was the community center.[10]

The community centre, many of which, in a sign of expanding aspirations among Singapore citizens, have now been redeveloped as "community clubs," was a site which incorporated both the legacies of colonialism and the energies of radical Nanyang Chinese political agitation in the 1950s. Several community centres existed before Singapore achieved self-rule in 1959, mostly as the result of private charitable initiatives. After 1959, the number of community centres expanded rapidly as a key element of PAP's attempt to create citizen-subjects by expanding the penetration of the newly legitimized democratic state. The centres were soon placed under the authority of a new statutory board, the People's Association, and quickly became a battleground between the social democrat and radical left elements of the party until the latter split off to form the Barisan Socialis.

The community centres sponsored a variety of activities, some more directly related to citizenship than others. They provided sports facilities and educational classes, as well as providing foci for Vigilante Corps and later National Service recruitment. Lee's speeches at community centres emphasized how study and physical self-cultivation were keys to the production of a disciplined citizenry. "Just a few weeks of training," he noted, "and they [Vigilante Corps members] hold themselves up erect: not stopping, not weak or flabby but with guts and gusto, and with cohesion. ... [S]lowly, first on a voluntary basis, every Singapore citizen must learn how to be a good citizen" ("The Vigilante Corps" 96). Race within the community centre was addressed, but often pragmatically, not deemed central to the self-fashioning of citizens. Indeed, for Lee, management of ethnicity seems initially to have been a purely strategic ploy, necessitated by the fact that his desired goal — the production of a homogenous, syncretic Malayan culture — was impossible in practice. In 1960, he noted in a speech to the Nanyang University political science society, "[the] ideal solution to a united Malayan nation would be to produce one race, one language, one culture, one religion. Since no one envisages the possibility of this happening, we have to do the next best thing, (i.e.) all speaking one language and sharing common cultural values although of different races and religions" (Talk to the Nanyang University Political Science Society 3). Such a vision of a homogenous, undifferentiated body of national citizens — a yearning for the "fusion of populations" of the nation of Ernest Renan[11] — has recurred sporadically, but less frequently, in public statements by Lee and other senior People's Action Party figures after independence. In a 1999 speech, Prime Minister Goh Chok Tong could still call for an effort by Singaporeans to "maximise the significant common elements of our different ancestral heritage" in order to create a "Singapore tribe" ("Will a Singapore Tribe Emerge?" 29).

In the late 1970s, however, PAP's vision of a modernity in which ethnicity was subordinate went through a radical transformation, and "race" again became foregrounded as a vital component of national self-fashioning. There are various explanations of why such a change occurred when it did, from the anecdotal to the political. At one level, it arose from a sense of crisis in the PAP leadership about the corrosive effects of modernity on Asian identity. Raj Vasil, for instance, quotes a senior PAP leader recalling that Lee's change of heart arose from a visit to the Bahamas in the 1970s. "There he was deeply influenced by the position of the blacks he saw. They spoke only English, even though in their own distinctive way. They had no language of their own and they had little left of their own culture, heritage and values" (65). Lee's notion of loss of cultural purity was bolstered by Goh Keng Swee's *Report on the Ministry of Education*, which stressed the perils of Westernization due to the creation of a generation of English-speaking Singaporeans (Vasil 62). In transnational terms, Lee's and Goh's unease found a philosophical solution in the philosophy of the American economist Ezra Vogel, who, from the publication of his influential *Japan as Number One: Lessons for America* onwards, has attributed Japanese economic success to a Confucian inflection of Weber's Protestant work ethic (Chua, *Communitarian Ideology* 35). On the domestic front, the folding of Nanyang University into the National University of Singapore meant the removal of the last bastion of modern Nanyang Chinese modernity independent of the state: there was now a need to placate Chinese-speaking intellectuals and to have a revitalized ethnicity work for the state.

While some of the initiatives of that period — for instance, the introduction of a course in Confucian ethics as part of a larger moral education syllabus offered in schools (Chua, *Communitarian Ideology* 185–6) — have not survived, most have prospered. Lee's renewed concern with ethnicity as discipline has resulted in several changes to the Singaporean political and social landscape since 1978. While English is now the medium of instruction in all Singapore schools which come under the purview of the Ministry of Education, Mandarin is now the official mother tongue of all Chinese Singaporeans, and it has become extremely difficult, if not impossible, for Peranakan children to study Malay as mother tongue at school. An unlooked for effect of the bilingual policy has been that a number of young Singaporeans of Sikh and Bengali heritage are now fluent Mandarin speakers, as their mother tongues were not immediately available to them at school. Since 1980, certain primary secondary schools, which have a history as Chinese-medium schools, have been designated as Special Assistance Plan (SAP) schools: students at such schools follow a curriculum that attempts truly functional bilingualism. Although a small number of private madrassahs do exist for the Malay/Muslim community, the state has not extended the SAP program to non-Chinese communities.

Since 1978, a government-sponsored yearly Speak Mandarin campaign has been directed at Chinese Singaporeans. Commencing as an effort to root out the use of so-called dialects, it has more recently been more firmly targeted at middle-class English-speaking Chinese. In 1994, when I first arrived in Singapore, I remember using Mandarin to ask for a stamp at a post office. The Chinese woman to whom I addressed my query could not speak Mandarin, and her neighbor roundly and rather smugly turned to her and rebuked her with the slogan of the contemporary Speak Mandarin campaign, "*Huaren shuo huayu*" (ethnically Chinese people [should] speak Mandarin Chinese). Recent manifestations of the campaign have tended to play upon guilt rather than shame. In TV advertisements in the 2001 campaign, hip Chinese-speaking Channel 8 and English-speaking Channel 5 sitcom stars drink tea, wave fans, and engage in games of *xiangqi*. The theme of the 2001 campaign, "Mandarin, Window to Chinese Culture," is rendered in more essentialist terms into Chinese: *huaren; huayu; huawen* (Chinese people, Chinese language, Chinese [written language and] culture).

The version of Chinese culture that the website promotes is in itself telling. While the campaign itself is promoted by Singaporean actors, and the site features one or two elements which refer to the multiracial and multilinguistic nature of Singapore, such as a series of cartoons about learning Mandarin featuring the popular character Mr Kiasu,[12] the site is curiously non-specific in Singaporean Chinese culture. Chinese ink-brush paintings are displayed with traditionally Chinese subject matter rather than the Malayan subject matter of Singaporean Chinese arts such as the Nanyang School. A further part of the site gives access to video clips from a dramatization of *The Romance of the Three Kingdoms*, and another section explains the roots of Chinese surnames in China but only gives the Hanyu pinyin transliteration of them based their on Mandarin pronunciation, as opposed to the "dialect"-based transcriptions used by the majority of Singaporeans. Even the sample Mandarin dialogues have an air of dislocation about them — the lesson on visiting a restaurant, for instance, is set in a high-class restaurant, because it would be almost unthinkable to use Mandarin for dishes known by their Hokkien names only in a local hawker centre. The most successful dialogues are those that discuss business, apparently for use in dealing with Taiwanese or mainland Chinese, and thus external to Singapore.

The Speak Mandarin campaign thus aims to use a certain high cultural, China-centred understanding of Chineseness to re-ethnicize subjects who have become unanchored from their cultural moorings in the winds of modernity. Re-ethnicization is here seen as providing an internal strength and cultural ballast that Lee felt was lacking in the English-educated of his generation. However, this re-ethnicization in service of the nation is done not by anchoring the subject within a lived past of Chinese culture in Singapore but paradoxically in exhortations to connect with an imagined Chinese tradition which is located elsewhere.

The Speak Mandarin campaign's notion of self-improvement (brief Mandarin lessons, Mandarin by telephone, self-help CD-ROMS, activities in shopping centres and community centres) is strangely mirrored in the mission of another organization, the Chinese Development Assistance Council. From 1981 onwards, the Singapore government has encouraged the formation of ethnically based self help groups: first MENDAKI, for the Malay community, then SINDA and the Eurasian Association, and finally CDAC. CDAC might seem anomalous, since the function of the first ethnic self-help group was to promote self-improvement among a disadvantaged ethnic minority; yet CDAC was instituted at a very particular moment and with clear objectives. Its formation was suggested by Singapore Prime Minister Goh Chok Tong in the immediate aftermath of the 1991 general election, when four opposition members of parliament were elected, apparently because of increasing alienation of Chinese-speaking and lower-income Chinese Singaporeans from successive People's Action Party governments. Although nominally independent, the CDAC has the prime minister as its patron and is led by a leading civil servant who is seconded from a government ministry (9). It is funded by an endowment and through a Central Provident Fund donation scheme from the monthly wages of all Chinese Singaporeans. Unlike the present Speak Mandarin campaign, CDAC specifically targets lower-income Singaporean Chinese, providing both tuition for students who are having difficulty at school, and subsidized courses to help unskilled workers upgrade their employment prospects.

Despite the support of the Chinese Chamber of Commerce, clan associations, and prominent individuals in the Chinese community, then, CDAC is not an organization that promotes Chinese culture. The fact that some of its courses are held in Mandarin or Hokkien is, in fact, entirely instrumental: tuition and upgrading courses are actually directed at enabling Chinese Singaporeans to enter a largely English-speaking world — that of transnational capital. CDAC and the Speak Mandarin campaign thus work to bring the disciplined Chinese Singaporean citizen into being in a process which has a fantasy of a mobile transnational Chinese subject, an "astronaut" who still keeps ties to the nation, as its ultimate goal. The affluent middle-class Chinese Singaporean, already functioning well within the market, needs the inner strength of a connection with Chinese culture — Mandarin may also give a helpful ability to function within the public space of East Asian business. The working-class Singaporean Chinese, for whom this connection to ethnicity in the private space of the home is presumed to be well established, needs equipping for his or her role in the market, which begins in but quickly extends beyond the nation.

Such constructions of ethnicity, however, are contested in Singapore. Theater in Singapore in recent years has constituted an element of an expanding public sphere which, if not quite fulfilling the conditions of Jürgen Habermas's "ideal speech situation" (Giddens 128) at least constitutes a third space with a capacity to destabilize hegemonic notions of ethnicity and nation. Three successful Singaporean plays over the last five years have addressed the disciplinary ethnicity I have discussed by writing shadow biographies of figures from Chinese tradition.

Bilingual playwright Kuo Pao Kun's *The Descendants of the Eunuch Admiral* was performed in separate English and Mandarin performances in 1996. The Eunuch Admiral here is the Ming general Zheng He, who led expeditions to Southeast Asia and indeed as far as Africa. The title is oxymoronic, and Singaporeans in the play live in a sterile environment in which material wants are satisfied but spiritual needs are not addressed. The play itself focuses closely on the process of neutering of a young baby destined to be a eunuch, in which a small thread is gradually tightened around the genitals over several months, while the nursemaid kneads and strokes them. For Singaporeans, then, there is a certain pleasure in the giving up of the political; rather than Lee's dramatization of ethnicized discipline as service to the nation, here we have such service figured as emasculation.

Tan Tarn How's *The First Emperor's Last Days* concentrates more closely on the act of writing itself. Performed at the Singapore Arts Festival at the time of the publication of Lee's memoirs, it featured four characters with wildly different motivations attempting to write the official biography of the first emperor of China, Qin Shihuang. Although the play's historical setting was clearly emphasized, the use of contemporary props such as notebook computers and video projectors by director Ong Keng Sen introduced a discordant note and focused reference upon the present. Thus the notions of the representation of a nation through the ethnicization of a single man's life, of disciplinary practices which centre on an individual body — never seen, always present — were repeatedly raised for examination.

Finally, the collaborative script for *One Hundred Years in Waiting*, written by Kuo, and three younger generation playwrights — Alvin Tan, Chong Tze Chien, and Haresh Sharma — opened up further questions. *One Hundred Years* tells the story of Sun Yat-sen's participation in the 1911 revolution in China and subsequent nation-building, largely through the eyes of his Penang second wife, Chen Cuifen. It is further complemented by a frame narrative, in which a modern Singaporean, engaged to play Sun in the making of a film about the national hero's life, struggles in his relationship with his partner, who is a civil society activist. Although many found the play too visually busy and emotionally empty, it does refer again to Chineseseness in Singapore, and ethnicity as discipline. The story of revolutionary sacrifice for the nation is turned inside out, in that Sun is seen to repress the private in service of the public. The frame narrative shows a modern Singaporean's uneasy relationship to "Chineseness" and the past: he cannot, even if he were to so wish, use Sun's example to assemble, in a modular fashion, his own ethnicity or national identification.

If there is any conclusion that we can draw from our consideration of disciplinary practices of Chinese ethnicity in Singapore, and their contestation, it is perhaps that the notion of Chinese transnationalism needs qualifying. First, transnationalism is not new: colonialism, indeed, was a particular form of transnationalism, and transnational identities are not automatically emancipatory, or post-national. The nation itself has always drawn on the transnational, and indeed often provided a means of embedding demands for cultural difference within a transnational system of capital flows. The "transnational desire" of much contemporary cultural commentary and theory is often a result of the particular national location of a migrant subject. Paradoxically, then, the transnational is frequently only comprehensible relative to the nation, and it may well be that it is often within the framework nation that it is fixed, transformed, and put to a particular local use.

Literature

5

Trans-East Asian Literature: Language and Displacement in Hong Ying, Hikaru Okuizumi, and Yi Mun-yol

Kristjana Gunnars

In her book *The Body in Pain*, Elaine Scarry works from the thesis that, as she says in her introduction, "Physical pain does not simply resist language but actively destroys it, bringing about an immediate reversion to a state anterior to language, to the sounds and cries a human being makes before language is learned" (4). The subsequent text of the book goes to great lengths to show how language and pain in the body interrelate. Her argument is that the whole possibility of narrative is destroyed by the undergoing of pain. But immediately upon returning to a state of normalcy, the act of language reaches for story. So, the idea of telling a story is inevitably a follow-up of having been deprived of language by physical pain.

This phenomenon is interesting because of the question of transnational literature; namely, when people migrate, there is inevitably a canvas of pain involved, and this has a direct effect on language. Specifically, there is a time in the migratory experience when story is not possible. One of the deprivations of migration, especially if it is forced migration, is narrative itself. When people put their lives together in a new place, one of the things they are reassembling is narrative itself. Seen this way, every story — and especially every novel, every book — is a triumph against the disassembling effect of pain. But it is also curious that there is a relationship, as Scarry points out, between certainty and pain. This is to say, as she frames it: "to have great pain is to have certainty; to hear that another person has pain, is to have doubt" (7). What I deduce from these comments is that narrative, once achieved, is also accompanied by the phenomenon of doubt, so that the process of telling a story, in particular one's own story, is an act (perhaps even of resistance) against rising doubt, because there is diminished pain in the possibility of speaking a story.

I want to discuss three modern, current novels (of the twenty-first century) in relation to this phenomenon of pain, especially historical pain, and language or narrative. One of the novels is *Summer of Betrayal*, by a young Chinese writer, Hong Ying. The second is a Japanese novel, *The Stones Cry Out*, by a young Japanese writer, Hikaru Okuizumi. And the third is a Korean novel called *The Poet*, by an already established Korean novelist, Yi Mun-yol. All of these novels were written in their original respective languages and translated into English. They all deal with historical pain related to politics and society and how such pain is generated, or inherited, from generation to generation. *Summer of Betrayal* is precipitated as a narrative by the attack on students and young people in Tiananmen Square. *The Stones Cry Out* is occasioned by the experiences of a Japanese soldier during World War II, and his attempts to lead a normal life afterwards. Finally, *The Poet* is about a much older story of a poet by the name of Kim, who is the grandson of an alleged political rebel and whose life of wandering is brought on by the tradition of punishing political rebels down to the third generation. This novel takes place in nineteenth-century Korea, and the poet is a historical figure whose name is Kim Pyong-yon, born in 1807.

In all three novels, the protagonist is completely undermined by historical events. Forces beyond the individual's control act upon the protagonist in such a way that everything is lost. By everything, I mean that which makes a person a person; that which constitutes a human being is dispersed in historical events. All three novels have a form of war to contend with, but on different scales. In *Summer of Betrayal*, the war is part of a government attempt to "clean up" in an upsurge of democratic forces inside the state. In *The Stones Cry Out*, the war is much more large scale, Japan's involvement in a world war, wherein the protagonist has experiences that completely disorient him. He has to shoot a colleague, and the psychological destruction he undergoes is about receiving two contradictory instructions and having to act them out. And of course in *The Poet*, the conflict is precipitated by civil war. The forces of rebellion are continually being subjugated by the ruling élite, insofar as the forces of traditionalism and rebellion have been battling each other throughout Korean history. An entire culture around betrayal, traitorship, and loyalty has been created and refined. However, each of these narratives explains how the conditions of war affect the individual. In all three novels, the exploration of that effect is deep, insightful, and devastating.

There is also an assault, in all three stories, on the poem and not just on narrative. In *Summer of Betrayal*, the protagonist is a writer, a student of writing, and she is deliberately trying to put her condition and mental state, and her political ideas, into words. *The Stones Cry Out* is, in fact, about a man who has become speechless, and his language has become the language of stones. He collects stones and is interested in the geology of stones. But they are his symbolic language, because words have simply failed for him. He is not communicating verbally. *The Poet* is of course about a poet and how the poet attempts to keep his language alive, in spite of the pain he is undergoing. In this case it is the pain of ostracism. My contention in all three novels is that emotional and psychological pain is also physical pain. While Elaine Scarry is discussing physical pain in particular, like torture and war, I believe this can be expanded to include emotional and psychological pain. Perhaps mental pain occurs in a less visible way, but it is nonetheless a phenomenon of the body and is felt by the individual as physical pain.

While none of these novels represents a migratory experience in an international sense, since all the protagonists are people who stay in their own countries and have their demise within those milieus, the phenomena they describe is something that can be transmitted to the migratory experience and to transnational literature. These three novels describe in detail the process of physical injury that leads to the loss of language and the disintegration of personality, which in turn leads to the serious struggle to re-acquire these. In general, my assessment is that all three protagonists of all three novels actually fail at reconstructing themselves, but this is a matter of interpretation. What you can say is that these modern narratives are tragedies. They explore the devastating psychological effect of injury to the body. This experience is exacerbated by the fact that the protagonists nonetheless love their countries or cultures or peoples. They wish to stay where they are but are cast out in a way from their mainstreams. So they are all in some way stories of the outlaw, or even of the lone survivor.

Hong Ying's novel *Summer of Betrayal* occurs in June of 1989, just as student demonstrators in Tiananmen Square are assaulted by the military. The protagonist is a young student, Lin Ying, who is in the writing program of the university and is living with a man who is in the process of getting a divorce. On this occasion of the military attack on Tiananmen Square, everything is thrown into confusion, and everyone is running to get somewhere, trying to escape bullets and tanks in Beijing. Lin Ying arrives home only to find that her lover is in bed with the woman he is supposedly divorcing. So into the political story comes the emotional story, and the scene of betrayal is enacted twice: once on a political level, and once on an emotional level. Lin Ying runs off again and is picked up by another student and taken to his dormitory, where she stays. There, she and all the other students and young people try to assess their situation, their level of safety, the democratic cause, and they try to put their lives together in a condition of uncertainty. Lin Ying is also putting her emotional life together, and now she has two lovers. Her sense of self is quickly disintegrating.

The whole novel is about that disintegration and about the place of the poet inside that story. So Lin Ying is not only a student caught in a dangerous political turmoil, but she is also a poet whose poetic voice is ultimately the central point and even target of all this swirl of betrayals and disorientations that are going on. Her quest is almost transcendental. It appears she is concerned about her love life and about her writing career. But in fact, what she is after is that which these other phenomena point to: "Lin Ying became aware that what she wanted at this moment was not a man who loved her; what she wanted was an unshakeable, immovable form of trust, the kind that could give stability in this upside-down world, an unchanging, steady diamond pivot" (13). When everything is thrown into question, the home life, the life of study, the career, the writing life, her life as a woman, what she needs is something to trust — whatever that represents. What will not change is a place of comfort in the world, as she says herself: " ... her childhood hopes for life did not seem so outrageous: a lamp glowing at the window, a spot of yellow warmth in a lacquer-black expanse of wilderness" (14). Security, confidence, trust: transcendental focal points that are going to elude her throughout.

She begins by becoming alienated, which is the opposite of that comfort she describes herself as wanting. Her alienation deepens throughout until, in the end, it has become complete. Interestingly, the whole concept of alienation is pitted against community and is connected with the idea of democracy. The students protesting for greater democracy are interested in greater individualism. Individualism implies the possibility of alienation. Lin Ying describes her take on this in a moment of self-reflection: "She had never been smooth or slick in social relations. She could not do things in the acceptable way. Moreover, she was fundamentally uninterested in doing anything in the acceptable way" (60).

Lin Ying's reflections on the condition of writing during this episode in recent Chinese history are interesting. Her problem with the disintegration of her career is closely linked to the disintegration of her political existence. The changes that the assault on the students represents are reflected in the changes that are happening for writing and publication. This is how she describes those changes:

However, many works that had been accepted by publications were now being rejected. If you wanted to publish, you had to write something in the "realism" vein that applauded the communist party. Or you could avoid reality entirely and indulge in folksy sentimentality, and the simpler and more transparent the writing the better. One couldn't put in any "avant-garde" twists and turns, and certainly not a drop of the dark rain of individualism. (66)

Lin Ying calls this a pressure to become a "white-washed poet" (66), and we learn that her income from writing is decreasing. It is interesting to compare this with the condition of writing in the so-called West, where you have the same phenomenon but some of it in reverse. That is, realism and sentimentality and simple, transparent writing are in fact also better sellers in the West than the so-called avant-garde or experimental. The main difference would be on the issue of individualism. In the West, everything that applauds individualism would be acceptable. What is at stake here, and what is very much connected to voice, writing, language, and the disintegration of these in a political environment, is the insidious, almost invisible, pressure that is applied on the writer by society, a society in change and in turmoil. There is very little, if anything, a writer can do about those pressures and the subsequent loss of voice that an insistence on integrity would result in.

But Lin Ying's uncertainty is manifold. It is reflected in her personal finances (her drop in income because of political pressures on writing) but also in her personal life. She has the sense, even before Tiananmen and the collapse of her relationship, that something is wrong. As she puts it, she is afraid that "her life might be built on air" (71), that a seed of uncertainty was already there before the crisis (71). She also reflects that writing, which is to say being able to narrate yourself and your story, while it becomes hard in a time of political turmoil, and harder still in a time of personal turmoil, and impossible under conditions of physical pain and torture, is, on all these levels, even harder for women. "Fate is never kind to women poets" is a comment made by Hua Hua to Lin Ying (74). So inside the general human story, there is a gender-specific problem. It is not easy to have a voice and be a woman. That seems to be Lin Ying's reflection, and about herself she says, "her life had been a long conversation with herself … " (90), as if that is all it has been.

As the novel draws toward the close, Lin Ying becomes more determined in her individualism and her sense of the betrayal of women in all of this. She declares quite late in the narrative that she wishes to be misunderstood, in fact. She is only able to be herself if she accepts the alienation she is undergoing. She says: "No. I will never depend on someone else's understanding to live my life. What will I become? A slave who behaves according to the kind grace of others? No, please, I would rather have misunderstanding. I am made of misunderstanding" (157). This is a story of disintegration, loss of freedom, and ostracism. The loss of community and loss of voice. The novel takes a strange turn at the end, when everyone goes to a party. There, Lin Ying herself sets off the transformation of what is supposed to be an artists' party into an orgy, by taking off her clothes and posing naked. Pretty soon others start doing the same, and in the end everyone is having sex, parading around nude indiscriminately, writhing on the floor. What has happened is that the whole artistic community has lost its voice, its community, its sense of certainty, and people have become, as Scarry says, "pre-linguistic," resorting to infantilized sexuality in the dark with strangers, in complete chaos. They are arrested, finally, and the novel ends with Lin Ying being carted off in a police car to join, for all practical purposes, her ex-lover, who has previously been apprehended. There is nothing more to be said, and the last line is simply that she is hungry. There is no intellectual life left in her. She is shattered, traumatized, and destroyed. It seems that no other end is actually possible for her, except for this downward spiral.

While *Summer of Betrayal* is exactly what the title says it is; the story of betrayal on many levels, the novel *The Stones Cry Out* by Hikaru Okuizumi is perhaps even darker, if that is possible. It is an extensively psychological story, but the issues are similar to those in Hong Ying's story. The protagonist, Tsuyoshi Manase, is a soldier during World War II. The telling is more sparse and almost frighteningly myopic. The tone has a Hemingwayesque touch, wherein only the most pointed matters are mentioned. There is stark realism and deceptive simplicity. Here, Manase has been traumatized by his war experience. He and some of his troupe end up hiding in a cave and realize they are surrounded and doomed. It appears that the young soldier Tsuyoshi has to shoot a friend and fellow-soldier who is dying in this cave. We do not learn the particulars about this incident. What we do know is that it haunts the young soldier. Though he escapes and survives and comes home to live what is supposed to be a normal life, this incident haunts the back of his mind and is capable of inducing great harm, which of course it does.

Into the shell-shocked soldier's life is injected a kind of metaphor of geology. Manase is fascinated by pebbles, stones, and is spending his life studying everything he can about geology and how stones come to be what they are. His theory is something he has picked up from his fellow soldier in that WWII cave, which is that any of earth's small stones contains the history of earth in it. It is a microcosm of the earth. The metaphoric value reflects on the personal history that the individual carries inside, presumably, the history of Japan. So he himself, in his existence, speaks volumes. He acts without his own knowledge, is betrayed by his own subconscious, and he sabotages and ruins his own life, because he cannot do otherwise. This extends to the story of his people, or so this can be deduced. The seeds of destruction are already there, in society itself.

There is a great deal of geology in this novel, but the story has Manase married with two sons and generally carrying on in a normal way. He constructs a workshop, where he goes every day and arranges his stones. He goes on expeditions to find new pebbles to add to his collection. Clearly, the stones and pebbles do not only act as metaphors of the self, the subject, the individual; they are also his language. When he is collecting them, organizing them, labelling them, he is in effect narrating an order into his life that is fundamentally in chaos, since what happened to him as a soldier has, in a serious and absolute way, disoriented him and caused him to psychologically disintegrate. He lives his whole life trying to put that self together, often, it seems, without knowing that is what he is doing.

Other stories of shell-shocked soldiers, like Virginia Woolf's *Mrs. Dalloway*, have the soldier simply committing suicide. But that would be too easy. This protagonist actually works at maintaining order in his life. He doesn't seem aware of what is happening, so he doesn't apparently realize how deep his disorientation is. As the story progresses it becomes clear, surprisingly, to the reader as well as to the protagonist himself, that he is the cause of his own doom. This has happened because of what he went through. When he studies the stones and geology, he is also looking for an answer to the unacceptable. He tries to make acceptable the unacceptable. His conclusion, or his discovery, calms him. That is, that "he understood that the world is created as it is and not otherwise ... " (53). Science is in itself comforting, because it simply presents what is, and that is what you accept.

It happens that Manase discovers a cave during his geological expeditions. He is psychologically unable to distance himself from that discovery. One assumes he has not been in a cave since that drastic wartime experience, when he had to kill that which he loved most. The horror of modernity is that, when he finds himself in a cave, much later in life, his mind is tossed back to the original cave. He no longer knows where he is or what he is. He thinks he is back in the original experience. While this is not spelled out, it is possible to project that he is exploring this cave with his son, who has become interested in geology. As a consequence, he thinks he has to shoot his son, but he does not know he is doing this. He comes back, the boy has disappeared, and everyone is out searching for the lost boy for many days.

The boy cannot be found, the search is ended, and it is only at the end that the reader realizes that Manase himself has caused this to happen.

The Stones Cry Out is a truly horrible tale of disintegration; but again, it is caused by wartime trauma, intense fear, physical pain, and betrayal, as well as the painful necessity of carrying out orders human beings are unable to carry out and stay sane. And of course, the victim not only loses his language — the ability to tell this story — but he loses his entire memory of it. The frightening thing about this story, therefore, is that once pain, even when only psychological, has become too acute, it departs from the memory altogether. Therefore, one cannot learn from experience when that experience is too difficult to remember. Therefore, the telling of these trauma narratives is an enactment of crisis. They must be told, and they cannot be told. This explains why there is such an emptiness behind the screen of words that constitutes this text. The depth seems to be missing — because it is missing. It is almost a flat portrayal of a psychological condition that one assumes is the modern condition. A very clear and concise essay on this matter, incidentally, by Primo Levy, is to be found in Geoffrey Hartman's collection from 1986, *Bitburg in Moral and Political Perspective*. Levy explains in "The Memory of Offense" how varied and complex the issue of memory is when connected to pain. Levy is talking specifically about the Holocaust and how it can be either remembered or witnessed. The essay seems to argue that such traumatic historical events cannot be remembered, because memory has numerous subterfuges and recourses to self-deception, which will always interfere. Nor can such trauma be witnessed, because, as Scarry has shown abundantly, it is impossible to concretely understand the pain of another, let alone transmit that understanding.

Yi Mun-yol's novel *The Poet* is fictionalized biography based on real history, and concerns the poet Kim Pyong-yon, who was born in Seoul in 1807. He was a member of the Kim clan, which was a powerful family (the Kims of Changdong). He died in 1863, only in his fifties, after having lived the life of a wanderer as a "people's poet" and about whom a great deal of folklore had grown. The precipitating event in Kim's life is the insurrection led by Hong Kyong-rae in Pyongan Province (1811–12), where his grandfather, Kim Ik-sun, is an administrator. He is captured by the rebels and changes allegiance and begins to collaborate with them. When he is recaptured by government forces, he is executed as a traitor. According to Korean custom, descendants of such political traitors, down to the third generation, must also be executed. When it comes to the grandson, the poet-protagonist, he finds he is not able to live as his birth would have demanded. Since he is an outcast anyway, he simply sets off on a homeless existence, wandering from place to place and living on alms or paying for his bread with poems.

The Poet is a harrowing tale of being outcast in one's own society, or being shunned in one's own home. People reject members of this family wherever they go. They cannot settle down in a community and live normally. So again, even though this takes place in the nineteenth century, we have a condition of modern alienation acted out in a traditional setting. The trauma involved is, interestingly enough, inherited trauma, unlike the other two novels under discussion here, in which the stories, even though politically induced, are extremely personal. For this poet-protagonist, Kim Sakkat (named for his famous bamboo hat), one trauma follows another and he comes up against traumatic and hurtful episodes throughout his life. The cumulative effect of his psychological pain is a great burden. As the translator, Chong-wha Chung, says in the "Introduction," Kim Sakkat lives the life of "self-imposed withdrawal from the light of the sun, the recognition that through no particular fault of his own he must forever bear the burden of an inherited guilt, an original sin" (vii).

There is an embedded reflection on punishment in this work of fiction which is quite interesting, given, for example, the history of punishment that Michel Foucault outlines in *Discipline and Punish*, that traces the evolution of the punishment of criminals from the physical (torture) to the non-physical (incarceration) form. In Foucault's words, the progress from torture and public beheading and related methods, to disciplinary technologies, is about turning from punishing the body to punishing the soul: "From being an art of unbearable sensations punishment has become an economy of suspended rights" (11). The poet Kim and his family are caught in such a suspension; deprived of the ability to work, live, and socialize normally, they undergo continuous re-formation, which is acted out always, at all times, from all sides. In this novel, it appears that when the law is changed so the descendants of the original traitor need not be executed any more, they still face an equivocal punishment. The poet reflects, as he says himself, "whether the leniency they had enjoyed [being exempted from a death sentence] had not in fact been intended to substitute an indirect and gradually inflicted social death for the immediate physical death demanded by the law" (36). There is a kind of capital punishment being enacted in the shunning that occurs. "Social death" is as devastating as actual death would have been, because the pain is no less for being psychological.

The whole feature of the poet running away and wandering from place to place and never settling down shows how he is able to avoid facing that shunning. That is also the only way he can continue as a poet. If he were to stay in one place and be a farmer like his brother, he would literally disintegrate and die, which is what happens to his brother. He would certainly not be a poet, because language would fail him, the same way language fails Manase in *The Stones Cry Out*. This whole novelistic dissertation is appropriate, because the poet has nothing but time to reflect on his condition and his method of punishment, and to reflect on the state and its rules. He is continually aware of the power of the state, which, as Michel Foucault points out, is the purpose of the enactment of punishment in the first place. The poet, in fact, "came to consider the state and its laws as nothing but latent violence" (47).

Here is spelled out, theoretically, what turns out to be realized fully in the other two novels, both of which take place over 100 years later: the state is symbolically violent, and symbolic violence is enacted on the individual in a myriad of ways. The individual is traumatized symbolically, all of which cumulates into forms of silencing. Foucault spells this notion out, when discussing the "punitive city," as a condition of continuous punishments on myriad of levels at all times: "This, then is how one must imagine the punitive city. At the crossroads, in the gardens, at the side of roads being repaired or bridges built, in workshops open to all, in the depths of mines that may be visited, will be hundreds of tiny theatres of punishments" (113). This method, which has as its model the "fable" rather than the school or the reformatory, is more effective, it came to be argued, than a simple passing moment of pain, and is more terrifying, in fact, than the public execution: "The great terrifying ritual of the public execution gives way, day after day, street after street, to this serious theatre, with its multivarious and persuasive scenes" (113).

Encased in the novel *The Poet*, just like in *Summer of Betrayal*, is a dissertation on the place and value of poetry in society. True poetry, as they are calling it here, is described in Yi Mun-yol's novel in the following monologue, which comes out of a conversation between the poet and another man:

> True poetry stands solely by its own worth. It doesn't have to grovel before the powerful, it has no need to be cowed in the presence of learning. It doesn't have to keep one eye on the feelings of the rich, it has no need to fear the hatred of the deprived. It is not to be measured with the yardstick of what is right, or weighed only on the scales of what is true. It is self-contained and self-sufficient. (116)

This is close to the reflections that the young poet in Hong Ying's novel is engaged in. When the so-called market has failed her because she is of the wrong persuasion in the wrong time, she can nonetheless be what she is because poetry is seen to be above the needs of society. It is seen to transcend rank, distinction, wealth, and so forth. Poetry is a completely independent being. The idea seems to be, in fact, that the poet needs to extricate himself or herself from society in order to maintain that poetic impulse and keep language alive — because society and its laws, punishing as they are, will inevitably silence the writer.

As the shunned poet Kim says himself, he eventually acquires "a strong inkling that there was a possibility for life to be full of poetry as such, and the notion that the true poet is one who has renounced everything" (123). This idea that one must have "life full of poetry" is what makes the story of the poet run. In other words, the narrator interjects: "Not all nonconformists are poets. But all poets are nonconformists" (124). This is exactly the conclusion the young poet in *Summer of Betrayal* comes to as well. And it is the tragedy of the stone-collector in *The Stones Cry Out* that he cannot not conform. Conforming kills him, because he has no language.

When language is connected to the idea of symbolic punishment, as discussed so thoroughly by Foucault, more and more layers of symbolic activity become possible. Even on the level of language itself, technologies of punishment are able to go on. As an example, I can point to an essay by Patrick McGee, which appeared in *Genre*, titled "Theory in Pain." This is a truly curious discussion, but with merit. McGee argues that critics and theorists, especially postmodern theorists, have the ability to "torture" the literary texts they examine. He sees this linguistic torture as a punishment by the academy and its systems of the poetic impulse. Therefore, on a strange and symbolic level, McGee is engaging in the same argument the young poet in *Summer of Betrayal* voices, as well as the ideas espoused by Kim Sakkat in *The Poet.*

As the story of Kim Sakkat the poet draws to a close, we find that he has left his wife and children to wander alone. As his son grows up, he goes searching for his father — and finds him. However, by this time, the father-poet's mind is so far gone, his condition as a wanderer is so settled, that there is no way the son can induce him to come home, which the son has set out to do. The son, Ik-kyun, slowly and painfully realizes what this is all about. He asks himself this penetrating question:

> Would he [the poet] be able to make clouds move and flowers bloom, once back in his own shabby room with its thatched roof? Would he still be able to live lofty and indifferent like some old pine tree or moss-covered rock, once supported by the labours of Ik-kyun, his wife, and mother, and doing his own share of trivial housekeeping chores? Would

his father still be able to be a poet, in the midst of cold stares directed at an old failure come home to prepare for death, or surrounded by a throng of third-rate poets drawn like moths around a light to the faded name of someone who in youth had been famous? Would he still be able to be a poet? (196–7)

The son realizes that the state and its laws would, in fact, eliminate the poet. And with it magic, and with it language.

So this is a story of learning to let go, and is very similar to Herman Hesse's novel *Siddhartha*. Hesse's narrative is about the sage learning to let go, even of his own child. In *The Poet*, the father-poet keeps trying to disappear and somehow sneak away from the son. But Ik-kyun always catches up with him, until he gives up, in the end. His final comment is: "The man moving away in the glimmering darkness was not his father. He was a poet, and nothing else. A poet tied down by nothing in the whole world" (198). The poet merges with nature, and disappears altogether as a member of society, or a member of a family.

These are devastating fictionalized treatises on the place of the writer in society, and the problem of freedom in relation to writing. There is a great deal here on discipline and punishment, and on trauma and language. What all three novels hammer home is the impossibility of conforming to what society, the state, has asked of you, and having the freedom of mind to speak or write with integrity, from your own heart. The suggestion seems to be that this dichotomy, or dilemma, will always exist. The settings in which these novels take place are starkly drawn, and are able to be so because of the extreme conditions in which the protagonists find themselves. But those extreme conditions only serve to highlight what is less obvious in Western novels, in which the myth of freedom is often just that: a myth. People suffer from the same dilemmas and paradoxes, only less visibly so, and there is greater self-deception involved. But at the bottom is the same question: Why can I not speak? I cannot speak because I have been damaged. The times, politics, the state, forms of punishment I have undergone, have all served to silence me. Therefore, these are stories of not simply the struggles of certain individuals to stay alive, quite literally. But they are narratives of the struggle of language itself to survive in what is clearly a never-ending series of forces and conditions of silencing.

6

Cultural and Culinary Ambivalence in Sara Chin, Evelina Galang, and Yoko Tawada

Petra Fachinger

At an art gallery opening for local Asian American women artists, a tall
white man in glasses, beard, and big hair bundled up into a ponytail,
hovers over a table full of sushi, chow mein, egg rolls, and teriyaki
chicken. He looks at me awkwardly and attempts conversation. "Did you
make any of the food? I notice you look kinda Asian." (Creef 82)

In "Notes from a Fragmented Daughter,"[1] Elena Tajima Creef, the "daughter
of a World War II Japanese war bride who met and married [Elena's] North
Carolinan hillbilly father one fine day in 1949" (83) addresses her sense of
cultural fragmentation, a product of her dual cultural heritage, as well as her
exoticization by European Americans. I am prefacing my article with an
excerpt from this text, as it links "Asian" food to female "Asian" ethnicity.
It also addresses cultural ambivalence. It is these two issues that I explore in
three short narratives: one by a Chinese American, one by a Filipina American,
and one by a Japanese writer who has been living in Germany for over twenty
years. Both food and the "authenticity" of language, as transmitters of culture,
are major themes in these texts. Sara Chin's "Below the Line," the title story
of her 1997 collection of short stories; Evelina Galang's "Filming Sausage"
from *Her Wild American Self* (1996); and Yoko Tawada's novella "The Bath"
(1991) focus on the experience of their narrators' negotiation between
cultures. All three protagonists are young professional women who have
chosen careers in the white, male-dominated culture industry and business
world. The price they pay for striving to play a part in this world is cultural

ambivalence. What I mean by cultural ambivalence is the feeling of being torn between two sets of values, specifically those upheld by the ethnic community and those espoused by the larger society. I argue that food imagery serves as a touchstone of identity in the three texts. Food also functions as metaphor in the portrayal of the three women's skepticism about textual authority. While all three protagonists have a "split" relationship with food, their work also exposes them to mediated language from which they feel alienated. Yet, they are also aware that by participating in the world of cultural consumption, they have had to make compromises.

While hungry women are recurrent protagonists in modern Chinese fiction,[2] in Chinese American literature those of the immigrant generation who attempt to survive physically and psychologically are often portrayed as "big eaters." This image of "big eaters" is rooted in the first generation's experience of poverty in China and reinforced by the challenge of survival in the harsh socio-economic environment to which they were exposed in the adopted country. Chinese American mothers of the immigrant generation have also been portrayed as "big talkers" and storytellers. As transmitters of culture, they are responsible for the preservation of Chinese history by passing it on orally to the second generation. In her pioneering study of alimentary images in Asian American and Asian Canadian literature, in which she draws on William Boelhower's theories of ethnic semiosis, Sau-ling Wong claims that Asian American alimentary imagery has "acquired unique nuances of meaning" (71). According to Wong,

> ingestion is the physical act that mediates between self and not-self, native essence and foreign matter, the inside and the outside. The mediating relationship is crucial: until eaten and absorbed into one's bodily system, food is no more than a substance 'out there.' [...] Physical survival is incompatible with a finicky palate; psychological survival hinges on the wresting of meaning from arbitrary infliction of humiliation and pain; survival of family and the ethnic group not only presupposes individually successful eating but may demand unusually difficult "swallowing" to ensure a continued supply of nourishment for the next generation. (26)

In contrast to the generation of big eaters and big talkers, young women in Chinese American literature have a complicated relationship with food and have lost trust in language. Many recent Chinese American texts by women have been concerned with eating disorders and with spiritual and emotional — rather than physical — hunger. Texts that come to mind, many of them first novels and short story collections, are Lan Samantha Chang's *Hunger* (1998), Patricia Chao's *Monkey King* (1997), Christina Chiu's *Troublemaker and Other Saints* (2001), Gish Jen's *Typical American* (1991) and *Mona in the Promised Land* (1996), Fae Myenne Ng's *Bone* (1993) and Mei Ng's *Eating Chinese Food Naked* (1998). In these texts as well as in the texts that I discuss in this chapter, "finicky palates" and skepticism about language often go hand in hand.

Having lost the immigrant creed of dietary stoicism, the palates of many second- and third-generation women portrayed in narratives from the 1990s have indeed become finicky. In many of the books mentioned above, food is a metaphor for the unsolvable conflicts between the generations as well as for inherited trauma. Daughters either become "hybrid eaters," that is, they prefer "Western-style" food to Chinese/Asian food, or they suffer from eating disorders, refusing nourishment altogether. Ultimately, those manifestations of conflict disrupt ethnic continuity. Many of the "hybrid eater" protagonists also have interracial relationships, a choice that is often represented as a rebellion against family tradition and ethnic loyalty. As these texts no longer relate an immigrant experience, emphasizing the differences between the "old world" and the "new world," they often portray the second and the third generations as victims of the traumatic experiences of their grandparents and their parents, as well as of the older generation's survivor mentality. Consequently, texts by the younger generation of writers focus on failed marriages — often interracial — abortion, sex, homosexuality, sexual abuse within the family, rape, suicide, mental illness and psychological disorders, particularly eating disorders, all topics that had previously been avoided in Chinese/Asian American writing. It may come as no surprise that the majority of these texts have been received negatively by first-generation readers. When asked about the reaction among Asian American readers to her portrayal of anorexic teens, and gays and lesbians, Christina Chiu admits that some members of the immigrant generation disapprove of her writing. She explains that older audience members have walked out of her readings, offended by the way some of her stories represent intergenerational relationships, because they expected "something a little more like Amy Tan; I know people like to draw those kinds of parallels" (Hogan 2–3).

Family dynamics and sibling constellations serve as backdrops against which the younger Chinese American women writers explore conflicts between the generations, concerns around sexuality, and emotional/psychological disorders. The most common sibling constellation explored in these texts is that of two sisters who, although they might be very close, develop in opposite directions; that is, one is more family- and community-oriented, while the other attempts to sever these ties. In Lan Samantha Chang's *Hunger*, for example, Anna who is working on a Ph.D. in Asian studies, stays in New York to take care of her ill mother while rebellious Ruth leaves the United States for France to begin a new life with a man who is not Chinese. The more responsible Sally in Patricia Chao's *Monkey King* marries and stays, like Anna in *Hunger*, close to her family, whereas the more selfish and promiscuous Marty travels the world. Similarly, of the two surviving sisters in Fae Myenne Ng's *Bone*, Leila takes care of Mah and Leon in San Francisco's Chinatown,while Nina, the youngest, moves to the opposite end of the country to live a life free from community and family obligations. In a more humorous and playful treatment of the two-sister constellation, Mona in Gish Jen's *Mona in the Promised Land* ironically arrives at an understanding of her "Chineseness" through conversion to Judaism, whereas her sister Callie, who plays the role of "good Chinese girl" (265), attempts to "re-discover" her roots by taking Cantonese classes and by wearing traditional Chinese clothes. In "Below the Line," Sara Chin gives this sibling constellation an interesting twist by constructing these opposing positions along gender lines. While May longs for family and ethnic community, her older brother Gary, a successful lawyer and entrepreneur, has left Chinatown behind.

When May takes refuge at her parents' house following a nervous breakdown, May's mother encourages her daughter to "eat, eat, better eat it all up" (146) — echoing Brave Orchid's motto that "big eaters win"— in the hope that food will restore May's mental balance. May suffers from what her psychotherapist has diagnosed as "serious boundary issues" (130). While Gary would prefer that May make more money at her job as an assistant video producer, her parents would like her to study law to duplicate Gary's success. A symptom of May's emotional imbalance is that she shops compulsively for "fresh and plentiful food in its raw state" (124), although both Gary and her therapist continue to admonish her to eat well before going out and to avoid Chinatown altogether. The attraction of Chinatown and of "authentic" food can be read as May's (sub)conscious resistance to her brother's "American" lifestyle. However, her compulsive shopping for Chinese food, more than she can eat, indicates her desperate attempt to fill the emptiness inside her. As much as May craves "authentic" food, she longs for "authentic" language. Overhearing a conversation of her parents in their native dialect, May wonders: "There was so little I remembered of the language I knew in deepest childhood. What metaphors made me throw my tongue away? I could almost taste the blood still. Was it chink, was it jap? After my early battles here with other people's metaphors, I would not speak the sounds closest to me. I went out instead and reeled in miles of other people's utterances, I spun their lives round my tape machine, I listened to their stories, and always, I kept a vigilant ear to what lurked beneath the surface, below the line" (145).

Although May is very close to her brother, she is simultaneously attracted and repelled by his worldview and his capitalist drive. Her description of her brother's personal history, that is, his re-enactment of the American myth of self-making, bespeaks admiration as well as an implicit desire to be different. What holds the siblings together, according to May, is their shared experience of racism: "We grew up where people called us commies, pinkos, japs, and every now and then they got it right: chink" (127). However, the siblings chose different strategies to counter hostility and othering: While Gary "fought his way through [...] and eventually created his own vision of what he was," May's way to retaliate was to throw "these words back at people who threw them at [her]" (128). May is aware of the connection between her early realization that language can be used as a weapon and as a manipulative tool in her career in the film industry. She observes:

> Cars crash, lips meet; in my business we're big on metaphors. We get paid by the metaphor. We dress the set, trim the lights, cheat the angles, doctor the story, *auteur* the film. Whatever needs doing, we do it, and the more the metaphors pile on, the higher we rise, maybe even to top billing on a marquee. Once there, who knows, the only thing left to do is to become an icon. A Marilyn. A Jimmy. Not anything smelling of incense, but an American icon. (119)

This observation reveals both May's awareness of her complicity in a world of make-believe and financial success as well as her ambivalence about it and gradual alienation from it. Participating in the mainstream culture industry empowers her to a certain extent, but she realizes that the sense of identity she gleans from it comes from a negative position. It becomes increasingly difficult for May to comply with the "American" way of manipulating reality and creating illusions. Her unease eventually spills into her recordings of video wills: "Strange contaminations started appearing spontaneously and totally randomly on my recordings. They appeared as faint but audible penumbras of electronic noise around certain peak levels of sound" (136). At the peak of her frustration with having to listen to and reproduce her clients' stories as "their hired ear," May bites into the ear of her sleeping boyfriend: " 'So this is what it's like to talk someone's ear off.' I pressed my teeth together suddenly; I surprised myself. I brought the taste of blood to my tongue" (139). This "vampire's kiss," as much as it is literally a manifestation of May's boundary issues, is also a sign of her refusal to continue "swallowing" the "wrong" metaphors.

Food and language are intimately connected in "Below the Line." May's access to both "authentic" food and to "authentic" language has been disrupted. Not only is May forced to "swallow" the stories of "incest, rape, murder, beatings" (135) before she decides to quit, but she also accuses her therapist of feeding, in succubus fashion, on the stories she tells her: "My doctor has been getting fatter and fatter right before my eyes. She fills up with all the stuff she hears from Gary, though she denies it. [...] My doctor has gained twenty pounds since I've been seeing her. She's ingested every word I've said, the conversations I've recorded, the meals I've cooked, the new things I've introduced to her" (141). By "feeding" her therapist "exotic" stories as well as by cooking "authentic" Chinese meals for Gary's clients, a favour that secures him major contracts, May becomes a "food pornographer."[3] In contrast to the first-generation "big eaters" who tell their stories for the sake of cultural continuity, May exploits rather than preserves her culture. While Gary transformed himself into a transnational entrepreneur — "he's been touted as the lawyer for the Pacific Rim" (124) — May struggles with her identity as a Chinese American woman.

In "Below the Line," as in many other texts by second- and third-generation Chinese American women writers, Chinese American men seem to have less difficulty situating themselves within the polarities of Chinese and American than do their female counterparts. Chin presents the reader with a range of possible Chinese American identities. "Below the Line" represents at least four positions from which "Chinese" identity is constructed in the United States along class and gender lines, time of arrival in the country, and the degree of assimilation. First-generation immigrants, like May's parents, who have lived in the country for decades and run small family-operated restaurants and businesses, are contrasted with working-class newcomers, represented by the hired help in the family restaurant, who do not yet speak enough English to function independently in American society. Within the second generation, the text differentiates between a transnational position, which is constructed as male, and an "in-between" position, which is constructed as female. The latter, although associated with loss and pain, comes across as ethically superior in its struggle to reconcile cultural heritage with life in the global economy.

The terms *transnational*, *cosmopolitan*, *hybrid*, and *in-between* are sometimes used indiscriminately to describe an individual's or ethnic group's cultural and political position outside the mainstream. Consequently, the concept of hybrid culture is often formulated in polemical opposition to the canonical concept of culture, as the hybrid is associated with counter-hegemonic and counter-discursive potential to resist and challenge a dominant cultural power and to subvert the status quo. In Chin's text, however, "transnational" is not equated with "hybrid"; neither is "in-between" automatically associated with oppositionality. The narrator/Chin is fairly critical of Gary, who as "operator on Pacific waters" (128) resides in a penthouse at the "lucrative edge" (126) of San Francisco's Chinatown. Gary not only manipulates and controls Pacific Rim capital, but because of his economic power, he also dominates his parents and his sister. Similarly, Fae Myenne Ng, like Chin a West Coast writer, criticizes globalization in *Bone* by charting both the fate of immigrant workers exploited by Chinese bosses within the Chinatown sweatshops and the exploitation of these entrepreneurs by wealthy multinational American companies. Some of the younger generation of Chinese American women writers mentioned above depict female characters in an in-between position that, in cultural and ethical terms, is the opposite of transnational cosmopolitanism with its disregard for local history and the complexity of material reality. Fae Myenne Ng's *Bone* demonstrates how precarious, if not fatal, the in-between position can be. Ona, the middle sister, a "dangerous mix" (51) of her sisters' personalities, is caught between the demands of the old and the possibilities of the future. She ends her unsuccessful struggle to balance her loyalties to her Peruvian-Chinese boyfriend and to her father by jumping off the roof of a Chinatown housing project. The danger lurking in the contested territory of both Chinatown and the Chinese American family is the loss of communal as well as of private history, a loss that May, unlike Gary, is also acutely aware of.

Sara Chin ends her story with an allusion to the climactic scene in Margaret Atwood's *Surfacing*, a text that, like "Below the Line," couples the problem of finding an adequate language with the quest for self-identification. Spending the afternoon at a nearby lake, May waits for a vision. When no "ancient Indian survived to this moment" materializes, she realizes that she will have to look beneath the surface (147). Touching the rocks at the bottom of the murky lake, she experiences a moment of rebirth in a liberating urge to surface. Significantly, this moment takes place in a location far away from Chinatown as well as from her parents. I read Chin's reference to Atwood's text as an ironic concession that "authenticity" can only be experienced in a mediated way.

Elena Romero in Evelina Galang's "Filming Sausage" works as a script supervisor in the shooting of a commercial for Danny Boy sausages. Like May, Elena finds comfort in food that links her with her family and ethnicity, food that is the site of shared history. Harassed by a white male director who "has a thing for Asian women," Elena arrives home after her second day at work to be welcomed by her boyfriend, with *pancit*,[4] which Elena's grandmother taught him to prepare. "Filming Sausage" juxtaposes in culinary terms a mainstream America that is "sausage in the morning, sunrise at the farm, spicy pork links, grandma, and love" (159) with an ethnically/culinarily diverse America. Elena responds to a colleague's observation that the director likes her because she is "Asian," by claiming: "I'm not Asian, I'm American." Yet she immediately modifies this spontaneous statement: "Well, Filipina American, really" (163). Elena's consumption of mainstream American food on the movie set, calamari and linguine at an Italian restaurant, and matzo ball soup at Millie's Matzo Madness underlines Elena's culinary ambivalence and signifies her cultural ambivalence too. "Filming Sausage," like "Below the Line," demonstrates that ethnic hybridity, as reflected here in culinary hybridity, does not come without loss and pain. Yet, although the two texts share the way in which their protagonists try to negotiate their identity as second-generation Asian women in American society, "Filming Sausage" also places itself self-consciously within Filipino/Filipina culture and literary history.

As much as Filipino/Filipina American writing can be read as part of the "Asian American textual coalition" (Wong), it can also be read as postcolonial literature, the Philippines having been the only Asian country subjected to systematic colonization by the United States. According to Oscar Campomanes and N. V. M. Gonzalez, because of this colonial legacy as well as the history of Filipino/Filipina immigration to the United States "many Filipino writers […] use […] various modes of ambivalence […] as sources of creative and oppositional energy. […] These ambiguities/discontinuities are demographically virtualized by the sheer fact of historic Filipino nomadism" (76). In the final story of *Her Wild American Self*, entitled "Mix Like Stir Fry," the narrator/Galang traces her own nomadic history in alimentary terms: "born on the very edge of the east coast of the United States of America, you've lived in many places, known your share of McDonald's and Wendy's lunches, dinners in an assortment of Chinatowns. […] Later, your parents planted you in the heartland, among wheat and corn. You drenched your share of grilled cheese sandwiches with bottles of chocolate milk" (181). Despite the narrator's culinary assimilation, she continues to be the Other, that is, an "Asian" of some sort. Occasionally, however, the narrator is addressed in Tagalog by an "American soldier who was stationed on Clark Airforce Base near Mount Pinatubo" because he is "somehow recognizing [her]" (183). This self-conscious deployment of (post)colonial history and the concomitant discontinuities and ambiguities can also be found in "Filming Sausage," which is narrated as a diary kept by Elena. In the concluding paragraph, Elena compares her body to the continent of Asia, thus drawing an analogy between the director's sexual harassment and colonization. However, in doing that, Elena, in an oppositional move, also "writes back" to the director, refusing to "swallow" his appropriation of her identity.

Elena is responsible for continuity on the job. She meticulously records the details of the shooting process as well as documenting everything the director says, as she has to ensure that clothes and props are the same for each take. The director becomes increasingly abusive once he realizes that Elena refuses to be sexually available. The sexual harassment makes it impossible for her to write complete sentences. Her notes become more and more fragmented, until she finally quits her job. While the director initially calls Elena "Ellen," thereby devaluating her Asian ethnicity, at the climax of their confrontation, he calls her "Asia," thus constructing her as radically different. Elena, in the conclusion of her journal, counters his racist remarks with a self-assertive statement of her Asianness:

> Look down the center of your body. What do you see? [...] Legs that begin just beneath your chin, stretching long and narrow like a strip of highway somewhere in the middle of desolate Nebraska. [...] Stare at your reflection, the contours of your face, the way your cheekbones sit wide and high, cocked at angles — the way your chin draws to a point and your hair feathers and frames your face like the Pacific Ocean borders Asia. You are Asia. The continent of Asia. Asia with long highway legs and blue-black hair. [...] You are an entire race of women. Chinese, Japanese, Filipina, Vietnamese. (180)

By retrieving the multiplicity of what constitutes "Asian" and by juxtaposing her own ethnicity with other "Asian" ethnicities, Elena not only highlights the uniqueness of her own ethnic background within the context of the story, but she also addresses coalition politics.

Notions of uniqueness and coalition are significant as the story portrays another "Asian" character: Keiko, the director's Japanese wife, who, so the text suggests, travels with her husband because she is aware of his womanizing. The fact that Keiko is not American born — the incompleteness of her Americanization is brought home by the presence of a "thick" Japanese accent (174) — can be read both as a reminder that only an ahistorical view could conflate Asian and Asian American. The fact that the director intends to cast Elena as the "other" woman affects Elena's relationship with Keiko, whose attitude towards Elena alternates between suspicion and hostility. Elena seems quite agitated by Keiko's dedication to her womanizing husband: "Tell her that you admire her for being such a dedicated wife, dedicated mother. Tell her you couldn't do what she's doing. [...] Look at the roots of her hair, they're dark and mis-colored, awkward as snow on the beaches of Hawaii. You want to advise her, 'Don't follow him, leave him.' Instead say, 'You must love him very much'" (174–5). Yet something in her perception of

Keiko hinders Elena from explaining the situation and showing solidarity. Although Keiko's portrayal remains sketchy, I would like to suggest a reading of Keiko as Elena's "racial shadow" (Wong) onto whom she projects her "negative" feelings about the "Asian" side of herself as defined by white males/ the mainstream.[5] Sau-ling Wong suggests "projection, a psychological process that (like bursting and vomiting) reverses the symbolic directionality of eating (introjection), keeps at bay the threatening knowledge of self-hatred. By projecting undesirable 'Asianness' outward onto a double [...] one renders alien what is, in fact literally inalienable, thereby disowning and distancing it" (78). One of the examples Wong cites is the silent girl in Maxine Hong Kingston's *The Woman Warrior: Memoirs of a Girlhood among Ghosts* whom she reads as the double onto which Maxine projects her negative feelings about being Chinese. Maxine acknowledges certain similarities between herself and the girl, for whom she feels nothing but resentment, such as the fact that they both wear unattractive clothes and that neither of them is good at sports. Most important, they share an inability to be heard. One day, Maxine corners the mute Chinese girl and physically assaults her to get a word, any word, out of her. After this incident, Maxine is afflicted by a mysterious illness that keeps her confined to bed for months. Wong concludes that Maxine must be repressing and projecting a "residue of racial difference which dooms Chinese Americans to a position of inferiority in a racist society" (89) onto the girl. When Maxine forces the girl to break the silence, she is seeking confirmation that her "fragile achievements in assimilation" will not be challenged by a "counterexample" (90).

Keiko's construction as hyperfeminine, dependent, and silent, as well as a finicky eater — she feeds on salad and seltzer — is juxtaposed with Elena's cultural ambivalence. The fact that Elena's attention is focused on Keiko's isolation and displacement, her status as the silenced "foreigner" who speaks with an accent and whose attempts to change toward her appearance look out of place, echo her own discomfort and loss of speech. Elena's spontaneous affirmation that she is American and not Asian, which she quickly modifies by conceding that she is Filipina American, indicates a split in her Filipina American identity. This split, however, is not inherent in the order of things but a result of a definition imposed by mainstream society. In her groundbreaking study *Articulate Silences: Hisaye Yamamoto, Maxine Hong Kingston, Joy Kogawa*, King-Kok Cheung observes: "Asian Americans should not have to *prove* their Americanness by distancing themselves as far as possible from their ancestral cultures. Trying to be American by going against what is stereotypically Asian only reinforces the norm dictated by the dominant culture. Hypersensitivity to the white gaze — whether it results in the internalization or the deliberate reversal of imposed definition — could shrivel the self" (18–9). While Elena's increased alienation at the movie set is reflected in her negligence toward her appearance — she attempts to make herself less attractive by wearing unflattering clothes — Keiko's "mis-colored" hair and "thick" accent reflect her own displacement. Although Elena is able to talk back to the film director, at least in her journal, by insisting that the indiscriminate use of the term "Asian" as imposed by the white majority is racist, she fails to show solidarity with Keiko because of her own cultural ambivalence. Read against the backdrop of Asian panethnicity, the "racial shadow" in "Filming Sausage" takes on an additional meaning. Yen Le Espiritu cites the limited Filipino/Filipina American participation in pan-Asian organizations and relates it to the perception of power relations within the Asian community — "Asian" often being equated with northeast Asian culture — as related to the perceived cultural "distance" of Filipinos/Filipinas from other Asian Americans.

Although Yoko Tawada, one of two women of Japanese descent to write and publish in German,[6] occupies a completely different diasporic location from that of either Sara Chin or Evelina Galang, her texts are also concerned with the exoticization of the "Asian" woman, language, and cultural negotiation. My intention in this chapter is not to universalize Asian women's experiences across countries and cultural groups. Yet, as I have been demonstrating, Asian women's literatures in "Western" diasporas do have much in common, especially in the ways in which they represent experiences of racism and sexism within and outside of their communities. Publishing both in German and Japanese and having established herself as a writer in both countries, Tawada leads a truly cosmopolitan life.[7] Her narrative style is quite different from that of any other writer of non-German ethnic background writing in German. The fact that there is no Japanese community to speak of in Germany — in contrast, for example, with the Turkish community, which has brought forth a number of successful writers — accounts for the uniqueness of Tawada's diasporic position. This uniqueness is reflected in her choice of topics and narrative strategies. Critics have commented on the fantastic and surreal elements, non-linear structures, and conflicting images in her fiction and literary essays. Some other trademarks of Tawada's prose are a predilection for narrative strategies that challenge the "Western" reader: defamiliarization, rewriting of ancient myths as well as of Japanese legends and fairy tales, transformation, and metamorphosis.

In "The Bath," a surreal account of alienation, the young Japanese narrator works as an interpreter for a Japanese/German business meeting that takes place in a fish restaurant. She points out that sole (the German word for it, *Seezunge,* translates as "ocean tongue" or "lake tongue") is her favorite European food. Not only does she like the taste, but she also imagines that this tongue will speak for her if words should fail her. However, she will not be able to rely on the sole's tongue to help her out, as one large fish was ordered for the whole party. To avert embarrassing moments arising from the cultural differences between the Germans and the Japanese, the narrator intentionally interprets incorrectly. Sensing the hostility of the Japanese businessmen towards her, she observes that a female interpreter is like a prostitute who sells her body to the occupation forces. While she is exposed to her countrymen's sexism, she is at the same time being exoticized by the German businessmen.

As the narrator's alienation grows, the lunch scene turns more and more grotesque. When a huge fish, whose white swollen belly looks like a woman's thigh, is being served, the narrator notices that its tongue has already been removed. She is relieved that everyone is silent during the meal so that she can take a break from interpreting. The narrator admits: "I'm not well suited to the task of interpreting to begin with. I hate talking more than anything, especially speaking my mother tongue" (16). Once the conversation resumes, the narrator observes that "people's mouths fell open like trash bags, and garbage spilled out. I had to chew the garbage, swallow it, and spit it back out in different words. [...] Everyone began to talk, using my mouth" (17). While the businessmen are "using her mouth," her stomach suddenly refuses to cooperate. She feels nauseous and begins to stutter. The group falls silent, and the narrator leaves the table. Alone in the bathroom, she feels an "ocean tongue" touching her lips. It slips into her mouth, plays with her tongue, at first tenderly, then more aggressively, until it bites it off and swallows it. As with May and Elena, Tawada's narrator's refusal to "swallow" leads to physical and emotional breakdown and temporary loss of speech. All three texts suggest that their protagonists need to find their own language as well as fight the colonization of their bodies in order to survive. Rewriting the (white) male text has become a common strategy for women of colour to (re)gain this autonomy.

In "The Bath," Yoko Tawada is "writing back" to Roland Barthes's *Empire of Signs.* In "The Written Face," Barthes describes the Japanese face as "reduced to the elementary signifiers of writing [...] the face dismisses any signified, i.e., any expressivity" (89). He expands on these thoughts in "The Eyelid," observing, "the Japanese face is without moral hierarchy [...] because its morphology cannot be read 'in depth'" (102). Barthes's reading of the Japanese face opens it to the kind of racist projections to which Gloria Anzaldúa draws attention: "The world knows us by our faces, the most naked, most vulnerable, exposed and significant topography of the body. [...] Since white AngloAmericans' racist ideology cannot take in our faces, it, too covers them up, 'blanks' them out of reality." According to Anzaldúa, "making faces" means "to put on a face, express feelings by distorting the face. [...] *haciendo caras* has the added connotation of making [...] political subversive gestures, the piercing look that questions or challenges" (xv). While Roland Barthes denies the "Japanese" face this power to signify and to subvert, Tawada's narrator denies the male gaze the power to "conquer" it. In another section of "The Bath," a male German photographer is taking pictures of the narrator's face for a travel agency and asks her if she could try to look a bit more Japanese. Xander, short for Alexander — whose name is reminiscent of another colonizer — returns disappointed the next day, telling her that her face is invisible in all of the pictures he took. He explains the disappearance of her face with her failure to feel sufficiently Japanese. Determined to be successful this time, he covers her face with white paint, defines her eyelids with a black liner, applies red lipstick, and puts additional black dye on her already black hair. Finally, the figure of a Japanese woman appears "etched onto the paper." The narrator glues this picture next to her mirror and compares it every morning with her mirror image. When she visits Japan shortly afterwards, her mother observes that her face has changed; it resembles the faces of the Japanese portrayed in American movies. The mother's observation can be read as Tawada's oblique reference to notions of the racial shadow. Yet Tawada's trademark deconstruction of signifying practices also seems to imply that both cultural context and perspective determine how a face/ethnicity/race is being read/constructed. In her literary essay "Don't Tell, but Europe Does Not Exist,"[8] in which Yoko Tawada playfully deconstructs notions of European cultural superiority, the narrator recalls having had a conversation with the character Xander from "The Bath" about whiteness. She notes that Xander sees his skin as a part of his body rather than as a metaphor. When he insists that differences in skin color are essential, she explains to him that it is not an inherent difference between skins that makes them look different but the light falling on the skin. Obviously, "The Bath" is much more concerned with problematizing (visual) representations of the cultural or ethnic Other than are "Below the Line" and "Filming Sausage." Compared to "The Bath," the two Asian American texts are stylistically much closer to the immigrant realism commonly associated with first-generation writing, or, in Wong's words, much more driven by necessity than extravagance. This difference can be explained by Yoko Tawada's particular diasporic location. Assimilation is really of no concern to her, as she will always remain an exotic outsider in German society. Furthermore, the fact that she has two literary careers, one in Japan and one in Germany, makes her perception of cultural differences and their representation truly unique.

I have attempted to show that negotiation of identity is the major issue in Chin's "Below the Line," Galang's "Filming Sausage," and Tawada's "The Bath." The protagonists' struggle for self-identification is set against the backdrop of the male-dominated culture industry and business world. May, Elena, and Tawada's narrator ultimately resist both being ethnically stereotyped as well as selling out to the mainstream. Yet the three texts are not about recuperating lost roots, heritage, or culture. Instead, they reveal how identity is a negotiation of terms and meanings, in which "authenticity," heritage, and culture are produced and re-articulated. Food and eating serve as the major metaphors for the protagonists' communication with the outside world. Focusing on their protagonists' culinary and cultural ambivalence, the texts undermine the assumption of the stability and coherence of "Asian" identity and indicate that there is no simple recipe for negotiation between cultures.

Acknowledgements

This chapter first appeared in *Modern Language Studies* 35.1 (2005): 39–48.

7

"The Tao is Up": Intertextuality and Cultural Dialogue in *Tripmaster Monkey*[1]

Jane Parish Yang

Many critics, noting the dialogic quality inherent in ethnic texts, have referred to Mikhail Bakhtin's ideas on dialogism in their analyses of Maxine Hong Kingston's works.[2] Bakhtin understood dialogism to occur when a privileged belief system or view is "relativized [and] de-privileged" by the appearance of an opposing viewpoint.[3] Although "not a dialogue in the narrative sense ... rather it is a dialogue between points of view."[4] The result of such a clash is what Bakhtin terms "double-voiced discourse" in which "[a] potential dialogue is embedded."[5] This mixed speech is what he further calls "double-accented, double-styled hybrid construction,"[6] which occurs when intent of the author of the original speech is bent or "refracted" to the intent of a second speaker "as if they actually hold conversation with each other."[7] Bakhtin recognized that in a polyglot world, "[l]anguages throw light on each other"[8] by undermining and undercutting any semblance of a stable core of meaning within a single tradition.

Texts that are the result of such contact between linguistic traditions can best be analyzed as sites where multiple voices, having absorbed values as well as subverting others, join in conversation. Such texts are examples of transnational literature, described by Azade Seyhan in *Writing Outside the Nation* as "a genre of writing that operates outside the national canon, addresses issues facing deterriorialized cultures, and speaks for those in what I call 'paranational' communities and alliances. They are communities which exist within national borders or alongside the citizens of the host country but remain culturally or linguistically distanced from them."[9] In Kingston's *Tripmaster*

Monkey: His Fake Book, the interplay of voices revolves around what Chinese, American, and Chinese American means, that is, the hybrid which results from the meeting of the two traditions: those of ethnic Chinese in America and those of mostly white, non-Chinese Americans.

If, as Robert Scholes asserts, "[a] text always echoes other texts,"[10] then the very title of Kingston's work, *Tripmaster Monkey*, draws the reader to the rebellious monkey figure from the 100-chapter late Ming Dynasty [sixteenth century] allegorical novel *Journey to the West*.[11] Monkey, whose religious name is *Wu-kong* (Aware of Vacuity),[12] after rebelling repeatedly against the Heavenly bureaucracy, does penitence for his crimes by serving as the chief disciple of the seventh-century historical Tang Dynasty monk Xuan-zhuang [also known as Tripitika or "Three Baskets (of sutras)"] on his pilgrimage to obtain the Buddhist sutras from India. Thus "Tripmaster" captures Monkey's role as pilgrim on the quest for the religious texts. But by appending *His Fake Book* to the second part of the title, Kingston seems to be claiming that her text is only an improvisation on the original Chinese text. Tripmaster can also carry reverberations of the Berkeley drug culture of the 1960s, of which the protagonist Wittman Ah Sing is a member.

The double identity of Wittman is inscribed in his very name. His Chinese-sounding surname is linked with the nineteenth-century American poet Walt Whitman by way of a personal name, Wittman. It is notable that his name can also be read as "Whitman I sing," a phrase extolling the famous poet, apt namesake for this would-be poet and reader of texts. A malcontent and visionary, Wittman trips through the Berkeley scene in the sixties, struggling to affirm that he is "deeply, indigenously here."[13] But both surname and personal name have been altered in the process of being Americanized (Ah Sing) as well as Sinified (Wittman). The Chinese surname is not quite a real Chinese surname, just as Wittman is not quite "the real Whitman." The protagonist remains somewhere in a third space between the two cultures, having absorbed part of both but having also subverted both. Wittman has become a hybrid growing out of both cultures, a new composite identity.

Equally prominent in this text is the protagonist's utilization of the American literary heritage as well as his experience about what it means to be a part of the corporate state in America. In other words, the dialogism in *Tripmaster Monkey* also centers on American ideology and competing ideological positions. The text is thus structured as a constant dialogue or inner war between the protagonist Wittman Ah Sing's competing identities as sixties artist and "working stiff,"[14] as he challenges or parodies the corporate culture around him. Sometimes the dialogue is between Wittman and the people he encounters; sometimes it is carried out between Wittman and the narrator, who challenges and queries Wittman on his behavior.

The very opening paragraph announces Wittman Ah Sing's alienation by appropriating the role, and therefore the name, of Ishmael from the seminal text in American letters, *Moby Dick*, as Wittman walks through the cold dank city of San Francisco. Describing this as-of-yet-unnamed Ishmael-type character tramping through the city streets, the narrator parodies the effusive nineteenth-century linguistic style of exclamation and exaggeration of Wittman's namesake, Walt Whitman, to open the novel on a mournful note. Listen to how the low moan and groan of the foghorn, heard first as "omen," is stretched out to "o-o-men," then slides into a Whitmanesque poetic transformation replete with "o" sounds and finally linked with his suicidal thoughts:

> Maybe it comes from living in San Francisco, city of clammy humors and foghorns that warn and warn — omen, o-o-men, o dolorous omen, o dolors of omens — and not enough sun, but Wittman Ah Sing considered suicide every day ...

A few lines later, the narrator notes that Wittman is not planning "to do himself in," which suggests that he was only acting out one of myriad of texts rattling around in his head as what the narrator terms "the run of his mind" takes possession of him. Indeed, the narrator further explains that here in San Francisco "[a]nybody serious about killing himself does the big leap off the Golden Gate."[15] Wittman was only performing the part in a text, not really choosing annihilation.

Despite the narrator's disclaimer, critic after critic has seen this opening paragraph as announcing Wittman's suicidal impulse.[16] But a closer look at the text will show that he is merely performing a role from the literary texts he has ingested, as this English literature major from Berkeley frequently does throughout the book, alternately becoming, for example, the monkey figure from the classic Chinese novel *Journey to the West*, "a convict on a locked bus staring at the sights on the way from country jail to San Quentin,"[17] or, on the way to the laundromat, slinging his laundry over his shoulder like a seabag and performing the role of the ghost of one of the five Sullivan brothers from the Second World War.[18] Thus, I prefer to view this opening scene as homage to Melville's *Moby Dick*, Wittman acting out the very same doleful mood Ishmael felt in the damp November in a New England sea coastal city before deciding to set to sea.

As a metaphor of exile, *Moby Dick* would be an appropriate text for this alienated Chinese American intellectual to perform, and Ishmael, the alienated outcast seeking integration and community on the sea and the sole surviving witness to the crew's ordeal, would be an appropriate character for Wittman to imitate. Indeed, the first chapter ends with the narrator's challenge to the reader to visualize in that opening line of *Moby Dick* — "Call me Ishmael"— more than just a white guy. If the person declaiming, "Call me Ishmael" were to be described as someone with "ochery ecru amber umber skin," Wittman pleads that the reader let it belong to someone other than "a *tan* white guy."[19] The narrator forces an acknowledgement of the reader's racist assumptions about the cultural figure of Ishmael as well as the assumed race of stage actors while at the same time creating a space for this Chinese American character of Wittman Ah Sing to be brought into our midst. Thus the Melville reference which opens this text ends the opening chapter by posing as an ongoing problem a twofold question about identity: is identity a fixed unity, or inherently fluid and unstable, open to shifts and hybridities?

Throughout the text, Wittman's performances continue to take place at sites of contested ideology; that is, at the junction of the two intersecting cultural traditions. When he begins reading his Rilke out loud on the bus, for example, he begins to fantasize that this may lead to a job as a reader on the Western railroads, reading out loud to other passengers to inaugurate them into celebration of a shared sense of American place. He would read to them the great texts of his American heritage — Steinbeck and Kerouac, Twain and Jack London, perhaps also Ambrose Bierce and John Muir. But his Asian ethnic heritage would compel him also to introduce texts outside the mainstream, diaries written by Japanese Americans of their experiences in relocation camps which he would be sure to declaim "in his fierce voice when the train goes through Elk Grove and other places where the land once belonged to the A.J.A.s."[20] Wittman's performance would thus result in a shift in cultural norms.

He further states he would omit from the usual American canon the writings of Frank Norris and Bret Harte, both of whom he terms "racist."[21] His Chinese side again would modify parts of his American heritage. Just as his American side would inform his choice of literary texts (while his Chinese side edited those choices), Wittman draws on his Chinese ethnic heritage when he comes to write the monumental play, a "talk-story" which ends the text and which ends up "defining a community"[22] through story. He invites acquaintances from all his various identities to perform in the in-progress play, which draws heavily from the legends and stories from China that he heard as a child, while also drawing inspiration from present-day America. Whether by redefining the American canon or introducing Chinese myths and legends to his non-Chinese American acquaintances and friends, Wittman takes on the task of devising and then performing in a new hybrid cultural enterprise.

The use of what I have seen as textual language and topoi appropriated from Whitman and Melville is what literary critic Homi Bhabha in *The Location of Culture* calls "[t]erms of cultural engagement, whether antagonistic or affiliative, [which] are produced performatively."[23] In other words, Wittman's performance of American texts, from his parody of Ishmael and appropriation of Whitman to his strong identification with literary texts inscribed in California place names, attests to his deep cultural engagement with America. Bhabha sees such imitation and appropriation as "on-going negotiation that seeks to authorize cultural hybridities that emerge in moments of historical transformation."[24] That is to say, the minority perspective is always reworking the received perspective of the majority, commenting on it, absorbing it, yet also challenging, revising, and undermining that very perspective as it makes a space for itself. For Bhabha, hybridity refers to "a subject that inhabits the rim of an 'in-between' reality."[25] And Wittman seems to be the perfect representation of that term, a deeply rooted American Chinese with affinities for both somewhat mutually antagonistic cultures.

Bhabha continues, noting that "[m]inority discourse acknowledges the status of national culture — and the people — as a contentious, performative space of the perplexity of the living in the midst of the pedagogical representations of the fullness of life."[26] Here, Bhabha attempts to describe the process of creating a hybrid culture amid lingering stereotypes. Never acknowledging the dominant national culture to be unyielding and fixed, minority discourse reworks, rewrites, and performs against stereotypical identities. Despite what "pedagogical representations" continue to teach the dominant culture about the minority within it, minority discourse not only rejects that depiction but actively struggles against it. It is not an accident that Wittman is offended when he encounters the FOBS (fresh off the boats, the stereotype of the Chinese in America in the minds of white Americans) in Golden Gate Park, as they are a reminder of how much distance separates the two ethnic Chinese groups, one deeply indigenous, proud to be fifth-generation American, and one just arrived off the boat, even as the sight of them mocks his attempt to identify with the dominant culture.[27] .

But it is also not by chance that Wittman chooses to resist the stereotype by wearing green clothing which accentuates his yellow skin, something he had always been warned against by well-meaning Chinese friends and relatives. Ironically, he wants to defy the stereotype by deliberately performing in accordance with it as he hoped "his appearance was an affront to anybody who looked at him."[28] It is as if, by playing to the stereotype on his own terms, he can decide when to resist, when to adapt performances, and when not to adapt. Disputing his "otherness" and unwilling to be an exotic object of another's gaze, he in turn defiantly gazes back.

In summary, by echoing texts from the nineteenth-century American canon which either celebrate or bemoan the national fate [Walt Whitman] and critique the lone, reckless individual [Melville], the opening narrative squarely sites Wittman in America. The narrator has located the protagonist in the performative time and space of American letters and American ideology, no matter what Chinese title — *The Journey to the West* — and rebellious figure — Monkey — she also appropriates. The journey of the rebel becomes that of Wittman Ah Sing, alienated hippie/beatnik of the sixties Vietnam War era, as he mocks and undercuts prevailing ideology.

After opening with this bravado echoing, extending, and finally muscling aside Whitman and Melville, the rest of the text is structured as an extended dialogue modulating among three or four or more sets of minds — the protagonist Wittman Ah Sing, Wittman's inner voice commenting on his own behavior, the people he encounters in his travels around the Berkeley scene of the 1960s, and the narrator — who reacts to Wittman's actions and words with mock rage, caution, or encouragement. The reader is thus presented with a complex interplay of voices, each allotted space to speak and be heard.

An early humorous encounter in the toy department of the store where Wittman works part-time illustrates the dialogic workings of the text. The first set of voices belongs to the dominant ideology — those of the customers trying to complete a commercial transaction without wishing to view their behavior as implicating themselves in what the sixties would call the "military-industrial complex." The second voice is the somewhat silent, ostensibly compliant Wittman; the third voice the inner noncompliant mind of the outwardly compliant Wittman; and the fourth voice that of the narrator, who disrupts the flow of her own narrative to ridicule the silent clerk, counter-pose questions to him, and critique his behavior. No conclusion or synthesis is drawn from these encounters, just as in a true dialectic all competing voices remain viable, though somewhat discredited, alternative views.

In Wittman's encounter with two women buying war toys, the reader can distinguish the four distinct sets of voices: those of the women as consumers ordering the salesclerk around, Wittman as polite salesclerk anxious to please the customers and make the sale, Wittman's internal voice raging back at the women against the capitalist war-mongering system in words he cannot say out loud, and the voice of the narrator sizing up Wittman's reaction. This complex dialogic interplay of voices begins with a query from one of the customers:

Two tourist ladies held a large toy before his critical eyes. "Would my grandson like this? What is it? How much is it?"

The two consumers demanding attention and answers confront Wittman. The reader is allowed access to Wittman's thoughts as he listens to their dumb questions. They have failed to read the labels or find the price tag. Wittman thinks to himself:

How come people leave their brains at home when they go on vacation?

But, of course, as polite working stiff, Wittman answers back to them patiently and points out the obvious from the package:

"It's a basketball gun," he said. "See? It says so right here, 'Basket Shooter.' You shoot this ball with this gun into this hoop here. It's a basketball game, but it's like a cannon."

As he explains how the toy works, he comes to the realization of what toy companies have begun to do and comments mentally:

No kidding. The fuckers were turning basketball into target practice.

Yet even as he realizes the sinister intent of the toy company, when he addresses the two women, he speaks only of the toy in its monetary value, appealing to the price-conscious consumer:

"It's the cheapest large toy we have."

It is at this point that a fourth point of view, that of the narrator, enters into the dialogic episode. Aware of his complicity with the capitalist system, the narrator assures Wittman in a soothing tone of voice that he is not being co-opted by the system, that his attempt to close the sale of a war toy for a young child has not cheapened him. The narrative voice intones:

Any job can be human as long as there are other people working in the same room as you. . . There are big people in small jobs, and small people in big jobs ... . The only wrong job would be where you have to be cooped up by yourself making some evil item, such as a bomb part, and never meet anybody. So here were this grandmother and her buddy giving him a chance to make this toy job human. Humanize them, as they said in the Cal Education Department, meaning one's contacts in the teachable moments during contact hours.

Wittman seems to be responding to the narrator's voice when he comes to a decision about how to behave when his beliefs are challenged. Ashamed of the charade, he decides to speak up against the war toy:

> "For the good of the kid, your grandson," said Wittman, "you should not buy him this thing that is really a gun ... . The harm comes from their pretending to kill. They learn to like the feel of weapons. They're learning it's fun to play war."
>
> "Are you one of those people against war toys?"
>
> "We didn't come in here to be lectured to."

At this point Wittman makes a rare confession, revealing his personal bias and forgetting that, as a cog in the capitalist machine, he should only be concerned with closing the sale:

> "Yeah, I'm against war toys. I'm anti-war. I'm looking after your grandkid better than you are if you're going to let him grow up to be a draftee."

The women, shocked that the clerk would violate the unspoken rule of salesmanship not to get personal in interactions with customers, speak up against his radical view. They assert their power by buying the war toy, which has offended Wittman so much:

> "We don't have to listen to this."
> "I'm buying whatever present I want to buy for my grandson. I'll take this — this Basket Shooter." She flipped out her charge card. "How much is it?"

With this one action of displaying her monetary power, the woman has reverted to her role as all-powerful consumer. Wittman, taking the cue, reverts to his original role as compliant clerk:

> "Fifteen ninety-nine," said Wittman, who discovered that his anger was mightiest when he was forced to be a spokesman for an inimical position.

The narrator, knowing full well his impotence in his role as clerk, mockingly urges Wittman to continue expressing his anti-capitalist views:

> Speak up against charge cards too, Wittman.

The narrator returns to her role narrating events, yet the sentence seems to end with Wittman's thoughts which sum up his reaction to the whole incident:

> Instead he wrote up the sale, let these women fuck over themselves and the kid.[29]

What is remarkable about this section is that it is not overtly marked with Chinese American minority discourse against the dominant culture. Rather, it is marked by minority discourse of another nature, that of sixties hippie culture striving to undercut the war economy and war discourse. Here we have Wittman presented as one who worries over the effects of the wrong kind of toys on the minds of the young. As American material values have triumphed over spiritual ones, he seeks to correct that situation somewhat by first speaking out, backing off when the women take offense, and finally reverting to his live-and-let-live policy.

Bhabha terms what Wittman encountered in the toy store as "affective experience of social marginality,"[30] leading him to express his frustrations over the workings of the capitalist system. Bhabha would view this clash between minority views and the prevailing ideology as "interrogat[ing]" the system.[31] It is clear that Wittman has interrogated the workings of the system before, but perhaps not when his loyalty was so divided. In this example, Wittman's marginality is due to his discomfort with the capitalist system, which even mindlessly produces war toys to sell to children, and not because of his ethnic background.

A further example of his engagement with — or disengagement from — American political culture unmarked by overt ethnic minority discourse occurs a bit later in the text when he attends a Mattel Company presentation of new toys for the next holiday buying season. Despite the fact that he has been booted out of management training because he tried to insert his hippie values into the program, Wittman accompanies another worker to the presentation. In this segment, the reader is again presented with multiple voices: Wittman's dialogue with the managers, the words of a few others who share his communitarian, cooperative view, Wittman's internal voice reacting to what is said to him, as well as the voice of the narrator full of irony explicating his behavior.

Bored listening to the Mattel Company representatives introduce their new toy line, Wittman begins to sketch out a random schedule over the next few weeks to skip work as he thinks to himself:

> Is it time to speak up and give this meeting some life?

What Wittman means by giving the meeting "some life" is to challenge the corporate assumptions at work. The narrator next steps in to explain Wittman's thoughts:

> Well, to tell the truth, the reason he was no longer in Management Training was that he had treated it like school.

Wittman's inner voice reacts to this information by interrogating the narrator in an innocent voice:

> It wasn't like school?

In reacting to Wittman's query, the narrator appropriates the steady voice of school teacher-like authority to explain how helpful he had been.

> He had raised his hand, and contributed to discussion.

The narrator frames his words and being helpful, though we as readers understand his disruptive behavior. We hear his actual words, which are, of course, really a challenge to prevailing business practices.

> "Do you give any goods, furniture, clothes, candy to the poor?"

The narrator continues to praise his actions as if they were positive.

> And he had tried to inform and give perspective —

But, the reader soon learns what "informing and giving perspective" means to Wittman when he explains to the gathering the company's past performance.

Although the relocated children were Japanese American and he does not overtly focus on their ethnicity, only the store's record of charitable contributions, the reader recognizes the covert allusion to an instance in America's racist history.

> "During World War II, this store gave dolls and toy cars to the 'relocated' children. But every girl got the same make of unsold doll, and every boy the same car. Kids don't like to get the same toy as the next kid. ... I move the next war we send a variety of individualized toys."

This last remark about the "next war" reveals his deep cynicism and rage, presented mockingly, at the American war machine. It then becomes clear that the manager has begun to speak, and we are presented with Wittman's questions back to what the manager said.

> "This isn't a voting meeting? What do you mean this isn't a voting meeting? I think every meeting in a democracy should be a democratic meeting. Robert's *Rules of Order* at least."

Next, the narrator reports his reply point by point to the manager. Note that the voice justifying the dominant position is absent, and we only hear its challenge.

A second mention of America's racist past is embedded in passing in the refutation by the manager.

> No, of course he wasn't being facetious. He wasn't asking for pie in the sky; he knew this wasn't the place for legislating that there be no more "Relocation" Camps and no more war, but they could pass resolutions. He most certainly had stuck to the subject at hand.

Wittman speaks up again in the meeting.

> "Doesn't anyone want to second my motion?"

The narrator again offers an explanation for what is happening.

> There had been others who got carried away; they too thought that meetings are places where one makes motions and seconds them and votes on them. See? He wasn't crazy.

We then hear the other people's words, which, of course, are crazy in a capitalist-driven economy.

> "I move that we operate on a profit-sharing plan." "Let's run this store on co-op principles." "Does selling candy to children contribute to their good?" "I move that the Sports Department stop selling guns and ammo."

This last line sounds like something Wittman would also offer. The narrator steps back in.

> He'd even won a few victories ...[32]

The ironic humor from this section comes precisely from the disparity among the various points of view. We hear the voice of a dissident railing against the American system of business profit while at the same time using the example of the relocation camps as a marker of racist policies. He is bringing up the company's record on charitable contributions not merely because this involves ethnic Asian Americans but also because he is a sixties California hippie trying hard not to sell out to the corporate world.

A final example joins Wittman's questioning America's lack of spiritual values with marked ethnic discourse. This excerpt juxtaposes two different systems of value by means of comic punning. The word "Dow," as in Dow Jones Industrial Average, is heard as the Chinese word *Tao* [more commonly written now as *Dao*], which means the path or way of nature. Wittman finds himself at a party in Oakland given by his friend Lance, an enthusiastic federal bureaucrat-in-training, complete with stock quotes ticker tape overflowing from his vest pocket. Having just confessed he was "canned"[33] from his most recent job, Wittman seeks consolation from his friend Lance, whose only inspiration is to draw the stock quotes from his pocket and pronounce to him that the economy is doing all right, thus suggesting that of course Wittman can easily find another job:

> "Utilities up a quarter-point," he said. "Burroughs down 1 3/8. Friday's Dow up 2.53 points in light trading on the Big board. The Dow for the week up six good points. Run with los toros, amigo."[34]

At this point, the narrator steps in to analyze Wittman's reaction to Lance's speech by explaining how Wittman's bilingualism in English and Chinese leads him to hear Dow as *Tao* [*Dao*]. The first word refers to an economic index to measure how stocks have appreciated for the material welfare of those lucky enough to own a portfolio — how much richer are we today, anyway? Against this economic measure is placed the concept of the Tao, the spiritual path in Chinese Taoism that leads one away from the material to a sense of an all-encompassing oneness with nature and the universe.

The narration reveals ironic intent by placing these terms side by side, allowing the reader to gain insights into the dissonance between the two values. By having the narrator ironically pretend that Americans measure their virtue daily, she in fact undermines that very belief system. Bakhtin's words, are apposite here: "Languages throw light on each other: one language can, after all, see itself only in the light of another language."[35] The whole context is changed and the whole debate is framed differently by bringing a moral sense to bear on the exchange by way of the bilingual punning:

Now, Wittman was susceptible to trance under the influence of numbers, and the evil name of Burroughs, Old Bull Lee, had been said in incantation. He heard: "The Tao is up." "Friday's Tao up 2.53 points," which is good; we were good today, not a hell of a lot better than yesterday, but holding steady and not backsliding, yes, some spiritual improvement. We are a people who measure our goodness each day ... A scientific people with a measurable Tao. Wittman felt pleased with himself, that he hadn't lost his Chinese ears. He had kept a religious Chinese way of hearing while living within the military–industrial–educational complex.[36]

What this narration has succeeded in doing is, again in Bakhtin's words, "casting a slight shadow of objectivization on that word,"[37] namely, how American citizens use the Dow to measure their well-being. Bakhtin refers to this as "introduc[ing] a semantic direction into that word which is diametrically opposed to its original direction. ... The word becomes the arena of conflict between the two voices."[38] By parodying American values in this way, the narrator has reframed the debate to highlight what she sees as a moral void in America, the fact that Americans do not care as much about their spiritual values as about their material ones.

In summary, the very title of Maxine Hong Kingston's novel *Tripmaster Monkey: His Fake Book* begs the reader to connect this fiction with the classic Chinese novel, *The Journey to the West*, while simultaneously warning that this text is only a frame on which to improvise. Yet what strikes the reader from the first page, as we have seen, is not the novel's close relationship to classical Chinese literature but the text's deep intertextual connections to the tradition of great nineteenth-century American writers Herman Melville and Walt Whitman evoked in one gargantuan sweep at the opening. Inclusion of the culture wars from the author's coming of age in the sixties further marks this as a text not centered on Chinese American issues alone.

Just as marginalized Berkeley graduate Wittman Ah Sing wants to "find someone to dig his allusions,"[39] so, too, does the narrator, who shows intimate familiarity with both Chinese and American texts, plant signposts for the reader to "dig her allusions." By displaying the self-conscious intertextuality employing deeply imbedded fictional motifs from both cultures — though I have dealt mainly with American culture here — the text has been transformed from what might have been mere surface cultural borrowing into a truly transnational literature.

In the end, Wittman acknowledges both his roots, entwined so tightly, like the Siamese twins Chang and Eng whom he invokes at the end of the novel,[40] that they couldn't be separated. Like his namesake Walt Whitman,

Wittman Ah Sing sees himself as the poet of the new age, the one central figure to bring the disparate elements of American society together. Yet the figure of Monkey from legends and texts also becomes a perfect metaphor for Wittman, who needs to be constantly on the alert in order to negotiate the American scene with his Chinese vision and hearing. A shape changer without a fixed identity, Monkey can alter his form at will to subvert the roles and lowly status assigned to him. With a word — *bee-e-een*! [change] — he could transform his identity and not be wedded to his roots. His power comes from his superior vision to penetrate noxious clouds that concealed the truth.

Much like Monkey, Wittman assumes various roles and masks within the society: Berkeley rebel subverting corporate America and aspiring poet whose inclusive vision demands that all be given places at the communal banquet table. Wittman refuses to stereotype or "racinate" anyone.[41] He writes a play, not narrative fiction, so actors can be of any race or color. His play-in-progress, a thread throughout the whole text, is an exercise in community building. Central questions that the play addresses are: what are the shared ghosts that make a community? And how does someone previously marginalized by the mainstream become a part of a community? How does one appropriate the discourse of a culture for present-day use? As the one who constantly puts on his "metaphor glasses,"[42] Wittman aspires to flesh out the shared traditions and intertextual meditations of his American and Chinese heritage.

The novel has further brought the question of cultural hybridity together with the dialogic principle. What is, after all, the center of American identity? Is it a fixed unchanging element, or is it inherently unstable, neither fully one thing nor wholly another but always in process as it is challenged and contested? The idea of a constant core ideology that defies challenge has been transformed by putting a self — in this case, Wittman Ah Sing — in relation to it and by teasing out a new transnational character who, because of the complementary qualities of being both American and Chinese, is stronger and more resilient. Wittman does not, after all, commit cultural suicide, as the text's opening montage makes plain. He draws strength from both traditions and makes his way toward helping to craft a new identity for the heterogeneous group assembled at the end of the novel.

8

Overseas Chinese Literature: A Proposal for Clarification

Laifong Leung

The expression Overseas Chinese (*haiwai huaren*) here is understood as referring to people of Chinese ancestry living outside mainland China, Taiwan, Hong Kong, and Macao. The term Overseas Chinese literature, *haiwai huaren wenxue*, contains two notions: Overseas Chinese-language literature (*haiwai huawen wenxue*) and Overseas non-Chinese-language literature (*haiwai fei huawen wenxue*). Despite the fact that both kinds of literature are written by people of Chinese descent overseas, they receive entirely different treatment by scholars in mainland China. The former has received much attention since 1979, with the introduction of well-known North American Overseas Chinese writers such as Bai Xianyong (b. 1937) and Yu Lihua (b. 1931) to mainland Chinese readers.[1] Up to 2005, thirteen international conferences on Overseas Chinese-language literature have been held in different cities in mainland China. Over a dozen universities and provincial academies of social sciences have established centers devoted to the study of works written in the Chinese language by Overseas Chinese writers. Journals such as *Huawen wenxue* (Literature in Chinese Language), *Shijie Huawen wenxue luntan* (Forum on World Chinese-Language Literature), and *Tai Gang yu haiwai Huawen wenxue* (Taiwan, Hong Kong and Overseas Literature in Chinese) have regularly published critical articles on the works written in Chinese by ethnic Chinese writers living in North America, Southeast Asia, Europe and elsewhere.

Mainland Chinese scholars have come a long way since the Cultural Revolution (1966–76) and the death of Mao Zedong (1976). They did not begin reading Chinese literature produced outside the Mainland until 1979. For the first time in mainland China, in the winter of 1979, the People's Literature Press published three anthologies of Taiwan literature: *Taiwan xiaoshuo xuan* (An Anthology of Taiwan Stories), *Taiwan sanwen xuan* (An Anthology of Taiwan Essays), and *Taiwan xinshi xuan* (An Anthology of Taiwan New Poetry), which immediately caught the attention of Chinese readers nationwide. *An Anthology of Taiwan Stories* became a best-seller in that year.[2] Realizing their three-decade long isolation, Chinese scholars tried hard to catch up with literature outside the Mainland. Naturally, they first turned to Taiwan and Hong Kong writers, for linguistic, geographical, and political reasons. The first conference held in 1982 in Guangzhou signaled the first fruits of their research on Chinese writers living beyond the Mainland borders. The title of the conference, "Tai-Gang wenxue guoji yantao hui" (International Conference on Taiwan and Hong Kong Literature) reflected their research focus. In 1986, because of an increasing knowledge of Chinese writing from other parts of the world (mainly North America and Europe), the name of the conference was changed to "Tai-Gang ji haiwai huawen wenxue guoji yantao hui" (International Conference on Taiwan, Hong Kong, and Overseas Chinese-Language Literature). In the fifth conference in 1993, in Lushan, Jiangxi Province, the name was again changed to "Shijie huawen wenxue guoji yantao hui" (International Conference on Global Chinese-Language Literature), and it has remained thus until the present day. The last change was significant. It shows mainland Chinese scholars' ambition to re-map Chinese-language literature from a global perspective. That is, instead of dividing Chinese-language-literature geographically into Mainland and non-Mainland parts, they view it as a worldwide construct. The underlying rationale is that "as an independent entity, Chinese-Language-Literature stands parallel to literatures in English, French and Spanish."[3] This seemingly broadened vision and scope, however, is still limited in its outlook. Although affirming in their critical discourse the significance and success of works written in Chinese, nothing was mentioned about those written by writers of Chinese descent in other languages.[4] The small number of articles on these works appearing in journals devoted to foreign literature studies may suggest that they are regarded as such.[5]

In November 1997, I was invited to attend the Ninth International Conference on Global Chinese-language Literature in Beijing. In my paper, I discussed works by Chinese Canadian writers.[6] During the discussion period, a scholar from Guangzhou pointed out that mainland Chinese scholars at an earlier conference had reached a consensus that literature not written in the Chinese language was considered foreign literature. In November 2002, when

I began gathering materials for this chapter, I wanted to know if there had been any change in the attitude towards literature written not in Chinese by Overseas Chinese. The answer I received from a young scholar of the Chinese Academy of Social Sciences was: "In discussions concerning the belongingness of literature not written in Chinese by Overseas Chinese, the conclusion reached by Chinese scholars was that it should be considered foreign literature."[7]

If one looks at the topics of study on Overseas Chinese-language literature covered by mainland Chinese scholars in recent years, one will notice that they tend to focus on such issues as identity, alienation, national consciousness, and nostalgia.[8] These topics also appear in works written in other languages by Overseas Chinese writers.[9] However, works not written in Chinese are mostly excluded from the research domain of mainland Chinese scholars, on several grounds (see below). This seems to be a narrow-minded attitude.

For one and a half centuries, the emigration of Chinese has resulted in over 50 million Overseas Chinese spreading all over the world. More and more Overseas Chinese, especially their descendants, have adopted the languages of their host nations as their medium of expression. Overseas writers of Chinese descent have written works of high literary quality in non-Chinese-languages and some have attained international fame (see below). As a result of increasing globalization and China's rapid pace in opening to the outside world, it is time for scholars in mainland China to modify their narrow view and to turn their attention to what overseas writers of Chinese descent have been doing with non-Chinese languages. To do so will not only enrich Chinese literature but also invigorate literary creation and research.

Writings by Overseas Chinese

In 1963, Tang Junyi (1909–76), a well-known Chinese scholar residing in Hong Kong, wrote three long essays lamenting the fact that terrible political and economic circumstances had caused the scattering of Chinese people like fallen petals and fruits (*huaguo piaoling*) to various parts of the world.[10] He regarded this diasporic situation as a great tragedy (which, of course, began before he was born and continues long after his death). Viewed from today's global perspective, Professor Tang's lament may appear gloomy. Today, as a large number of Chinese readily migrate to different parts of the world, what they write and in what language they write will have an impact, directly or indirectly, on the Chinese cultural landscape.

Those Overseas Chinese writers who use their mother tongue as a medium of literary expression are usually first-generation immigrants who grew up in a Chinese cultural environment and received Chinese language education. Even though these writers have lived in their adopted countries for many years, their behavior and worldview, to various degrees, still bear the imprint of Chinese culture. They publish their works in mainland China, Taiwan, and Hong Kong, as well as, though less often, in Chinese language magazines in the adopted country. But it is through the readership in mainland China, Taiwan, and Hong Kong that they build their writing career. This applies to many Overseas Chinese writers who immigrated to North America, Europe, and elsewhere.

However, the ability to write Chinese is not always restricted to first-generation immigrants. In Southeast Asian countries that have a long history of Chinese immigration and a tradition of teaching Chinese language in school, many second- or third-generation Chinese descendants can write in Chinese. This is further made possible because many Overseas Chinese in Southeast Asia have a tradition of sending their children to attend school in mainland China. After the Communists came to power in 1949, most South Asian Chinese sent their children to Taiwan, and recently, again, back to mainland China. The cultural ties with the ancestral land help maintain the use of the Chinese language as a literary medium. A prime example is the scholar and poet Wong Yoon-wah (b. 1947), who was born in Singapore, educated in Taiwan and the United States, and now teaches in Taiwan.

The situation in North America is less favorable. Far fewer in number and very scattered, North American Chinese live for the most part in an English-dominated environment. It is not easy for the North American-born second generation to speak fluent Chinese, let alone write in the language. Therefore, second-generation Chinese writers, such as Maxine Hong Kingston and Amy Tan, mostly choose English as their medium of literary expression. Of course, there are a few first-generation immigrants who master the English language and who can write in both languages. Prominent early examples include Lin Yutang (1895–1976), Li Jinyang (b. 1917), and recently, Ha Jin (b. 1956).

Thus, the situation for Overseas Chinese writing in the global context is that there are those Overseas Chinese writers who write in Chinese and those who write in other languages. In the following, I briefly discuss the development of Overseas Chinese-language literature and Overseas non-Chinese-language literature in North America. I attempt to show that a one-sided emphasis on either will lead to an incomplete picture of literature by Overseas Chinese. It will be a great loss for China to ignore Overseas Chinese writing in other languages.

Recent Overseas Chinese-Language Literature in North America

Relocation from one place to another is often a stimulus for literary writing. But this only applies to those who can write. Early immigrants from China, most of them poorly educated, had little opportunity to record their emotions, thoughts, and experience.[11] Foreign students from China then became the élite who could write their experience, though they were much preoccupied with China. A number of writers and scholars of the May Fourth era, such as Hu Shi (1891–1962), Chen Hengzhi (1890–1976), Xu Zhimo (1896–1931), and Wen Yiduo (1899–1946), who studied in the United States in the early twentieth century, and Lu Xun (1881–1936), Guo Moruo (1892–1978) and Yu Dafu (1896–1945) who studied in Japan, made a significant contribution to the development of modern Chinese literature. After the World War II, the first group of Chinese students to experience dislocation was students from Taiwan who landed in North America from the 1950s. In the 1960s, the emergence of fictional works focusing intensively on the lives of Chinese students in the United States resulted in the genre of foreign-student-literature (*liuxuesheng wenxue*) being established. Yu Lihua was acclaimed the founder of this genre after she published a number of stories and novels. She was immensely popular among Overseas Chinese throughout the last four decades of the last century and is still active. Her novel *Youjian zonglu, youjian zonglu* (Seeing the Palm Trees Again*)* (1966),[12] which captures the feelings of rootlessness through the intellectual hero's predicament, was widely read in Hong Kong, Taiwan, and elsewhere. When it was published in mainland China in the early 1980s, it immediately caught the attention of readers who, since 1949, had been cut off from the outside world.

After 1979, China under Deng Xiaoping (1904–97) began the Four Modernizations drive and adopted a policy of sending students and scholars abroad to study. In 1988, the number of students sent to the United States reached 25,000, only 1,000 fewer than those from Taiwan.[13] After the June Fourth massacre in 1989, over 30,000 students and scholars from mainland China chose to remain in the United States.[14] In 1995, over 220,000 Chinese students were studying in the United States.[15] Beginning in the late 1990s, even middle school and elementary school Chinese students could study abroad, and their numbers continue to increase.

Because of the drastic differences between mainland Chinese and North American societies, these students who came to study in the United States and Canada encountered much greater culture shock than those from Taiwan and Hong Kong. The psychological impact of this culture shock is vividly depicted in the book *Liuxue Meiguo* (Studying in the United States) (1996) by Qian Ning (son of Qian Qishen, former Chinese minister of foreign affairs), who writes, "In China, many people are eager to get to know what they thought of as Western thinking and culture. However, once they come to the West (United States), they immediately feel that the greater impact on them is not Western thinking and culture but the material world of the West (United States) which forms the basis of Western thinking and culture."[16] Such reactions to the West have resulted in works expressing great curiosity about the new material surroundings.

The foreign-student literature written by students from mainland China started almost thirty years later than that by students from Taiwan. However, the late appearance was just in time to fill the space left by the gradually ageing writers from Taiwan. The large number of mainland Chinese students throughout the United States and Canada has become a new force in the foreign-student literature genre. Apart from stylistic differences, after the 1990s, the typical themes of earlier foreign-student literature such as love, identity, national consciousness, conflicts among foreign students themselves, and clashes of values between East and West, have been extended to or even replaced by a greater variety of concerns, such as struggles at the workplace, and the lives of illegal immigrants. These works tend to emphasize the realization of individual potential (which was suppressed under Communist rule), the adjustment to newly acquired freedoms, and the search for wealth and fame — usually not thematic concerns for writers from Taiwan. Works such as *Manhedun de Zhongguo nuren* (A Chinese Woman in Manhattan, 1992) express the idea of aggressively making use of every means for personal success.[17] *Beijingren zai Niuyue* (A Beijinger in New York, 1991) dramatizes the characters' initial struggle to survive in the United States and their loss of moral values in the quest for material wealth.[18] These works, set in the United States, became immediate best-sellers in mainland China. A television series based on *Beijingren zai Niuyue* became a hit. This was after Deng Xiaoping launched his more radical economic reform in February 1992 in Shenzhen, the special economic zone near Hong Kong. The combined impact of the open policy, the economic reform, the development of the media, and the subsequent changing popular taste of the readers boosted the sales of this kind of Overseas Chinese-language literature.

Another aspect of the later foreign-student literature is the use of the Internet. During the months leading up to the June Fourth massacre and after, mainland Chinese students studying in North America used the Internet to communicate among themselves. Afterwards, they continued to use it as a channel of communication on things ranging from political matters to buying and selling cars, as well as literary creation. In websites such as *Fenghua yuan* (Maple Garden), *Xin yusi* (New Words), and *Huaxia wenzhai* (Selected works from China), and many others, literary works of various kinds appeared daily. For the first time, mainland Chinese writers could publish their own thoughts and feelings without going through the red tape and censorship of the Chinese editorial bureaucracy. More gratifying is that their voices can reach anywhere in the world instantly. Most prolific among these Net writers is Shao Jun (b. 1960, Qian Jianjun), who came to study economics in the United States in 1988 and published the first Chinese story "Fendou yu pingdeng" (Struggle and Equality) on the Internet in 1991. He actively promotes the use of Internet in writing. Recently, a collection of essays was published about his works.[19] The transnational nature of Chinese-language literature is certainly greatly enhanced by the Internet.

At present, post-secondary institutions such as Fudan University, Nanchang University, Shandong University, Shantou University, Ji'nan University, Tongji University, Zhongnan Finance and Economics University, and Fujian Normal University, as well as research institutes such as the Guangdong Social and Sciences Academy, and the Chinese Academy of Social Sciences in Beijing have established research centers for studying Overseas Chinese-language literature. A six-volume collection of foreign-student literature was published in Shanghai in 2000.[20] Other multi-volume collections of Overseas Chinese-language writers are also under preparation.[21] What must be pointed out is that the research undertaken by mainland Chinese scholars seems to be confined to literary works in Chinese by first-generation immigrants (except for Southeast Asia, where the teaching and use of the Chinese language has a long tradition among Overseas Chinese.)

The Development of Overseas-Non-Chinese-Language: Literature in North America

It is almost 100 years since the first Chinese living abroad began publishing works in the language of the adopted country.[22] In the early 1900s, Sui Sin Fa (pen name of Edith Eaton [1867–1914]) began publishing stories in English in the United States.[23] In the 1930s and 1940s, Lin Yutang published many books and stories in English.[24] In the mid-1970s, Chinese American writing became well known with the publication of Maxine Hong Kingston's *The Woman Warrior* (1976).[25] Also very successful was Amy Tan's *The Joy Luck Club* (1989), which became a best-seller and was subsequently made into a film.[26] As successful popular novelists, they continue to enjoy recognition in North America.

At the same time, in Canada, a century and a half after the arrival of Chinese immigrants, a number of fictional works by Canadian-born ethnic Chinese writers began to receive acclaim.[27] Evelyn Lau's *Runaway* (1989),[28] Sky Lee's *Disappearing Moon Café* (1990),[29] Denise Chong's *The Concubine's Children* (1994),[30] Wayson Choy's *The Jade Peony* (1995),[31] and Paul Yee's *Ghost Train* (1996)[32] were either nominees for prizes or award winners.

In the 1990s, these North American ethnic Chinese writers were joined by recent immigrants (most of whom came as students) after the Cultural Revolution in China. In English, these students or dissidents wrote autobiographies or similar works exposing the dark aspects of Chinese Communist rule. This kind of writing concerning the Cultural Revolution had its beginning in 1972, with Ken Ling's gripping account of his Red Guard experience in *The Revenge of Heaven*.[33] But it was not until the appearance of Liang Heng's autobiographical work *Son of the Revolution* (1983)[34] that the devastating results of the Cultural Revolution on individuals and families became a prime theme for writers from similar backgrounds. From the mid-1980s to the late 1990s, there appeared in the West many works of similar nature, such as Nien Cheng's *Life and Death in Shanghai* (1986)[35] and Rae Yang's *Spider Eaters* (1997)[36] in the United States; Jung Chang's *Wild Swans* (1991)[37] in England; Li Yan's *Daughters of the Red Land* (1995),[38] and Ye Xingting's *A Leaf in the Bitter Wind* (1997)[39] in Canada; and Lulu Wang's *The Lily Theater* (2000)[40] (first published in Dutch) in the Netherlands. Other works such as Ying Chen's *Ingratitude* (1998),[41] originally written in French, was nominated for the Femina Prize in France. In France, Dai Sijie's *Balzac and the Little Chinese Seamstress* (2001),[42] also originally written in French, was a best-seller and made into a film. In the United States, Ha Jin's *Waiting* (1999) won the National Book Award, and his recent novel *The Crazed* (2002) brought Chinese American English writing to a high level.[43] These works are significant for at least two reasons. First, they were written in English (or other European languages) and thus were accessible to readers worldwide; and secondly, most attain a high literary quality.

Their international fame is a matter of envy to mainland Chinese writers who (even perhaps household names inside China) are hardly known outside. Except for a few — Mo Yan (b. 1956), Liu Heng (b. 1954), Su Tong (b. 1963) — whose works have been adapted into films (*Red Sorghum, Judou,* and *Raise the Red Lantern* respectively) by well-known directors such as Zhang Yimou (b. 1948) and Chen Kaige (b. 1949),[44] most are little known outside mainland China. Even popular names in mainland China such as Wang Anyi

(b. 1953), Zhang Xianliang (b. 1936), and Wang Meng (b. 1934), despite having some works translated into English,[45] cannot match the fame of Jung Chang and her book *Wild Swans*.

Among other things, I can see one similarity between the works written by the later immigrants and the North-American-born ethnic Chinese writers. The North American-born ethnic Chinese writers attempt to reconstruct a Chinese American ethnic history through retelling the bitter struggles of their ancestors and their own often unhappy childhood. Family history plays an important role in their works. Works by recent immigrants from mainland China overwhelmingly use the autobiographical approach to express themselves. They reconstruct from memory their personal and family sufferings caused by the Cultural Revolution and other political campaigns, as well as their coming to terms with the past. Both groups of writing embody three stages: expose, resist, and re-establish. In both cases, the disasters of China forced people to leave. For the North American-born Chinese writers, it is the disasters of the late nineteenth and early twentieth centuries; for the recent immigrants, it is the disasters of the second half of the twentieth century.

Overseas Non-Chinese-Language Literature Not Recognized in China

Works of non-Chinese-language literature are generally considered part of the literature of the adopted country. However, they are not just that. They also have links with China. One clear item of evidence is the fact that their stories are mostly about people of Chinese ancestry. If so, why are they not recognized by mainland Chinese scholars? I suggest three reasons:

First, mainland Chinese scholars seem to think that only works written in the Chinese language are authentic; works written in other languages are automatically considered foreign literature. This view arises from the idea that only *Hanyu*, the language used by the Han majority in China, is the acceptable language.

Secondly, mainland Chinese scholars tend to say that not many people in China know foreign languages. This, too, cannot be an excuse. One only needs to look at how many scholars in the foreign literature division in every provincial academy of social sciences and how many foreign language departments exist in universities throughout the nation. Of course there are far fewer than those working in the field of Chinese literature, but the number is certainly not negligible. Actually, in the past twenty years, many mediocre novels in English have been translated into Chinese. But many quality works written in English by ethnic Chinese have been ignored.

Thirdly, some autobiographical works written by Overseas Chinese writers are critical of the current government and hence they are not translated into Chinese, or it is asserted that these autobiographical works by exiled Chinese writers are merely versions of the "literature of the wounded" (*shanghen wenxue*) of the late 1970s and early 1980s, and so they are not worth mentioning when Chinese literature has already entered the so-called "post-modern era." The first reasoning shows the damage caused by censorship on literature, which does not need further elaboration here. The second reasoning shows a rigid and inadequate view of literature, and represents a slightly camouflaged advocacy of censorship. The question is: who has the right to put an end to the scrutiny of historical events? It would generally be agreed that the greatest work of literature coming from Napoleon's invasion of Russia in 1812 is Tolstoy's epic novel *War and Peace*, which he wrote about half a century after the events described. If and when a monumental and magisterial literary presentation of the Cultural Revolution in China appears, then and only then will its nature, its form, and its style — and its language — be evident.

The problem lies in the rigidity of thinking: drawing a boundary, putting writers and their works that fit one's conception inside the boundary, and excluding those that don't fit. "Going into the world" (*zouxiang shijie*) has been a popular expression in mainland Chinese cultural circles since the mid-1980s. In order to make Chinese literature known to the world, foreign language organizations in mainland China specialize in the translation of Chinese literary works into foreign languages. Yet works already written in foreign languages by ethnic Chinese writers overseas are not being recognized.

The essential condition for maintaining Overseas Chinese-language literature is to foster the Chinese language. However, if one looks at the distribution of Overseas Chinese, one must admit that, except for Southeast Asian countries like Malaysia, Singapore, and Thailand, which have a large proportion of Chinese and a long tradition of teaching Chinese in schools, elsewhere, in North America and Europe, it is not practical to expect the second generation to be able to write Chinese. If Overseas Chinese-language literature is limited to the first-generation immigrants, the prospect of the next generation writing in Chinese is rather dim. For that reason, it seems all the more important to encourage Overseas Chinese writers to write in whatever language they wish.

The narrow-minded mentality imposed on Chinese intellectuals since 1949, and enforced by successive political campaigns — particularly the Anti-

Rightist Campaign (1957), and the Cultural Revolution — seems to have a lingering effect on them. The one-sided emphasis on learning the Russian language, and the rejection of English and other European languages under the Communist rule, sadly and seriously hampered their ability to carry on a dialogue with the outside world. As the historian S.A.M. Adshead wrote memorably about the Tang Dynasty, "China was the middle kingdom, not in the exclusive sense of having nothing to learn from the rest of the world, but in the inclusive sense of being able to learn anything."[46]

In conclusion, I would like to suggest tolerance and acknowledgement of diversity in the discussion of Overseas Chinese literature. In particular, I wish to propose that Overseas Chinese literature be understood as comprising two parts: Overseas Chinese-language literature, and Overseas non-Chinese-language literature, both of them representing potentially valuable parts of Chinese literature in a broad sense.

Film

9

Crouching Tiger Hidden Dragon: (Re)packaging Chinas and Selling the Hybridized Culture in an Age of Transnationalism

Jennifer W. Jay

In 2001, numerous international awards garnered by Ang Lee's *Crouching Tiger Hidden Dragon*, together with its resounding box office success, marked an age of transnationalism and globalization in Chinese film culture and identity.[1] When observed as the flow of culture and the dynamics of the world economy, the concept of globalization embraces the inclusionist ideals of cross-culturalism and boundary crossing.[2] The dominance of Western culture inevitably makes Westernization a part of the transnationalizing process, as seen in the making and reception of the film, variously described as a Chinese fairytale, a tragic love story, and the auteur's boyhood fantasy world of *wuxia* (martial chivalry). In order to examine the question of cross-culturalism, border crossing, and Westernization, we first need to have a handle on what Chinese configurations of identity and culture are portrayed in the film. In this chapter, I look at how Ang Lee rounded up the talent among the Chinese diaspora and China to construct a transnational China of individual turmoil, family tensions, social conflict, and a Confucian patriarchal ideology — all present in his *Pushing Hands* (1992), *Wedding Banquet* (1993), and *Eat Drink Man Woman* (1994).[3] I argue that this transnational China of hybridized Western feminism and dialogue is marketed as the conglomerate Chinese culture that derived from the *wuxia* genre of popular culture, fantasies of gravityless martial capabilities, and a landscape of varied geography and blurred ethnicities.

Creating (Transnational) China: Rounding up the Diaspora Talents

The US$15 million budget for *Crouching Tiger Hidden Dragon* amounts to the biggest budget for Chinese film (Schaefer 2001), but it is modest by Hollywood standards and certainly by itself would not have been adequate to recruit the film's large pool of talent from the Chinese diaspora and China. These individuals, of Chinese ethnicity but most living outside China, welcomed the opportunity to work with the Taiwan-born auteur, who made no secret of his commitment to win an Oscar®. When *Sense and Sensibility* did not get nominated for an award for directing in 1996, Ang Lee apologized to Taiwan, promising that his next Chinese film would win international awards (Shih 2000, 94 citing *Chinese Daily News*). Indeed, *Crouching Tiger Hidden Dragon* brought home the Golden Globe's Best Director and Best Foreign Picture awards. Although the film was the official entry from Taiwan, Ang Lee shared the honor with the Chinese film industry from Taiwan, China, and Hong Kong with his public statement: "I think the achievement is an accumulation of all the endeavors that all Chinese filmmakers have put in over the years. I think it is a great thing that such a cross-cultural event can happen ... and I'm just very happy I'm participating in that" (CNN.com 2001).

With the exception of the scriptwriter, James Schamus, the production team and actors who created *Crouching Tiger Hidden Dragon* hail from the Chinese cultural zone that includes the overseas Chinese diaspora. Tim Yip (Oscar® for art direction), Peter Pau (Oscar® for cinematography), and Yuen Wo Ping (Oscar® for martial arts direction) are from Hong Kong; together the three designed a continuous landscape with the aesthetics of traditional Chinese paintings. Pulsating from the landscape is the rhythm and music composed by Tan Dun (Oscar® for original musical score), who was born in China, worked in Hong Kong, and now makes his home in the United States.[4] Taiwanese American Yo-Yo Ma's cello and Hong Kong/American CoCo Lee's title song enhanced the beauty of the landscape and heightened the poignancy of the plot.

Film critics on location in China commented on local technicians communicating in Mandarin Chinese while the art direction and martial arts teams shouted their instructions in Cantonese. At the Oscars® ceremony, Peter Pau and Tim Yip acknowledged some names in Cantonese. Mandarin is the language of *Crouching Tiger Hidden Dragon*, but the presence of the different accents of the principal actors, rather than seen as a weakness of the film, is actually quite appropriate, given the fact that the characters they play, Jen,

Lo, Shu Lian, and Mu Bai came from various parts of China. The popular Hong Kong star Chow Yun Fat (Li Mu Bai) lives and works in Hong Kong but has already ventured into Hollywood in *Anna and the King* (1999). Born in Malaysia and now living in Hong Kong and in the United States, Michelle Yeoh is known as a *gongfu* film star in Hong Kong and American box offices (*Tomorrow Never Dies*, 1997). Both labored through their lines with a Cantonese accent, but Michelle Yeoh had a more difficult time because, not reading Chinese, she learned her lines through *pinyin* romanization. Taiwan's Chang Chen has a Taiwanese accent, and Beijing's Zhang Ziyi (Jiaolong) speaks Mandarin with the same Beijing accent used by the minor characters.

The fact that the production team and the actors come from the Chinese diaspora and China is nowhere more evident than in the appearance of the names in the film credits and film reviews. The Chinese order of names is consistent, the surnames appearing before the personal names. But the English listing varies according to the romanization system chosen, and the order of the surname depends on the country where the individual currently works. Ang Lee, born in Taiwan and living in the United States, has a Taiwan romanization and lists his surname last; Chang Chen, born in Taiwan and working in Taiwan, uses the standard Wade-Giles romanization and lists his last name first, as do the Taiwan scriptwriters Wang Hui Ling and Tsai Kuo Jung. China's Zhang Ziyi, similarly, lists the last name first, but the *pinyin* romanization used is different. Chow Yun Fat and Yuen Wo Ping have the Cantonese romanization, as used in Hong Kong, and they list their surnames first; but Tim Yip and Peter Pau, who also live in Hong Kong, list their surnames last because of their non-Chinese personal names. Because they live in the United States, Michelle Yeoh and Yo-Yo Ma list their surnames last, but Tan Dun has chosen to continue using the traditional Chinese order of his surname, although he now works in New York.

In this wide assortment of principal talents, all are identifiably of Chinese ethnicity, but only Zhang Ziyi and Tan Dun have actually lived in China. The director, art director, cinematographer, and other principal actors constructed and articulated a China of stunning landscape and martial chivalry through the shared experience of popular culture, derived from reading *wuxia* novels and/or watching and/or making previous martial arts films. Martial chivalry is based on the imagination of an underworld, or *Jianghu* (literally, rivers and lakes), where moral fighters call upon justice and righteousness to rid the public of bandits and corrupt fighters, to support the underprivileged and avenge personal wrongs. Because the *Jianghu* world operates with its own principles of vigilante justice, it often collides with government authority and can be considered a culture of resistance. But in *Crouching Tiger Hidden Dragon*, there is no tension or collision between the *Jianghu* underworld and government authority. The China portrayed here is not plagued by domestic or international politics; instead, it is a transnational China with fantasized superhuman strength and gravityless walks on walls, balances on bamboo trees, and leaps over water and rooftops — martial skills believed to be acquired through transmission from masters and/or from secret manuals.

Constructing/Configuring a Transnational China

From Novel to Screenplay: Characters and Plot

In his acceptance speech at the Oscars®, Ang Lee describes his team pursuing "… a China that is fading away in our heads." This China is derived from Wang Dulu (1909–77), a native of Beijing, whose *wuxia* novels have been noted for the intensity of emotions rather than by their display of martial arts.[5] The novel *Crouching Tiger Hidden Dragon* (*Wohu canglong*) is the fourth part of a five-part saga of four entangled relationships that take place in three generations. The relationship between Yü Xiulian (hereafter, Shu Lien) and Li Mubai (hereafter, Mu Bai) is dealt with in the second and third parts of the saga, so *Wohu canglong* focuses on Yü Jiaolong (Delicate Dragon, hereafter, Jen) and Luo Xiaohu (Little Tiger, hereafter, Lo), whose names and secrets provide the title for the novel and film. After reading the novel, Ang Lee wrote the précis and gave it to his usual scriptwriter, James Schamus, who worked with two writers from Taiwan to turn the novel into a script. An academic who does not know Chinese but who understands Hollywood and film critics, Schamus is valued for his intuitive grasp of the Chinese script (Ma 1998, 168).

The resulting screenplay is generally faithful to the original novel in characterization. The principal and minor characters are portrayed with remarkable accuracy, particularly in holding back emotions and hiding secrets. The love between Shu Lien and Mu Bai is doomed by traditional social values and martial chivalry, and the relationship between Jen and Lo is destroyed by class differences. Jen's theft and pursuit of Mu Bai's Green Destiny Sword serve as the unifying sub-plot in both the novel and the screenplay.

But to transform Wang Dulu's complex 763-page Shakespearean tale into 120 minutes of screen time, Ang Lee and his scriptwriters had to adjust the plot. One change involves omitting sub-plots, one example being Lo's tragic family background and his Han Chinese ethnicity. The number of characters is reduced by blending personalities, as in the character of Biyan huli (Jade-eyed Fox, hereafter, Jade Fox) being combined with that of her husband Gao

Langqiu, who was actually Jen's literary and martial arts tutor in Xinjiang. Another example is the combination of Mu Bai's master, Jiangnan He (Southern Crane), with the latter's sworn brother, Yaxia (Mute Fighter), who was killed by Jade Fox.

Mu Bai's death and Jen's leap from the mountain represent the most drastic changes from Wang Dulu's novel. In the novel Jade Fox dies early in the plot and she is killed by Shu Lien and not by Mu Bai (Wang Dulu 2000, 3.129). In fact, Mu Bai survives the other three principal characters twenty-one years later, at the conclusion of the five-part saga (Wang Dulu 1985, 17.1132). But Mu Bai's screenplay death is a more powerful symbolic statement of the same tragedy — the impossibility of intimacy between Shu Lien and Mu Bai, plagued as they were by guilt and repression.

The screenplay has Jen jumping off Wudang Mountain in south China, leaving open the question whether she has committed suicide. In the novel, however, Jen jumps off Miaofeng Mountain, outside Beijing, to perform ritualistic filial piety to bring about the recovery of her father from illness. The jump here is just a way to leave the family that she had shamed; as she had planned, she survives her jump, has a last rendezvous with Lo before disappearing and later giving birth to their son in the deserts of Xinjiang (Wang 1985).

Inclusionist Geography and Ethnicity

Apart from the characterization and plot, Ang Lee has preserved Wang Dulu's expansive and inclusionist view of China's diverse regions and ethnicities. Although much of the plot takes place in the capital, Beijing, the characters traverse the deserts and oases of Xinjiang's Taklamakan in the northwest, and scale the mountains and bamboo trees of Anhui and Hubei provinces in the south. In addition, Wang Dulu's novel has Jade Fox operating her banditry from Yunnan Province in the southwest.

It is not surprising that multiple ethnicities should exist in a diverse geography such as China. Indeed, we observe a bandit gang composed of ethnic groups in Xinjiang, and in Beijing we see ethnic differentiation of Manchu and Han groups. Both Wang Dulu and Ang Lee blur the ethnic differences and focus on the similarities in rituals, for example, those of marriage. Although the Han women bound their feet as an ethnic and civility marker (Ko 1997, 9), both Han and Manchu women sport natural feet in the film and much of the novel. Another case in blurring the lines of ethnic differences is in Ang Lee's conversion of Lo into an unspecified and collective non-Han minority. He also appropriates the Beijing superstition of jumping off a mountain to bring about the recovery of sick parents and recycles it as a non-Han myth that Lo describes to Jen. In both the novel and screenplay, the Manchu, Han, and Lo's unspecified ethnic groups are shown with mutual trust and without the racial and ethnic tensions one would have expected in Qing China. Thus we see Shu Lien and Mu Bai in close friendship with a Manchu aristocrat, entrusting him with a valued Han Chinese sword. Such incidents can be seen as examples of border crossing in the inclusionist perspective of China's ethnic diversity, as reflected in both the novel and the screenplay.

Chinese Identity and Culture: Confucianism, Buddhism and Daoism

In an inclusionist China of blurred ethnicities, the core culture embraces Confucianism as the dominant ideology. Despite being set in eighteenth-century China, where minority conquest and political tension occurred, the story has no wars or natural disasters that exert external pressure on the characters. The conflict is in the individual mind as it relates to family and social norms, as dictated by the dominant ideology that cut across the lines of ethnicity, class, and gender. In negotiating their way through Confucian norms and Buddhist and Daoist alternatives, the characters become the architects of their own tragic circumstances.

In the Confucian social order that we observe in the film, the principal characters are subjected to Confucian conformity and hierarchy. For example, marriages are arranged by parents and elders, who must be obeyed according to Confucian obligations of filial piety. After being enticed by the *Jianghu* underworld and acquiring martial skills, Jen could not live the prescribed life of an upper-class wife, nor could her aristocratic upbringing allow her to defy her parents and marry a former bandit, Lo.

Equally doomed is the long-enduring love between Shu Lien and Mu Bai, both belonging to a lower class than Jen's. Shu Lien's betrothal to a man she had never met, but who later became Mu Bai's friend and who died in the *Jianghu* underworld before the marriage took place, destroyed any chance of a union with Mu Bai. The Confucian patriarchy treating the betrothal as an actual marriage, Shu Lien becomes an unmarried widow who offers incense to her late betrothed's altar at her home. Whenever Shu Lien and Mu Bai meet face to face, the intersecting values of the individual (love), family (filial piety), and society (*yi*, righteousness) reaffirm Shu Lien's ambivalent status, as reflected in her hairstyle. Her hair is piled up in a chignon as is characteristic of married women, but one thin braid brushes against her shoulder, perhaps to show her maiden status.

In *Crouching Tiger Hidden Dragon*, Buddhism and Daoism are offered as alternative ideologies, but although they bring psychological relief, they are not effective in overturning the dominant Confucian rules. Daoist notions of harmony, peace, and balance seem to pervade through the natural beauty and the tamed discipline of animals in the landscape. Daoism is brought to us disjointedly as bits of philosophical aphorisms, as shown in the following examples: "Be strong yet supple, that is the way to govern"; "The more you want to repress it, the stronger it gets"; and "Sharpness comes from dullness." Although Xinjiang and the *Jianghu* underworld seem to offer freedom from the constraints of Confucian rules, allowing untrammeled exercise of emotions, such freedom is ultimately unattainable in the experience of all four principal characters.

Mu Bai in particular is in the deepest conflict with his emotions, despite drawing upon Buddhism and Daoism as alternative ideologies. Confucianism makes intimacy with Shu Lien impossible, but Confucian public obligations still entangle him and his Green Destiny Sword in military chivalry against corrupt bandits in the *Jianghu* underworld. At Wudang Mountain, he engages in physical exercise and practices the Daoist style of martial arts, but the Buddhist discipline and the philosophy that he dispenses prove unable to remove the inner turmoil of his emotions. The following are examples of Buddhist aphorisms in the film: "The things we possess have no permanence"; "What we do not possess is real"; and "Mu Bai, the name, sword, martial skills, manuals, everything is illusory." He describes to Shu Lien that during meditation he had once reached a realm where space and time faded, but he could not let go because he was held back by a matter of the heart, or his unspoken love for Shu Lien.

The strong prevalence of Confucianism is the reason why no one in the film could defy Confucian social norms and achieve Daoist freedom and Buddhist discipline, resulting in the impossibility of resolving the inner and social conflicts without tragic consequences. But the presence of all three ideologies, which are often seen as markers of Chinese identity and culture, also construct the core components of a transnational China.

Globalizing Transnational China

Marketing and Explaining the Film

In portraying this transnational China, Ang Lee sought to "respect the promise that *wuxia* makes to the Asian audience, which is a fantasy of power, romance and morality" (Chute 2001). However, this highbrow martial arts film did not overwhelm the lukewarm audiences in China, Hong Kong, and Taiwan. The criticisms of the film ranged from the non-standard Mandarin spoken by three of the principal actors, to the plot being too complicated and the martial arts being too boring compared to the speed and violence of Hong Kong *gongfu* films. Another comment is that the film is too Westernized, and indeed Ang Lee admits that serving up *Crouching Tiger Hidden Dragon* is like educating the Western diet with chop suey before introducing authentic Chinese food in a Chinese American restaurant (Chute 2001). But it is this Westernizing touch that has generated a more enthusiastic global audience in North America and Europe.

Marketing the film early was the first step in enticing the Western audience; this was done by inviting foreign film critics to the shooting in Beijing and the Gobi Desert a year before the film screened commercially in the West. The importance placed on publicity can be seen by a US$7 million advertising budget in a film that cost only US$15 million to make (Liu 2001). Sony Picture Classics hired a 13-year-old to construct the film's impressive official website; the bonus is the additional advertising by the boy himself, who advises that people his age should go and see the film (Liu 2001).

But much of the publicity was done by Ang Lee himself, according to Michael Barker, co-president at Sony Picture Classics: "… Ang went around the country and spoke to everyone … . One of the keys to success was that he put as much work into promoting the film as he did into directing it." In an interview, Ang Lee challenges the Western audience to accept *Crouching Tiger Hidden Dragon* as a transnational film and culture, as he speaks about a more inclusionist world: "I think as globalization is happening more and more, at the same time people cherish their individual cultures more…. In the course of 15 years, I find the world has become more embracing. It's progressing. Now we'll see if we can break into the multiplexes" (Kirkland 2000).

From Screenplay to Translation and Subtitles

One crucial step in selling *Crouching Tiger Hidden Dragon* as a global film and culture involves using Western notions to translate the dialogue into English subtitles. The subtitles could not simply be literal translations, as James Schamus states: "There are so many layers and echoes and meaning and poetry that are simply nonexistent for westerners, and it was really important to avoid that to keep the flow of the movie going" (Kaufman 2001). To make the subtitles user-friendly, Schamus used a minimum of English words so that the viewer's interest remains focused on the screen action. The reduction is achieved by simplifying both the names of the characters and the dialogues, at the sacrifice of accuracy. Those who understand Chinese may read the resulting subtitles as describing not a transnational China but a Westernized hybrid China.

The translation and simplification of the names reflect a flexible adaptation in pronunciation and romanization. Yü Jiaolong becomes Jen, and Luo Xiaohu is translated as Lo, Liu Taibao as Bo, Cai Xiangmei as May, and Biyan huli as Jade Fox. Perhaps in order to retain some Chinese touch, Xiulian and Mubai are not translated, but they appear as Shu Lien and Mu Bai, in transcriptions that are easier for a Western audience to pronounce. Jen's fiancé Lou becomes Gou in the subtitles, in order not to confuse this name with Lo, her lover from Xinjiang.

Simplification and reduction are also applied to the translation of the dialogues, which turn out to be rather accurate in tone and intent although not in literal meaning. For example, in the scene under the bamboo trees, after Mu Bai has just taken away the Green Destiny Sword from Jen, he hollers, literally, "Kneel and recognize me as your teacher." The tone is appropriately translated as "Kneel!" Jen's response, literally, "you are dreaming" is even more skilfully translated as "Never!" In another case, when Shu Lien congratulates her employee on the birth of his daughter, he replies, literally, "it would be good if she has one toe like yours," which Schamus more effectively translates as "I'll be happy if she's half as strong as you are."

The most Westernized rendering of the dialogue occurs when Mu Bai, dying in Shu Lien's arms, says literally: "I would rather wander at your side, be a ghost in the wilderness for seven days; and even as I drift into the darkest place, my love will not let me be an eternal lonely spirit." The subtitle renders a very free English translation: "I would rather be a ghost drifting by your side as a condemned soul than to enter heaven without you. Because of your love, I will never be a lonely spirit." A literal translation would be too cumbersome for a Western audience not familiar with the Daoist and Buddhist concepts of ghosts and the dead. But bringing in the Western notions of the condemned soul and entering heaven without a loved one is too foreign to the traditional Chinese palate. This translation appeals to the Western audience, providing an obvious example of Westernized hybridity in the film.

Another hybridity that appeals to the Western audience is the three-minute long title song, "The Love Before Time," with music by Tan Dun and lyrics by James Schamus. Sung in English by CoCo Lee in the middle of showing the film credits, the song is a moving testimony of unforgotten love in the expansive backdrop of the North Star, sky, mountains, and oceans. The fact that it is sung in English in a film that is totally in Mandarin Chinese is a hybridity in itself. In the Cantonese version of the film, the song is titled *yueguang airen* (Lover in the Moonlight) and sung by CoCo Lee in Mandarin. The song portrays a sleeping lover who wakes up in the moonlight; the lyrics bear no resemblance to the English version. Because it is the same film, one wonders why translation is not used, as in the subtitles. Could it be that the English version would not appeal to the Chinese audience, and so new lyrics had to be written in Mandarin?

Women, Feminist Sensibilities, and Sexuality

In the globalization of transnational China in *Crouching Tiger Hidden Dragon*, another Westernizing process can be observed in the focus on women, the depth of emotions, and feminist sensibilities — a combination found in Wang Dulu's novel but made much more emphatic in the film. Indeed, as Schamus states, "From an Asian point of view, the emotional content is quite new for the genre. And the emphasis on female subjectivity and the concerns of the women characters are absolutely revolutionary" (Kaufman 2001).

Women dominate the film with their presence and strong personalities, and all principal and minor characters display their own emotions and unique life experiences. The characters include a cross-section of society and reflect several generations: a newborn baby girl, a girl acrobat in the market, the teenaged Jen and May, Shu Lien in her late twenties, Jade Fox and Jen's mother in middle age, and Shu Lien's housekeeper in old age. Trapped in emotional turmoil, Shu Lien still functions effectively as a successful career woman managing a security courier service. Jen's mother is shown as an upper-class wife conducting herself with dignity, but her emotions could be as repressed as those of Shu Lien.

We could say that the film minimizes gender differences, or even note that gender crossing has occurred in the portrayal of these women as equal, if not superior, to the men in physical strength. Physical endurance can be observed in Jen and Shu Lien, who engage in the longest fighting sequences of the film; another example is seen when Jen sends dozens of male fighters into defeat at the restaurant. When Jen emerges dressed as a man, even Shu Lien does not know of the disguise until she pulls a woman's hairpin from Jen's hair.

Although no physical frailties of women are shown, femininity and tenderness are communicated through the traditional roles of women, as when Jen lies in bed with Lo, and Shu Lien drinks tea with Mu Bai. And despite their strong personalities, the women weep and cry profusely, as shown in

May when her father is killed, in Jen when she visits Shu Lien to get a change of clothes, and in Shu Lien when Mu Bai dies.

No character in the film intrigues the Western audience more than the feisty Jen, whose embedded name of "Dragon" is masculine and unusual for a girl in traditional China. The courtship fighting sequences with Lo in Xinjiang readily bring out the rare chuckles in the film audience. Jen's pursuit of her comb and the symbolism of love that the comb represents in the film are not found in Wang Dulu's novel; by writing the comb into the film, Ang Lee succeeds in making the character of Jen more innocent and more like a spoiled teenager in the West. Her range of personalities certainly invites Freudian analysis: gentle, unmarried upper-class young lady trained in artistic and literary talents; passionate lover with Lo; and cold, calculating thief and fighter against her tutor (Jade Fox), friend (Shu Lien), and strangers. In the film, Mu Bai fears that Jen's lack of moral discipline, when combined with the martial techniques that she had hidden from even her parents, would turn her into a poisonous dragon, or an evil force, bringing disaster and chaos to both society and the *Jianghu* underworld. We observe a hint of this ruthlessness when Jen cuts Shu Lien's arm and continues the attack, after Shu Lien gives her a chance to return the sword and escape unharmed. In sum, Ang Lee has made Jen into a more innocent and likable personality than what was intended in Wang Dulu's novel.

The flexibility of the script is demonstrated by adapting the original roles to the strengths of the actors. Chow Yun Fat had agreed to do the film when the role of Mu Bai was rather small, but Ang Lee later carved out a larger and more mature role because of Chow's status as a star. And because Chow is not trained in martial arts, the fighting scenes were also reduced in intensity (Schaefer 2000). As the filming progressed, Ang Lee made Jen's role sexier, as he perceived that Zhang Ziyi, despite being a neophyte actress, could handle the film's sexuality better than he had expected. These changes led to the creation of a subconscious and mutual attraction between middle-aged Mu Bai and the teenager Jen. This relationship is shown in the scene in the cave, when the disheveled Jen challenges Mu Bai: "Is it the sword you want, or me?" An agitated Shu Lien, who feels that her relationship with Mu Bai is threatened by Jen, implores Mu Bai: "She is not our concern. This will pass very quickly. She'll get married." Shu Lien betrays her jealousy and possessiveness in the fighting sequence with Jen, when she sternly warns: "Don't touch it. It's Li Mu Bai's sword!" The sword here is heavily charged with the Western notion of phallic symbolism; Shu Lien here is seen fighting for her relationship with Mu Bai rather than for the sword.

The tragic unfolding of the relationships between Mu Bai and Shu Lien, and between Jen and Lo, constructs the epic love story that the Western audience extracts from the film. The keen observer will notice that Ang Lee squeezed in a more simple love that can be actualized. This is the relationship between Bo and May, whose paths crossed when her father tried to arrest Jade Fox. Bo and May occupy much larger roles in Wang Dulu's novel than in the film.

Conclusion

When *Crouching Tiger Hidden Dragon* won mainstream awards, Ang Lee and Tan Dun attributed the success to crossing boundaries, and popular film critics talked about the "marriage between translatable cultures." In discussing Ang Lee's other films, literary critics have referred to "the politics of flexibility" and "flow" (Shih 2000, 86). According to Shih, *Sense and Sensibility* and *Ice Storm* did not receive recognition, because "racism disregards Ang Lee's strategic flexibility and universal appeal as irrelevant at crucial moments in the production of meaning. The Academy Awards' exercise of gendered and racialized minoritization is the moment of arrest, a nodal point, in the process of flow" (Shih 2000, 98). Now that Ang Lee's film has taken home four Academy Awards®, the breakthrough or flow has certainly taken place. What flows through the film is the transnational China created by Ang Lee's team of largely diaspora talents; what propels the flow is the process of Westernization associated with marketing transnational China as a global film culture. What is marketed remains identifiably Chinese, the dominant Confucian culture and actors of Chinese ethnicity acting out a *wuxia* epic of doomed love and emotional turmoil. Indeed, this transnational China, despite being Westernized and hybridized, retains its Chinese identity and culture in the eyes of the global film audience — approachable but still exotic, intriguing but accessible through subtitles.[6]

10

Father Knows Best: Reading Sexuality in Ang Lee's *The Wedding Banquet* and Chay Yew's *Porcelain*

January Lim[1]

> But with all my pictures, I'm always dealing with the same theme — the conflict between personal freedom and social obligation, especially in a changing time.
>
> Ang Lee, "In Person"

> Ultimately, I feel that great theater raises core questions, questions about our humanity and our place in the world.
>
> Chay Yew, "Fusion"

In "Coming Out into the Global System," Mark Chiang states that the closet "signifies the deviation from ethnic identity that must be covered up" in *The Wedding Banquet* (379).[2] For Chiang, it is clear that "all of the younger generation of Chinese/Taiwanese in the United States are engaged in the masquerade of authenticity insofar as none of them are capable of enacting the forms of tradition that the older generation continually seeks to re-create" (379). Drawing upon Chiang's idea that the closet is "a function of ethnicity as well as sexuality," I want to explore further the trope of the closet, a masquerade of normative gender and sexual identity by the younger generation of the Chinese diaspora in America and Britain, who are unable to maintain the traditional, axiomatic heterosexual configurations (379). The closet, I suggest, also applies to the older generation in the Chinese diaspora who are invested in patriarchal imperatives and "Chineseness." I choose two works, a film and a play, not because they individually or together exhaust the field of questions regarding race, gender, class, labor, and sexuality, but because they will allow me to throw into relief the concept of performance, an enactment of sexual identity in the body, which permeates the narratives and involves all the main characters who act out already-scripted subject positions. Throughout my discussion, I deploy the concept of the closet to inform an analysis of the film and play and the ways in which they articulate same-sex sexuality and affirm patriarchy in relation to questions of power, identity, and Chineseness.[3]

My reading of Yew's *Porcelain*[4] and Lee's *The Wedding Banquet* focuses principally on the way both stage an interracial relationship and show that the father figure occupies a role that calls for an ongoing reinterpretation of patriarchy in light of geopolitical realities. Openness is not a feature of Chinese culture in these two works, and the closet works as a strategy to maintain "face" in the diaspora. *Porcelain* was first staged at the Etcetera Theatre Club in London on May 12, 1992, and *The Wedding Banquet* was first shown at the Berlin Film Festival in February 1993 and released in the United States in the same year. In these two works, I focus on the lies, silences, and denials that dominate the patriarchal family. In particular, I adopt Eve Sedgwick's theorization of the closet, extending the deployment of the closet to the diaspora to inform an analysis of the disciplinary mechanisms that function to produce and preserve intact the heteronormative definitions of a sense of "Chineseness" in the diaspora.[5] As Chiang has rightly put it, homosexuality is not only a forbidden subject in most Asian communities, it is also something that does not warrant any discussion "because it is only a *problem* for white people: 'it' is a white *disease*," and in Hong Kong, for instance, the "colloquial word for a gay man is simply *gay-loh* (gay fellow)" (378). The first section of this chapter takes up the preservation of an idealistic, masculine Chinese identity and the issues of patrilineality, by attending to the film's use of gender differentiation and the concept of closetedness. In the second section, I argue that the closet in Yew's play gestures to the tension between public sex and containment. To begin this analysis, I turn to the question of Confucian thinking and the idea of Chineseness.

Confucian Values, Filial Piety, Chineseness, and *The Wedding Banquet*

The Confucian political philosophy is foregrounded in patriarchy, a structure that is based on stratified relations. In the Confucian hierarchical system, status is defined clearly and conduct is guided by propriety, which requires submission to and acceptance of authority. This leads to asymmetrical communication and interaction between father and son, husband and wife, superior and subordinate, teacher and pupil, and so on. In *An Introduction to Confucianism,* Xizhong Yao contends that Chinese scholars conceive of Confucianism as containing elements that contributed to Chinese and East Asian modernity, despite their acknowledgement of the tension between Confucianism and social reality (266). In the pantheon of Confucian ethics, the most important values are unquestioning allegiance and obedience of subjects to authority. It is not my intention to delve in detail into Confucianism and neo-Confucianism; rather, I focus on the salient elements of Confucian ethos such as acceptance of authority, filial piety, and familial orientation, for the purpose of highlighting the investment of the closet in the diaspora, a closet of secrecy that stabilizes the gender and sexual identity of the characters who violate Confucian taboos such as same-sex romance or erotic practices and interracial romance.[6]

The concept of filial piety is complex, comprising a range of virtues such as moral obligation, respect toward the elders of the family, and fraternal deference. Basically, filial piety can be defined as "a natural feeling of responsibility and as an expression of gratitude which makes good the pains the parents took for their child" (Roetz 54). As Roetz has put it, "the survival of Chinese culture has been attributed to the influence of *xiao,* filial piety" (53). If *xiao* represents the basic power in which to perpetuate the Chinese nation, then *The Wedding Banquet* ceaselessly reinstalls the concept of filial piety for this purpose: care and obedience toward the parents, "primary to the father" (Roetz 54). The film takes pains to reiterate the son's care for his father, for example, by showing Wai Tung sobbing quietly in bed and begging Wei Wei not to let the father know that she is not having a baby. Clearly, the film portrays the mother as a submissive wife to the father, and Wai Tung as an obedient son who respects his parents, especially his father, as central to a sense of Chineseness in the diaspora.

In order to locate and analyze the trope that constitutes Chinese identities in the diaspora and the social and cultural contexts of transnational Chinese practices, however maligned and vexed the term has become, I invoke an imagined category like "Chineseness." I do so even while acknowledging that such an identifier works to perpetuate an essentialist identity, an identity that elides the materiality of class, gender, sexuality, place of birth, language, and religion, which Chinese people must negotiate historically and geographically.[7] For a transnational entrepreneur élite such as Wai Tung, family and *guanxi* (particularist relations) provide him with "access to inside information and commercial contacts" in the diaspora (Nonini and Ong 21). It is no surprise that the mother is disappointed and upset with her son's casual treatment of the marriage ritual. Thus Chineseness here is based on filial piety, family values, communal ties, and *guanxi* relations that are crucial to Wai Tung's economic success in the diaspora. His investment in the closet becomes a necessity; it is literarily the father's, mother's, Wai Tung's, Simon's, and Wei Wei's business. While the generation and valorization of bloodline kinship by Chinese immigrants point to a political taxonomy of exclusion, it might be understood as a resistance to the dominant culture that refuses to accept them. What is at issue, then, is that the rationale for bloodline purity operates as a way, though fraught with difficulties and contradictions, to arrive at some kind of common historical cultural identity to counter racial oppression and cultural hegemony. In the context of *The Wedding Banquet,* filial piety takes the form of Wai Tung closeting his sexual orientation and fulfilling his father's wish. To be sure, Wai Tung manages to perform heteronomative masculinity, to effect biological reproduction, and to maintain his romantic union with Simon, which is no mean feat for a gay man in the diaspora.

In his insightful essay on *The Wedding Banquet,* David L. Eng points out the new, non-stereotypical way in which Lee portrays a gay Asian American man who moves "toward an incipient queer and diasporic formation," but argues that this potentially groundbreaking representation remains "ultimately unfulfilled" (44). Following Eng, I would argue that the narrative underwriting of Wai Tung's sexual identity is one of need, the need to be closeted in order to produce an authentic ethnic identity that evacuates homosexuality. Although the film enables the reimaginings of Asian American men, particularly in the character of Wai Tung, the reimaginings rest on heteronormative ideologies marked by gender hierarchy, in which women as well as Simon are subjected to the authority of father and husband. Assuming the role of Simon's bourgeois husband and later as a heterosexual groom in the wedding banquet, Wai Tung is at once man and father. Wai Tung can have the cake and eat it, that is, enjoy an intimate relationship with Simon and, simultaneously, perform a sanctioned identity by seeming to have a heteronormative reproductive family. So, in the end, the full spectacular exercise of the wedding banquet is invoked as public performance for the diasporic community, maintaining the movie's heterosexual resolution. However, I think it is important to take note that the narrative — though comedic and innovative — works to re-establish a modified patriarchal law and to reinstate conservative notions of gender boundaries, even as it reframes Wai Tung's identity outside of the heterosexual paradigm. In particular, Wei Wei's eventual freedom from her Third World status through her pregnancy indicates that her corporeality and sexuality are bartered for her security, cultural belonging, and legal status in America.[8]

According to the filmic narrative, Wei Wei, the feisty, bohemian artist, undergoes a transformation in which she becomes a domesticated housewife and a nurturing mother. From this perspective, the film conveys an imagined patriarchy and a conservative notion of womanhood, which inform a femininity associated with motherhood and submission. Wei Wei represents an aberrational character, a woman who is not "wife material" for Wai Tung. Central to the narrative is the construction of Wei Wei as a liberated, sexually available woman, whose subjectivity must be delimited and disciplined to maintain the stability and order of social relations in the diaspora. Titillating in its play with Wei Wei's open sexuality, the film is adamant in enacting the change in her behavior by regulating her desire and displacing it from the sexual register to the maternal. When the film first shows Wei Wei in her sweltering loft, her seductiveness, her perspiration-soaked clothing, and her come-on directed at Wai Tung are at once out of place in received Confucian notions of identity and morality, and exceed the boundaries of femininity. Her aberrational splitting from traditional femininity legitimizes the discipline that is needed to subdue her. Taking swigs of vodka from the bottle, engaging in disappointing erotic encounters with all kinds of men in an attempt to secure a green card, and declaring to Wai Tung that she fancies him — "It's my fate. I always fall for handsome gay men" — Wei Wei spells trouble, notwithstanding her physical beauty as a heterosexual object of desire. It is precisely the surplus signification Wei Wei embodies that must be contained and managed, according to the narrative logic of Confucian ideology, so that she becomes, or at least performs the role of, proper Chinese woman, dutiful wife, and nurturing mother.[9]

Whereas Wai Tung's physical relationship with Wei Wei is merely instrumental, his relationship with Simon is one of affect, romantic love. The marriage between Wai Tung and Wei Wei represents a function of the closet, which is to conceal Wai Tung's sexual identity and to preserve the institution of the family in the diaspora. Indeed, Simon represents the apotheosis of the perfect partner, a romanticized ideal, for Wai Tung. The cinematic narrative depicts Simon as a character performing normative gender roles and guaranteeing harmony in the domestic space, a space that is stabilized around heterosexual norms. Occupying the place of a caring partner, Simon is required in the narrative structure in order to position Wai Tung in the masculine role and to closet his sexual identity. Working as a physical therapist, Simon complements Wai Tung, a busy, driven real-estate entrepreneur, with his domestic skills that include whipping up a candlelight dinner, and cooking an Asian gourmet dinner for the Gao family, a culinary expertise that the domestically challenged Wei Wei passes off as her own. Besides managing the affairs of the home, Simon even arranges the dubious wedding, thinking that it will give Wai Tung a big tax break, appease his parents' anxiety about their son's marital status, and provide Wei Wei with a green card. In cultural terms, it is Simon rather than Wei Wei who represents the movie's locus of stability. To put it simply, what appears to be a violation of heteronormativity — Simon's queerness — simply secures its power.

To mark Simon's sexual identity as concealed, the film includes two scenes of him in the bathroom.[10] The first scene involves Wai Tung talking on the phone with the mother, who tells him that she and his father are coming to America for his wedding. While this conversation is going on, the camera lingers on Simon in the bathroom, enclosed and circumscribed by the cubicle. The second scene occurs in a bathroom at the restaurant after the wedding banquet and before Simon drives the father and mother home. Simon faces the urinal, but the camera films his back, which covers him from view, and pans around the facilities after he walks away from the urinal. Crucial to these shots of Simon in the water closet, especially within the patriarchal imaginary the film articulates, is their function of keeping Simon's sexual identity in the closet, even though he is out in his community. The washroom, then, is symbolic: these scenes make visual the closeting of Simon's relationship with Wai Tung, who fails to live up to the traditional Chinese expectation of marrying a nice Chinese girl.

In return for his staying in the closet for the sake of maintaining Wai Tung's ethnic and sexual identity within the Asian diasporic community, Simon is readily accepted by the father as another son. This is demonstrated when the father gives him a red packet containing money on his birthday, a gift signifying Simon's contractual agreement with and complicity in the father's secret.[11] Although the film contains this contractual exchange by displacing Simon's acceptance with the aura of romance, it implies that his taking care of Wai Tung, that is his conjugal servitude, is a condition of the contractual familial agreement.

Before I discuss the role of the father in the diaspora, I want to address Wei Ming Dariotis and Eileen Fung's interpretation of the father's raised arms when he is frisked by an airport security attendant "as a gesture of surrender, of one generation's sacrifice for another" (202).[12] What escapes this argument is the logic of the father's knowledge of the staged wedding, his approval of Simon, his understanding of homosocial bonds, and his assurance of getting an heir. As such, I do not read the lifting of his arms as an indication of surrender; rather, I read it as a victory, as a moment of "father knows best." In an economy of patriarchal succession, the father himself escapes from an arranged marriage to join the army, but ultimately fulfills his filial duty of producing an heir. Now that patrilineal duty is passed to Wai Tung in the diaspora, the father can fly home, knowing that his lineage is secured and the loving care between his son and Simon is restored.

The Omnipotent Patriarch

But what kind of man or father is Mr Gao, whose attributes might seem to be his ill health and delicious passivity? As a retired general, Mr Gao wields tremendous power in the family, despite his silence. It is certainly no accident that the father's status in the army is revealed to the audience through the mother: "He was a general commanding tens of thousands of soldiers." Louis Althusser asserts, in "Ideology and Ideological State Apparatuses," that the army constitutes one of the components of the Repressive State Apparatus, which "functions massively and predominantly by *repression* (including physical repression), while functioning secondarily by ideology," in order to "ensure their own cohesion and reproduction, and in the 'values' [the Army and the Police] propound externally" (74; original emphasis). Given this proposition, the film already positions the father in the forefront of the narrative, for his productive role and stature extend beyond commanding an army of soldiers to commanding his family. The army represents an overarching hegemonizing institution with a load of historical weight behind it, playing a crucial role in the formation of social order.

It is, of course, Lee, who mobilizes the narrative motif of the respectable paternal authority and disposes him to the veneration and submission of his family and Old Chen in the diaspora. So, Old Chen, the father's jeep driver for twenty years, is called on to formalize the heterosexual union in the film. Assuming the role of the father's "servant" in the diaspora, Old Chen demonstrates deference to the retired commander (he bows to the father and insists on standing before him) and reminds Wai Tung of his filial obligation.[13] More importantly, he facilitates the rigor by which the sexual closet must be preserved when he mobilizes the wedding banquet ritual so that the father will not lose face in the diaspora.[14] Striking in the narrative is the fidelity and fraternal sentiments between the father and Old Chen, even as their relationship is anchored in the hierarchical order of patriarchal society. I would argue that the father's concern for genealogical transmission and his acceptance of his son's transgressive sexuality might be brought out by drawing together the homosocial and fraternal elements in the film. The father's endorsement of the same-sex romance between his son and Simon is facilitated by his own homosociality — his ties to Old Chen. Old Chen, positioned subordinate, reminisces upon his service to the father during the war. The power difference between the father and Old Chen might be read as a turn-on in homosocial relations, that is, the social and military hierarchies are sites of erotic investment.[15] The father's homosocial bond to Old Chen is resolved by an appeal to the loyalty of a soldier to a commander, an allegiance that continues well after the war is over. Within the Confucian patriarchal social system, the father and his son are unable to make choices openly, so that both have to dissemble and closet their knowledge of the strength of homosocial and homosexual bonds. Mr Gao's performance of unknowing when it comes to his son's sexuality makes explicit that his family's status in the diaspora is based on wealth, privilege, and established sexual mores as a technology of power. In this narrative, there are talkative women and silent men. The mother might be doing all the cajoling and talking; however, at any time when the father decides to speak his word is law.

The Wedding Banquet, I suggest, legitimizes the closet in order to secure patrilineal transmission and to sustain the normative constructions of masculinity and femininity, which underlie relationships of power, race, and sexuality. On its face, The Wedding Banquet appears to be a narrative about familial relations, but it is a carefully constructed work.[16] Amid the diasporic reality of challenging cultural and social changes, the film keeps the ideal of paternal, masculine power well alive: it is the father figure of Mr Gao — "I watch, I hear, I learn" — and his looks of disapproval that Wai Tung, Wei Wei, Mrs Gao, and Simon reverently fear and attempt to please, demonstrating that the father continues to wield tremendous authority. The closet, then, satisfies the father's excess privilege and desire to perpetuate both family lineage and ethnic identity in the diaspora through the exploitation of Third World reproductive labor.

Porcelain

Chay Yew's *Porcelain* focuses on the father's power and role in the relationship of his Asian son with a white man. Yew dramatizes the immigrant father, ashamed and devastated by his son's sexuality and crime of murder, disowning him, and offers us the figure of Dr Jack Worthing, cloaked in the drag of heteronormative moral authority, begging the question of his sexuality. Drawing upon the concept of the closet, I suggest that the play tellingly elaborates same-sex sexuality in relation to questions of ethnic identity, pathology, social control, and power. Considering Chinese cultural aversion to publicity and resistance to same-sex relations, the father's need to enforce the closet within the diaspora is even more urgent in the play *Porcelain* than in Lee's film. John's male-centered sexual practices constitute a transgression of the traditional definitions of Chinese community and its established perimeters concerning sexuality.

Whereas the closet in *The Wedding Banquet* works to conceal queerness, the closet in *Porcelain* points to the tension between public sex and containment. *Porcelain* is not quite as glossy as, and is more intense than, *The Wedding Banquet*. The language used in the play to describe the detail of erotic exchange is abrasive, but it brings to bear the realities of a lived experience. The trajectory of the play follows John Lee, a 19-year-old British Chinese[17] boy waiting to attend Cambridge University, who cruises the public restroom scene looking for love. John's lover, William Hope, is a 26-year-old builder who identifies himself as a heterosexual man but participates in same-sex erotic intimacy in public restrooms. Feeling that his heterosexual male identity is threatened by John's sexuality, William ditches John and returns to meeting strangers at the public restroom in Bethnal Green in East London for quick trysts. For William, returning to this practice serves as a way of disavowing a relationship with John and his own queerness. The jilted John shoots William six times, turning the white porcelain urinal in the restroom red. Immediately after this murder, the media conduct interviews with various individuals, transmogrifying the murder into a sensational documentary of an Asian killing a British man. Then enters Dr Jack Worthing, "one of the least liked criminal psychologists in the business," who interrogates John and decides that the young man be put in jail (*Porcelain* 17).

As a theatrical retelling of *Madame*[18] *Butterfly* and *Carmen,* with the Asian man sitting in his jail cell and saying, "I've finally got Will all to myself now," *Porcelain* unsettles the audience's presumptions of codes of behavior for Asians (110).[19] Giacomo Puccini's libretto presents a recognizable representation of the demure, faithful, and silent ideal Asian woman, a Butterfly who plays out all the erotic, exotic, and imperialist fantasies of Western men. Chinese pop music, Puccini's libretto, and *chinoiserie* are popular Asian signifiers of colonial fantasy, and Puccini's opera is a popular piece of music for evoking an "erotic fantasy" for white men (Fung 124). William asserts from the outset that the music of *Madame Butterfly* is his favorite, revealing that his relationship with John is predicated precisely on a perspective aligned with the opera whose theatrical function it is to circulate the romantic sentiments embodied in the Japanese geisha, a model in which racial and sexual fantasies intersect. Contrary to the conventions of the Madame Butterfly legend, a trope that continues to circulate as an instrument for the oppression of Asian women and gay men, with a gruesome twist the play counters the stereotype of the submissive Asian woman killing herself for a man, after learning that he has married an American wife. Will's death, of course, has specific dramatic functions: it underscores John's refusal to play the role of the tragic Butterfly in cultural terms, and at the same time critiques the West's intrigue with Asian culture as "rooted in ignorance" (*Porcelain* 32).

Rejecting the discursive representations and essentialist notions of Orientalist fantasy, John debunks stereotypical expectations twice over: first by not conforming to the image of the accepting victim, and second by not appending himself to the list of Madame Butterfly's necrology. As the play depicts an Asian man committing a homicide, an act that goes against the dominant culture's racial stereotypes of the "model minority," it uses John as a perverse figure of resistance[20] and offers an ongoing process of rethinking the power politics of race and sex in interracial relationships in all their complexities.[21]

Viewed in this light, *Porcelain* is a necessary play, laying bare the messiness of appearance and reality, of identity politics and diasporic communities, which are threatened with implosion of racial, political, social, and sexual tensions.[22] To the politically conservative Asian communities in the diaspora, John is bad boy karma, and his flouting of the law, participating in illegal sexual conduct and killing Will, seem morbidly twisted.[23] The shooting scene, for instance, represents radical, shocking behavior, unexpected from one who seeks social approval from the Asian diasporic community and the state. John's "*disruptive excess*," to borrow Luce Irigaray's term, threatens the hegemonic heterosexual system, a system that has already excluded him racially, culturally, and sexually (78; original emphasis). However, his excess also represents a resistance to the status quo of closeting his sexual identity and desire because he refuses to be oppressed by it. As the cultural identity and representation of Asians in the diaspora is in constant flux, I read Yew's portrayal of John's excess as an attempt to reinvent new narrative strategies emerging in the early 1990s, pushing the envelope in order to address the concerns of Asians living in the diaspora.[24]

Politics of Gay Space

To insist on a normalization of heterosexuality, however, requires active management and policing of non-normative sexual desires, as shown in the dwindling of public erotic locales in Britain (*Porcelain* 46). The presence of an attendant in the public restroom also gestures to the technology of surveillance, which effectively renders the waning of same-sex erotic encounters within the closet. Arresting individuals for "public indecency" and "police entrapment" in public restrooms comprise the strategies deployed by the fathers of culture, a culture that endorses only heteronormative reproductive coupling, to crack down on non-normative sexual practices (*Porcelain* 64, 65).

Such assaults on non-normative sexualities also rely on a disciplinary regime that includes an inscription in law of the prohibition of homosexual practices, and Yew's play comes at a time that prefigures a reform in British legal history in 1994, when British MPs would vote on the Sexual Offences (Amendment) Bill. Specifically, I take the Foucauldian concept of power to punish and discipline beyond the walls of the mental asylum and prison, and uncover its new investments, particularly those that center on bodies practicing non-normative sexual conduct. To be sure, prior to the reign of Queen Victoria, gay sex was punishable by death.[25] Although the specter of punishment by hanging was gone, male homosexual relation was made a crime in 1885. It was only in 1967 that British MPs voted to legalize consensual gay sexual activity, formalizing the age of consent at twenty-one. In spite of the decriminalization of homosexuality, there remain the laws against consenting homosexual activities such as buggery, indecency, cruising and propositioning men, and procuring, which are considered offenses (Tatchell 84–5). Following this legislative restriction, if a man over twenty-one has consensual sex with a man under twenty-one, both have committed an illegal activity, an offense that implies criminal prosecution and custodian sentences. One of the reasons for the age of consent is to protect children from older predatory males. The *1967 Sexual Offences Act* specifies that males must be over twenty-one, in order for them /to conduct their homosexual behavior in a private space. In addition, the act states that a lavatory is a public convenience used by the people, and thus consensual gay sex is deemed illegal in the public washroom.

Operating in the interests of protecting the health and morals of society and sustaining the heterosexual matrix, the fathers of the law capture, or rather, strenuously contain, queer space by invasion and criminalization: social cleaning, police harassment, and deployment of stigmatizing rhetoric. It was not until 1994 that the British government made an amendment to the age of consent to eighteen. And in 2000, the government invoked the *Parliament Act* to bypass the House of Lords, an appointed body of English aristocrats, and sent the *Sexual Offences Act* to the Queen for royal approval. Since then, the age of consent for same-sex sexual relations has been lowered to sixteen. In the early 1990s, however, social cleaning operated as a form of interventionist panoptic system that marginalized and stigmatized homosexual erotic exchange.

Father of the Law²⁶

What the play depicts as the initial deficiency of John's masculinity (his effeteness) amounts in fact to an excess of exteriority, a failure to contain or closet his sexuality. John's sexual and racial encounter with William, the murder, and the cruising itself also evoke contempt and censure, as evident in Dr Worthing, whose typologizing impulse revealed to an investigative reporter from the Channel Four news team, an artsy and liberal television station, corresponds to the intensity of institutional and informal racism and homophobia in contemporary Britain:

> I think — personally, between you and me, I think this whole case is — sick. Public sex is an offense. Murder is an offense. Well, let me put it in simple words — a queer Chink who indulges in public sex kills a white man. Where would your fucking sympathies lie? Quite open and shut, isn't it? (*Porcelain* 27)

As a criminal psychologist located within the lineage of Enlightenment figures, in the sense that he embodies the Western value of rationality, Dr Worthing is willing to give the lowdown on a young gay British Chinese man's erotic pursuits to an in-your-face journalist only if Channel Four prepays him £1,000: "I'm sure there are other news shows that will want first dibs on this story" (*Porcelain* 16). Notwithstanding his self-serving impulse, Dr Worthing's voice is the voice of heteronormativity, the dominant voice of culture and the law. As an Enlightened figure, Dr Worthing is supposed to be liberated from the grips of "tradition," as his intellect has the ability to reason, question, and transcend the tenacious conventional power structure, and to emancipate individuals from different kinds of prejudice.

Dr Worthing, however, does not invoke a sense of optimism. Rather than a forward-looking psychologist, Dr Worthing is a retrogressive "heterosexual white male," who insists that he has never "cottaged,"²⁷ that is, had sex in a public restroom, and is "definitely not Oriental" (*Porcelain* 27). In effect, John's violence becomes a racially and sexually conditioned characteristic, as Dr Worthing alludes to this understanding when he remarks to the reporter: "It's just that I have nothing in common with those types, you know" (*Porcelain* 28). What is underscored in the media interviews is a technology of racialization as it is interimplicated with heteronormativity, that is, white and straight, not "Oriental" and gay. To put it simply, Dr Worthing underscores a distinction between John and him. As a British Chinese excluded from Dr Worthing and the community's imaginations of sympathy,

John is an absent presence in social, sexual, and political representations. In short, John shifts from invisibility to hyperembodiment in the play. Intrinsic to the criminalizing logic of the interrogation, as conducted by Dr Worthing, is the specter of government involvement and the characterization of John as pathological, a characterization that relies on racially embedded stereotypes of irrationality.

Reading Dr Worthing's interrogation of John in its social, cultural, and medical context, it is possible to theorize how same-sex erotics are insistently contained in the play. The confession that Dr Worthing attempts to extract from John, then, operates within a larger discursive sexual economy: John's killing of William emanates from the excess that his desire signifies, which must be regulated in order to maintain the dominant cultural order and coherent heterosexual contract. At the same time, Dr Worthing's voice transforms John's sexual excess into surplus value as it sensationalizes his "crimes" into a form of television entertainment, providing the audience with the knowledge and secrets of race and sex. To put this another way, Dr Worthing's attempt to contain a regulated sexual excess in turn produces excess as surplus value.

John's confession, that is, his act of speaking out, is turned into a performance and spectacle, and the various commentaries offered by a variety of radio stations point to Foucault's concept of power that operates through the production and proliferation of discourses. Extending Foucault's idea of Christian confession as producing sex as a disclosure of truth that is predicated on pleasure, I suggest that the play brings to bear the use value of inner, raw, authentic feelings, the "errant fragments of an erotic art that is secretly transmitted by confession and the science of sex":

> We have at least invented a different kind of pleasure: pleasure in the truth of pleasure, the pleasure of knowing that truth, of discovering and exposing it, the fascination of seeing it and telling it, of captivating and capturing others by it, of confiding it in secret, of luring it out in the open — the specific pleasure of the true discourse on pleasure. (Foucault, *History of Sexuality* 71)

John's disclosure of his brief affair with Will, a speaking out of his sexual history that involves the body and mind, then, generates pleasure among listeners and viewers. The tedious process that is involved in eliciting the disclosure of truth and sexuality, as evident in John's initial silence and Dr Worthing's persistent coaxing and concoction of a romantic affair with Suzanne, only enhances the pleasure of the secret sexual act between John and Will. In short, the disclosure process is always already implicated in an asymmetrical power relation of domination and submission, the father of authority demanding the truth of sexuality, a discourse that purportedly represents the truth of John's moral and psychological standing.

Part of Foucault's research is to critique the authority of experts and to repudiate the voices of mediators. By narrativizing the disturbing story of John's "crime of passion" (*Porcelain* 111–2), the mass media, together with clinical psychologist, Dr James Christian, a figure that recalls the Christian Church, and criminal psychologist, Dr Worthing, mediate, evaluate, and offer an "inside look" at the *real* thing, at a British Chinese male closeted away in the public restroom and later, incarcerated in jail. As Dr Worthing at the helm gives the media his "daily dealings" with his client and puts John's sexual identity under intense public scrutiny, the so-called "Lee murder documentary" staged and circulated by Channel Four not only makes good spectacle; it renders visible the anxiety of racial difference and erotic exchange between men, as evident in the dangers and threats that lurk in the terrain of the porcelain urinal (*Porcelain* 15). Previously a spatially compressed world for male-centered erotic interludes, the public water closet becomes a site in which John's sexuality, an excess that overflows the containment of the closet, is subject to the surveillance and social discipline of Dr Worthing. Sentencing John to life without parole is always, ultimately, a disciplining of both race and sexuality as a potentially disruptive problem, as a threatening excess.

Bodies in Transit

Dr Jack Worthing, who calls *The Importance of Being Earnest* (1895) a "play about people pretending to be other people just to get laid" (*Porcelain* 22), invokes intertextual echoes with Oscar Wilde's play and its encoded homosexual allusions. Specifically, I want to consider the way Wilde's play pivots on identity. Characters are never what they appear to be: Jack pretends to be virtuous Uncle Jack Worthing in the country and adopts the name Ernest when indulging a life of pleasure in the city. It is important, then, to understand the erotic undertones of Dr Worthing's secret double identity in the context of Wilde's play.

One of the essential preoccupations in *The Importance of Being Earnest* is the issue of names and naming, which has implications for a nexus of contacts, desire, and sexuality. If social and professional life is a kind of visceral spectacle, a site with political implications, it is significant that, in Yew's play, Dr Worthing presents himself in the media as "the technician of behavior who must measure the punishment for the corrective effect it will have — on the guilty party or others," to borrow Foucault's phrasing ("Talk Show" 140). It is no accident that Yew names a psychiatrist after a character whose identity is highly suspect, especially given that, in Wilde's play, Jack Worthing is found in a black leather handbag that is placed in the cloakroom at a railway station. In Wilde's play, the concealment of identity is at issue — in the handbag, in the cloakroom, and in the dressing room — gesturing to the already closeted body in transit. Timothy d'Arch Smith takes up this idea of double identity by citing the final sonnet from John Gambril Nicholson's homoerotic ballad, "Of Boys' Names."[28] As Smith suggests, the name "Ernest" is a coded word for homosexual desire, and by extension, the Ernest in *The Importance of Earnest* is an allusion to the double life that Jack Worthing is living. In Wilde's play, the double lives of his characters permit them to emancipate themselves from the constraints of society and the Victorian policing of physical desire and intimacy. While the play registers the mobility of Jack's identity transitions, his tactics of manipulating the disjunctures in space (town and country), and his circumvention of the strict codes of late Victorian morality, he lives in a period of tremendous anxiety about morality, miscegenation, racial health, male same-sex love, and sexual identities. Yew's allusions to Wilde's play suggests that bodies and identities continue to be subjected to discursive inscription and control within a nexus of power relations in contemporary Britain, where the power of domination that Dr Worthing has over John is misrecognized because of the psychiatrist-patient relation. At the same time, such allusions suggest that, despite his protests otherwise, Dr Worthing is closeted, a closeting that enables him to traverse in and out of his sexual identities, taking pleasure in the confession he elicits from John for ostensibly disciplinary, heteronormative purposes.

It is worth noting that the barrage of media blitz and moral panic resulting from John's crime uncannily mirror the tabloid excesses of Wilde's homosexual scandals and courtroom trials in 1895 under the *Criminal Law Amendment Act of 1885* that legislated against homosexual liaisons. The objective of this critique is not to recover the actualities of the late Victorian age but to offer a way of reading those discourses and the apparatus of legal, medical, and social enforcement that continue to exert ideological force in the twentieth century. Dr Worthing seems to promote the state regulation of sex, but his name recapitulates the fact that he is a master of duplicity, which means that he is interested in dissecting sex only insofar as it lends itself to respectability, self-righteousness, and monetary gains. Reading the literary and historical allusions to Wilde's play, it is possible to see how Ernest and Jack Worthing transmogrify into the face of Dr Worthing. In this manner, the violence of the British state reverses upon itself, and the criminalization of John's sexual transgression, illegitimate sex practice, and homicide refracts back upon a contaminated and hypocritical version of law and governmentality.

Father of the Nation

The web of identifications in *Porcelain* extends beyond Dr Worthing's identification with Wilde's Jack Worthing. A network of associations between Mr Lee — John's father — and Mr Lee Kuan Yew, the former prime minister of Singapore from 1959 to 1991, is inscribed in the family name "Lee."[29] Specifically, I want to use the father of the nation to think about the relationships constructed between the body and the nation in the play. John's father, Mr Lee, is an especially evocative appellation, given it is also the surname of Lee Kuan Yew, the founding father of the nation. Yew names John's father Mr Lee, a name connecting the cultural force of Singapore and Britain. Foucault's notion of a "technology of sex," which has been implemented by the bourgeoisie by the end of the eighteenth century, is worth elaborating as a way of comprehending Lee Kuan Yew's control of procreation and sexualization of the female body (*History* 116). The "technology of sex," Foucault continues, "made sex not only a secular concern but a concern of the state as well; to be more exact, sex became a matter that required the social body as a whole, and virtually all of its individuals, to place themselves under surveillance" (116).

Both Geraldine Heng and Janadas Devas have provided much insight into state fatherhood in Singapore, approaching the treatment of nationality, sexuality, and race, with a consideration of "the nation's father of founding fathers, Prime Minister Lee Kuan Yew" (108). For all its procreation logic, the state father's "autonomous birthing of a nation" (Heng and Devan 112) also subjects the citizens to what Tim Davis would call "the panoptic gaze" that "exists in the form of heterosexism and internalized homophobia" (287). Transgressive sexuality, however, differentiates John from Lee's Victorian ideas of masculine manhood.[30] If received ideas of women's sexuality, understood as a site of reproduction, have shifted, threatening Lee's absolute power, John's non-procreative sexuality violates the law of the father, pointing to the emerging crisis of definition of the male body. However, in "denouncing and speaking out" the sources of power in the play, Yew is engaging in a Foucauldian discourse of struggle: "it is because to speak on this subject, to force the institutionalized networks of information to listen, to produce names, to point the finger of accusation, to find targets, is the first step in the reversal of power and the initiation of new struggles against existing forms of power" ("Intellectuals" 79). Lee's obdurate severity makes him an authority in Singapore, but John's father's paternal authority is rendered ineffective in Britain, and, so, in the diaspora. John's father, by contrast, loses control of his son, whose sexuality is not productive and, worse, is uncontainable within the closet.

The Father in the Diaspora

John's sexual transgression further points to the disintegration of the Lee family, a sacrosanct institution diminished by a son and a daughter who fail to live up to the expectations of filial piety and Chinese culture which is, at the same time, under siege from the mass media. Whereas filial piety, a value associated with Chineseness, appears to remain unscathed by the forces of modernity in *The Wedding Banquet,* it seems to fall apart in *Porcelain.* In *The Wedding Banquet,* the father deploys the "closet as a form of protection" (Lane 270), of cultural institutions exemplifying "Chineseness," and upholds the heterosexual imperative for the community to see. In *Porcelain*, the closet, as a site of erotic engagement, registers the tension between heteronormative public morality and the threatening elements of male-centered sexual practice. For Mr Lee, his son's sexual transgression stands outside a procreative framework and brings shame to the family, and his unfilial behavior, that is, his failure to honor his father, also bespeaks a steady erosion of paternal authority. When a reporter from Channel Four wants to interview Mr Lee to do a "special documentary" (*Porcelain* 54) about John, the distressed father denies eight times having a son, and, finally, renounces his son: "No son! No son! My son is dead" (55).

Family ties bear social import in the diaspora, but they turn out to be elusive and capricious, as the paternal figure vested with authority proves to be just a nostalgic romantic illusion. The father-son relationship represented in this scene, then, is seen as a symbolic manifestation of the conflict between the young and old generations within the diaspora. In fact, John's parents never visit him in jail because they are "too embarrassed to come" (*Porcelain* 109). In diasporic Britain, John's father is utterly distraught by his fissured family, specifically his disobedient son and daughter, both of whom adopt a decentered lifestyle and have no sense of shame. In sharp contrast, the father figure in Lee's *The Wedding Banquet* occupies a supreme position in the patriarchal system, commanding respect from his family.

By rendering public what is necessarily silenced in order to sustain the heterosexual construct in the community, *Porcelain*'s focus on public restroom male-centered erotic practices constitutes a resistance to the ways Asians in the diaspora are represented in the dominant culture and a critique of the hegemonic containment of male homoerotic desire. The play shows the closet as a site of sexual excess and the impossibility and failure of containment. The play subverts the seductive portrayal of Asians as model minority and depicts the tension between desire and normalization: the closet is the locus of horror, the site where the inexplicable terrors of same-sex desires can be scrutinized, and where Dr Worthing strips John of his humanity and diminishes him to his sexual practices. In *The Wedding Banquet,* the closet functions to sustain a supposedly inviolate ethnic identity within the diaspora; but *Porcelain* breaks the silence about the question of same-sex sexuality in the diasporic Chinese community, responding to the histories of sexuality and race, taking into account a nexus of conflicting discourses and desires. The play poses questions about the legitimacy of reproductive apparatuses, disrupting the paternal's voice by showing that, in the spaces of the diaspora and away from the hegemony of the nation's father, procreative sexualities are unstable.

11

The Cinema of Tsai Ming-liang:
A Modernist Genealogy

Mark Betz

The cinema of the Taiwanese filmmaker Tsai Ming-liang arguably has been neglected by Western scholars in favor of work by other East Asian filmmakers, including those working within the context of the New Taiwanese cinema of which Tsai might be considered tangentially a part. This chapter seeks to go some way in redressing the balance and aims to stimulate further interest in Tsai within the Western academic arena of work on East Asian cinema.[1] My approach to Tsai's films derives from a position of expertise in postwar European art cinema. For me, what is striking about his visual style and narrative approach is that they evince a contemporary, East Asian filmmaker working explicitly within, and in many ways extending, the modernist project of postwar European cinema's various new waves.

Such a recognition has not been lost on others, and when I began working through the English-language criticism on Tsai Ming-liang, I thoroughly expected to find comparisons to other European art filmmakers. I was surprised, however, by the sheer volume of and insistence on such comparisons, which have served many as a sort of shorthand to evoke for Western viewers unfamiliar with his work the particular rigor of his narrative style and the likely experience of viewing it. But the comparisons rarely depart from shorthand. One unauthored online article situates Tsai among his predecessors of the so-called first wave of Taiwan's New Cinema, Hou Hsiao-Hsien and Edward Yang, when it claims that just "as Hou was often compared to Ozu and Yang to Antonioni, Tsai has been labelled 'the Fassbinder of Taiwan'" ("Love, Life and Lies"). Chuck Stephens finds in Tsai's second feature, *Vive L'Amour* (1994), an "oppressive, Antonioni-derived sense of urban, architectural nausea," and in the ways the film's three main characters "manage to skirt and dodge and eventually collide or nearly miss each other … an almost Tati-esque choreographic grace" (21). But Toh Hai Leong has gone the furthest in this exercise, referencing Tsai's "austere Bressonian images" (48), his sparse dialogue "(more sparse than in Bresson's *L'Argent*)" (50), his real time and slow pacing that are "nevertheless involving and hypnotic, especially to those familiar with the work of Antonioni or Chantal Akerman" (50), and with complete aplomb he even asks Tsai himself "if the master of displacement of emotion and narrative, Michelangelo Antonioni, was his greatest influence" (48). Despite getting a few noncommittal words from the director on the matter, Leong has no qualms subtitling his piece "The Taiwanese Antonioni."

Moving from shorthand to longhand, one can script a much fuller and, I think, generative portrait of Tsai's relations to European art cinema of the 1960s and 1970s. In casting and approach to character, theme and tonal quality, formalist rigor and visual style, and reflexivity with respect to specific postwar European art films and to the medium itself, Tsai's films construct many roads of inquiry that lead, at least to this scholar's admittedly over-saturated eye, to modernism. Like Ingmar Bergman, Antonioni, Federico Fellini, and several of the young directors of the French New Wave (especially Jean-Luc Godard and François Truffaut), Tsai favours an artisanal or theatrical troupe approach to casting: his features contain very few characters, and they are played by an only slightly larger stable of actors, creating the sense of an ongoing and consistent creative project immediately recognizable to auteurist critics. While his third feature film, *The River* (1996), was in production, Stephens was already reporting that Tsai's small filmography constituted "a trilogy … concerned with alienated longing … in contemporary Taipei" (22); Tony Rayns seconded the assessment (15), but hindsight shows they were jumping the gun. For all five of Tsai's films fit this description, with Shiang-chyi Chen as a female love interest in two, Kuei-Mei Yang an independent though lonely young woman in two, Hsiao-Ling Lu a mother in two, Tien Miao a father in three (and a salesman in a fourth), Chao-jung Chen a handsome boy of the streets in three, and Kang-sheng Lee the young antihero (and usually son) of all five. Not even Bergman's use of Max von Sydow, Fellini's of Marcello Mastroianni, Antonioni's of Monica Vitti, or Truffaut's of Jean-Pierre Léaud (who makes a cameo appearance in Tsai's *What Time Is It Over There?* [2001]),[2] can approach the single-mindedness and rigor with which Tsai has cast Kang-sheng Lee as his cinematic alter-ego, and has returned time and time again to the love triangle, the impossible heterosexual couple, and the dysfunctional nuclear family as his social units of investigation, sometimes all in the same film.

Of the many formal similarities between Tsai's films and art film narration, I will here point out only a few. Fiona A. Viella has stated in an article on *The River* that the "cornerstone of Tsai's style is minimalism and ellipsis," founded on the salient use of "the mid-shot or wide-shot without cutting the scene" and leading to an overall aesthetic that is "uncluttered" yet "exacerbates the sense of being confined and entrapped by one's environment":

> Tsai renders this contemporary urban malaise and profound isolation in a starkly materialist mode. So much concentration is placed on bodies simply performing their necessary actions, framed from a distance, that a distinct rhythm emerges. A certain 'beat' of the everyday, so that the same amount of effort that goes into cooking a meal and ironing a shirt goes into a shower at the sauna or an anonymous sexual exchange.

What we have here is nothing less than the aesthetic of cinematic realism extolled by André Bazin in the films of the Italian neorealists and taken as far as many thought it could go in the mature work of Robert Bresson and Carl Theodor-Dreyer or in Chantal Akerman's *Jeanne Dielman, 23 Quai du Commerce, 1080 Bruxelles* (1975) to an actual working method: flat acting style and attenuated characterization; long takes and *temps mort*; minimal camera movement, and then rarely unmotivated; sparse dialogue and little to no use of non-diegetic sound; alienated protagonists circulating without aim in a modern urban environment. Such formal rigor across a body of work may be found in the *oeuvres* of several modernist directors, but not in any young contemporary ones I can think of, and never with such consistency.

The much commented upon reflexivity of modernist art finds in Tsai's films a most willing and able subject, as filmic references, implicit and explicit, exfoliate into a kind of uncontrollable vine creeping up and over the edifice of European art cinema's apogee in the early 1950s through the early 1970s, with the French, as the title of his second film suggests, the most insistently covered. The nameless and lonely male and female protagonists of *The Hole* (1998), Tsai's fourth film, call to mind the similar metanarrative game playing of Alan Resnais in his first two features (*Hiroshima mon amour* [1959] and *Last Year at Marienbad* [1961]), and the combination of silence and an inverted, opened umbrella as a means to collect debris while chipping away at the hole from above are lifted quite obviously from Jules Dassin's French thriller *Du Rififi chez les hommes* (1955). The male-female-male love triangle of *Vive L'Amour* reworks Truffaut's *Jules et Jim* (1961) and Godard's *Bande à part* (1962) and *Une femme est une femme* (1963), albeit with considerably less exuberance. And the conceit of inexplicable incapacity or character stasis evokes the dissection of table manners common to the late surrealist work of Luis Buñuel in *The Exterminating Angel* (1963) and *The Discreet Charm of the Bourgeoisie* (1972) or the tortured chamber dramas of Bergman's films in the 1960s.

Less explicitly but no less crucially, all of Tsai's work addresses to some degree image making or visual fascination and pleasure (voyeurism) or fantasy projection — the constitutive basis of cinema as a medium that is particularly attuned to intense psychological experience and affect. (*The River* contains a film-in-the-making-within-a-film, and a real-life filmmaker, Hong Kong's Ann Hui, playing a director.)[3] Finally, what separates Tsai's artistic practice (as well as those above) from the avant-garde proper and situates it within a modernist constellation is its forthright examination of the workings of narrative as opposed to effecting its outright destruction, to expose the rhetoric of narrative causation that may leave characters often powerless but never completely out of the picture.[4] Water appears in all his films as an obvious symbol and counterpoint to character relations or psychology. But it also at times leaks into the realm of narratology itself, assuming the role of narrative agent either left vacant or unable to be taken up by characters, blurping up from unseen reservoirs or raining down in unrelenting downpours, forcing characters to connect in a fluid circuit of exchange by turns comic and tragic.

When Kuei-mei Yang, who plays the female protagonist of *Vive L'Amour*, opens up her own floodgates in the film's celebrated final scene, during which she sobs without comfort or end for a full six minutes, the European modernist film project is as inescapable a referent as is her own character's powerlessness and despair. Chuck Stephens suggests that *Vive L'Amour* was originally "planned as a 'comedy' about romantic isolation à la Eric Rohmer's *Le Rayon vert*" (1978) (21), but the audacity of this ending and the overall treatment of the young modern woman warrants the Antonioni comparisons most clearly at the same time as it moves them into new aesthetic and global territory. Whereas Antonioni's endings often lead to the virtual annihilation of subjectivity along with narrative in favor of spectacle, space, and the image itself (*L'eclisse* [1962], *Blow-up* [1966], *Zabriskie Point* [1970], *The Passenger* [1975]), Tsai's never dispense with either subjectivity or narrative, and instead stitch them together in such a way as to create a new couple or connectedness between almost painful embodiment and real, particular, time and space. In actually crying for six minutes in a medium close-up continuous take, the actress Kuei-mei Yang forces the viewer to attend to her real presence at a specific moment in an actual space, an incomplete park nonetheless and incongruously opened to the public in the center of Taipei: "In the loud decibels of her wails and moans, one can hear the clanging of cement mixers, and the shuffling bustling noises of early morning joggers and commuters" (Leong 51). The existential quality of the characters' existence in this and other Tsai films indeed evokes European art cinema, but the films' equal insistence on spatial and historical inscription bears examination of a slightly different sort. The homelessness of *Vive L'Amour*'s three young protagonists is both a spiritual and a real condition. As Woei Lien Chong, among others, has pointed out, "The film is a barely veiled comment on the housing situation in Taipei, where speculation during the building spree in the 1980s drove prices sky-high, leaving many big apartment buildings standing empty while youngsters remain[ed] homeless" (Chong 91). The empty wastelands of meaningful human relationships are not simply symbolized by the spaces of modern Taipei; they are grounded in them. Kuei-mei Yang's tears flow in that moment, from the urban space itself.

Many have commented on how Taiwan's New Cinema is concerned with its country's unresolved and complex national identity, to a degree that suggests not so much a national allegory being played out through subjectivity and narrative as a nation *as* a subject and *as* a narrative. Under martial law until 1987, faced "with censorship and repression, caught between east and west, modernity and tradition, the Taiwanese adopted a pragmatic materialism and existentialism," writes one anonymous critic ("Love, Life and Lies"). Chris Berry finds in the sad young male character of *Vive L'Amour* "an excessive significatory complex implying the Taiwanese condition as an existential homelessness" (2000, 197) and cites Hou Hsiao-Hsien's 1989 film *City of Sadness* as kind of counter-foundation text for Taiwanese national identity, in that it signifies the particular hybrid postcoloniality and cultural liminality of Taiwan "as less a relation between inside and outside and more as an internal condition; a threatening but simultaneously dynamic fracturing within Taiwanese society" (1992, 42, 45). Tsai Ming-liang's personal circumstances add a further dimension to the torsion of Taiwanese national identity as it appears in these writings: Malaysian-born, Tsai moved to Taiwan at the age of twenty, and his diasporic experience of displacement has led at least one theorist to read the filmmaker's working through of these themes as a borrowing of the language of Europe to speak this experience — a kind of "double modernity," of Taiwan on the one hand, of Tsai's diasporic presence in Taiwan on the other.[5] And this provides us with some explanation for the confluence of human and spatial emptiness where there should be fullness in Tsai's films, set not just in Taiwan but more specifically Taipei: soulless video arcades and cram schools in *Rebels of the Neon God* (1992); luxury buildings and columbaria in *Vive L'Amour*; a vacant market in *The Hole*; and in all, motorbikes and scooters and barely furnished flats in apartment complexes rather than homes. As Chong puts it, "[H]omelessness as a physical and spiritual condition of today's Taiwan youth is a permanent theme in his films" (Chong 85).

While it is valid, then, to see Tsai's project in relation to European modernism, it is equally important to realize how embedded this project is in Taiwanese cinema and culture. Tien Miao, who plays the father figure in three of the films and has a cameo in another, is recognizable to local audiences for his appearance as a younger man in scores of swordplay movies, including King Hu's *Dragon Inn* [1966] and *A Touch of Zen* [1969].[6] Tonglin Lu argues that

> Taiwan New Cinema directors ... were driven by their desires to transgress conventional filmic forms in their respective cultures ... . Hou Xiaoxian [Hsiao-Hsien] and Edward Yang ... went much further in this respect than most of their colleagues ... . [T]hey succeeded in creating their own cinematic "languages," often defined against previous mainstream genres, namely, ... Taiwan escapist-melodramatic cinemas. This emphasis on formal innovation, partly inspired by postwar European cinemas, distinguishes them in the history of Chinese cinema ... . (9)

Tsai has gone even further in this enterprise than his colleagues: while he embraces the formalist experimentation of European art cinema, he does not reject the popular genres and forms of Chinese commercial cinema in the way Hou and Yang conceivably do. On the one hand he is taking very seriously the Chinese family melodrama as his primary genre, in which "the symbolisms of food and house are used to create an atmosphere of intimacy, while carefully avoiding the exaggeration normally associated with melodrama: understatement and restraint are quintessential" features of not simply modernist film but of a popular Chinese genre (Chong 83). In "analyzing Tsai's visual idiom," Chong finds that it is based on both foreign models and on a "reversal of well-tested generic conventions of traditional Chinese small-scale family melodrama," and that the "backbone of his style is the innovative and sophisticated manipulation of the familiar symbolisms of food and house" (Chong 82). The "sharing of meals, ... cooking, sweeping the floor, chopping wood — in short, the maintaining of the household in a material sense" — function in the Chinese family melodrama to demonstrate intimacy in an indirect way and to symbolize "the maintenance of the household in the social sense" through "both the nourishing of the body and the physical maintaining of the house" (Chong 83). The homelessness of the young characters in *Rebels of a Neon God* and *Vive*

L'Amour, then, refers to an existential condition *and* a concrete socio-economic phenomenon *and* a reversal of local generic expectations. As the characters move almost somnambulistically through their life's dull paces and spaces — "kitchen, restaurant, bathroom, bedroom" ("Love, Life and Lies"), themselves the now-familiar terrains of postmodern cinema (e.g., *Pulp Fiction* [1994]) established via the groundwork of modernists like Godard, among others (e.g., *Masculin-féminin* [1966]) — social functions have been replaced by purely bodily ones.

Eating food together is rare in Tsai's films, and when it is shown it is to demonstrate the absence of a familial or social contract as opposed to a presence. In one scene in *Rebels of a Neon God*, the father, in catching his son playing truant from the cram school he is slaving away as a taxi driver to fund, attempts to make a connection with his morose son by suggesting they see a movie and then stopping at a street stall to have a bowl of fruit together. While the son "silently eats his fruit in his usual sullen manner, his father looks at him from the side and puts a few pieces of fruit from his own bowl into his son's to express concern: A helpless attempt at communication" (Chong 86). By the time of *The River*, the father no longer even attempts to connect with his son by sharing food: at a similar street stall, the father eats from his own bowl, asks why the boy is not doing same, then physically turns away from him when he receives his answer: the son cannot, his neck is too sore. In this remarkable film, the generic themes of family duty and tradition and the modern conditions of alienation and sexual release without emotion are combined with mysterious elemental forces (disease, water) as narrative agents and a modernist visual style so rigorous and ascetic as to hybridize the family melodrama into a new form — the art melodrama.

Even in Tsai's second and fourth feature films, in which the father-mother-child familial triad is not present as such, rituals of foodtaking and housekeeping are of central concern and the family melodrama a ghostly inferential presence. The gay stereotype of the sad young man of 1950s Hollywood, played by actors such as James Dean and Montgomery Clift, is ubiquitous in Tsai's films, and I would go so far as to see *Vive L'Amour*, with its three protagonists — streetwise clothes hawker, female petty bourgeois, doleful closeted gay man — as a reworking of the tragic alternative nuclear family enacted by James Dean as father, Natalie Wood as mother, and Sal Mineo as son in that decaying family estate in the second half of *Rebel Without a Cause* (1955). For Chris Berry, the sad young man in this and other Asian films of the 1990s is "a local reinvention that draws upon and resonates with regional cultural antecedents" by propping their meanings "upon the widespread modern interpretation of the broad Confucian family-based culture as one where space outside family and family roles is dystopic and anomic rather than liberating" (2000, 188).

> The writings and debates about the conception of the self in East Asia
> ... tend to agree that in pre-modern cultures heavily influenced by
> Confucianism, the self was understood not as an autonomous and
> internalized personality or character but as a socially and relationally
> defined role that one tried to assume ... . Within this system, the only
> place of the individual outside family roles is that of the outcast, the exile,
> the social derelict ... . [or, in the case of Tsai,] modern day realist
> portrayals of the lonely romantic. (2000, 190)

The homelessness of the romantic young Tsai protagonist is taken to a new level in *What Time Is It Over There?*, insofar as it is doubled into both male and female strands, one of whom (female) moves literally out of the nation/ family/home, the other of whom (male) imagines her movements in a wholly other space by repeated viewings of Truffaut's *The 400 Blows* (1959) as well as through a literal marking of time. The ghost of the family melodrama is made material in this film, in the form of the male protagonist's dead father, to whose memory his widow dedicates herself in particularly poignant scenes of loss and disavowal.

For Berry, the figure of the sad young man may indeed be alienated from other people, but he is not alone, and here we can begin to understand why Tsai's modernist project is so interesting when read through the context of Chinese modernity. The origins of modernity have long been attributed to European expansion in Amerindia, and "[d]espite its often ambiguous nature and emphasis on changes, the centrality of the Western world in the discourse of modernity has essentially remained unchanged" (Lu 2). If Chinese modernity has its roots in the May 4th movement of the last century, and involved a discourse of European Enlightenment and progress in place of the Tao or Confucianism, the transformation of Taiwan by the Nationalist government "from an agricultural society in the early 1960s to a labor-intensive, export-oriented industrial society in the 1970s, and then to a high-tech-based, capital- and knowledge-intensive consumer society in the 1980s" (Lu 18) has brought with it the breakdowns in traditional family structures and the unstable and shifting new identities that Western Europe experienced in its two great explosions of modernist art making, the 1920s and the 1960s.

The danger, of course, in considering a contemporary East Asian filmmaker like Tsai in relation to modernist aesthetics is that one finds oneself in the sticky territory of the mapmaking of aesthetic forms, a clearly chronological mapping that charts the emergence of modernism and postmodernism at different moments for different media, but also and more dangerously a geographic mapping like that undertaken by Fredric Jameson. The goal of Jameson's analysis is to get to the truth of the fundamental global realities that are the absent cause of individual experience in the era of modernism and postmodernism, a cause that these eras cannot represent directly but only in distorted and symbolic ways, such as allegory. But in doing so, he also enforces a kind of a Western economic stagism that demarcates *a priori* a twentieth-century cultural object as premodern, modern, or postmodern based on when and where it is produced. In his conflation of the terms of political economy with those of aesthetic and cultural periodization, Jameson thus privileges the objects of the First World, which must necessarily be postmodern because they are coterminous with a late capitalist political economy, over those of the Third World, which cannot be postmodern because they are the products of a less developed political economy. Aijaz Ahmad in 1987 was the first to call him on his making of essentializing statements like "all third-world texts are necessarily … to be read as … national allegories," but Jameson has not shown much evidence of changing his mind: on the very first page of *The Geopolitical Aesthetic* he suggests that a Taiwanese film directed by Edward Yang, *Terrorizer* (1986), "seems to raise the question of the belated emergence of modernism in the modernizing Third World, at a moment when the so-called advanced countries are themselves sinking into full postmodernity."[7] Such historical and geopolitical segregation not only myopically views "developing" Third World cultures as always following in the aesthetic footsteps of the "advanced" Western cultures, which blaze new aesthetic trails as inevitability as they do capitalist ones — a myopia that leads to expressions such as "The Taiwanese Antonioni." It also fails to see the degree to which historical time is palimpsestic and dispersive in all cultures and how aesthetic forms may be translated across cultures in multiple circuits of exchange and appropriation. Neither essentially economic nor bound to the strictures of historical or geographic stagism, realist, modern, or postmodern aesthetics must be considered in terms that pay attention to the complex interplay of discourses at work in any given historical moment and any given culture.

It is in these terms that I locate what I consider Tsai's important intervention in the discourse of modernism in cinema — a very conscious intervention, and one that is not simply a product of his discursive position within a Taiwan in the advanced stages of modernisation. In his essay "Beyond Eurocentrism: The World-System and the Limits of Modernity," Enrique Dussel suggests "transmodernity" as an alternative to modernity or even postmodernity. Transmodernity emphasizes cross-cultural exchanges instead of one-way changes imposed by the center upon its periphery. And it is a starting point for me for coming to understand just how Tsai's modernist project might not only be read, but also, perhaps, *used* to interrogate how film studies continues to read the European modernist cinemas of the 1950s through 1970s in a myopic way. The more obvious, and I think safer, route is just to consider Tsai a postmodern artist, as Tonglin Lu or Chris Berry do. The latter argues that the "alienated young people" of much contemporary East Asian cinema "are symbols of a post-modern era" and "the modernist, progress-oriented teleological model of development largely forgotten" (197). And a film like Tsai's *The Hole*, with its ironically staged, catchy and kitschy song-and-dance numbers, is not an easy one to bring in line with a modernist aesthetic program. But the fact that these musical numbers are all culled from European cinema's period of high modernism, that they, in the words of the director, "show my subconscious aspiration for the 50s and 60s" ("Love, Life and Lies"), suggests that even this film has something of that old modernist nostalgia — not nostalgia on the part of the characters and the filmmaker for meta-narratives, for progress, but nostalgia on the part of *the film itself* for something of the seriousness engagement of modernism (I think Wong Kar-wai's *In the Mood For Love* [2000] is another germane reference here). Indeed, it is the concrete materiality and alienating separation of the adjacent spaces in *The Hole* that the film itself, as the hole, wishes to puncture, to bridge, to move back and forth through and beyond. And here the formerly soulless apartments of Tsai's Taipei finally show themselves to be soulful, endowed with narrative agency, will, and empathy — here space can even dream, as in those all-singing, all-dancing fantasy sequences.

If Tsai's modernism is one so inextricably bound to its historical and geographic context — Taiwan, Taipei, a now always in the process of becoming — then seeing it in such terms may allow for a rereading of Western European cinematic modernism of the 1960s, which has not tended to be read in relation to the specific geopolitical shifts contributing to its own sense of alienation — the rise of the European Economic Community and internationalization on the one hand, decolonization and the racination of European culture on the other.[8] If one begins here, it is entirely possible to find in Tsai's cinema an exemplar for further study of the unfinished project of modernism. Finally, if to name is to begin, then I would press for a renaming: no more monikers such as "the Fassbinder of Taiwan" or "the Taiwanese Antonioni," nor even the dubious residual status of something like "the Last Modernist," as two recent monographs on Alexander Kluge and Theo Angelopoulos would have it. Why not, simply, "the First Modernist"?

Postscript

At the time of first writing of this article, Tsai's most recent films, the short *The Skywalk Is Gone* (2002) and feature *Goodbye Dragon Inn* (2003), had not yet been released, and I subsequently viewed them at the Times London Film Festival in November 2003.[9] In both I find confirmation of my reading of Tsai's film practice as a continuing dialogue with modernism, as well as his own *oeuvre*. Taipei-bounded *The Skywalk Is Gone*, in which a young woman searches for a street vendor who used to sell watches on a now-gone overpass, interfaces intertextually with Tsai's third and fifth features: the young woman is played by Shiang-chyi Chen, the main female character of *What Time Is It Over There?*, and she is looking for the main male character of the same film, played by the ubiquitous Kang-sheng Lee; both of these actors first appeared together in *The River*, wherein they met on an outdoor escalator and later engaged in sudden, passionate sex, and an identical shot of the same escalator (leading up to Mitsukoshi Department Store) opens both *The River* and *The Skywalk Is Gone*. *Goodbye Dragon Inn* is the most insistently self-reflexive and metafilmic yet of all of Tsai's work, in that its scenario involves the last screening in Taipei of the Taiwan-based director King Hu's *Dragon Inn* and casts Kang-sheng Lee once again, this time as a projectionist (unseen except for the last few minutes of the film, after the screening has ended), as the ghostly puppet master in charge of the cinematic apparatus — a privileged role. Ghosts (perhaps) appear in the forms of Tien Miao and Shih Chun, nameless spectators of the film-within-the-film, in which they themselves appear now as images of the past, more dynamic, more fantastic, than the static and material present of the film's near-real-time unfolding. In this sense, *Goodbye Dragon Inn*'s first line of dialogue beyond that of the film being screened — "Do you know this theatre is haunted?"— carries both enormous weight and relief, emerging from the otherwise ambient soundtrack of noises from the theater spaces as if from outside the world of the film itself, and spoken as it is after fully forty-five minutes of reel time, more than half the length of the film itself. Kuei-mei Yang is present as well in a small role (as is Hsiao-Ling Lu in *The Skywalk Is Gone*) and provides one of the film's brightest comic moments: noisily shelling and eating nuts, she renders the almost deserted theater a treacherous obstacle course to move around in, as the floor, the aisle, the stairs, everywhere is covered by the detritus of her incessant snacking.

But *Goodbye Dragon Inn* offers some evidence of changes in Tsai's foci as well. As with *The Hole* and *What Time Is It Over There?* equal emphasis is laid on male and female isolation and desire with attendant double plot lines, and the female protagonist is essayed by Tsai-regular Shiang-chyi Chen; but the male lead is no longer Kang-sheng Lee but a young Japanese actor, Mitamura Kiyonobu, whose goals are split between trying to watch *Dragon Inn* without the annoyances of his few fellow spectators impinging on his physical and/ or aural space and in forging a gay encounter with another young man, an activity which takes him quite literally outside the space of the screened film. Here is a metafilmic scenario that is almost entirely interested in exploring the peripheries of spectatorship: the various distractions in the theatre vying for attention with the film itself; the practices of looking and desire not directed at the screen but in spite of it. The doorways, stairwells, passageways, toilets, all of the spaces external to the screening space itself are what nonetheless service it and its patrons, and in fact structure the film-going experience. As in all of Tsai's films, the space is not devoid of human agency, but here that agency resides primarily in the occupations that make the show possible, pared down to the bare essentials: projectionist and ticket-seller/ house manager. As played by Shiang-chyi Chen, the latter comes across as a kind of Mouchette (cf. Bresson's film of the same name [1966]), defined as she is by the sound of her feet as she works through her various tasks for the evening, the slow and tortured clomp of her lame steps echoing with cavernous emptiness through grimly utilitarian spaces on her last night of employment. The poignancy of her isolation is condensed in her failed gesture of communication with the projectionist in another Tsai trademark — the sharing of food, in this case a steamed bun — but their only connection exists at the level of film language: the conclusion of *Goodbye Dragon Inn* consists of the chores she and the projectionist perform after the screening is over, separated by space but not time as they are crosscut together. When all is accomplished and the theater closed down, he leaves by scooter and she by foot in the ubiquitous downpour of Tsai's Taipei. Another frustrated end, another potential beginning — for the characters, for Tsai, for Taiwan, for film, for modernism.

12

Sentimental Returns: On the Uses of the Everyday in the Recent Films of Zhang Yimou and Wong Kar-wai[1]

Rey Chow

[I]n reality there is no tree — there is, however, the pear tree, and apple tree, the elder tree, the cactus — but there is no tree. Thus cinema will not be able to "reproduce" (write) a tree: it will reproduce a pear tree, an apple tree, an elder tree, a cactus — but not a tree. Exactly as in the primitive cuneiform languages. Therefore, does the language of cinema, which is the product of a technology which has come to determine a human epoch, precisely because it is a technology, perhaps have some points of contact with the empiricism of the primitives?

Pier Paolo Pasolini[2]

The Everyday as a Problematic in Film

The everyday: an open, empty category, one that allows critics to fill it with critical agendas as they please. This is why both its defenders and its detractors can use it to stake their political claims, either as the bedrock of reality, the ground zero of cultural representation, or as a misleading set of appearances concealing ideological exploitation, a collective false consciousness. For these reasons, it is perhaps less interesting simply to unravel the argumentative pros and cons around the everyday as such than to consider specific uses of the everyday in representational practices, which in this essay I shall do with two examples of contemporary Chinese cinema. I have found it productive to approach some of the key questions involved with Pier Paolo Pasolini's theorization of cinematic signification.

1. Chow, Rey. Sentimental Returns: On the Uses of the Everyday in the Recent Films of Zhang Yimou and Wong Kar-wai. New Literary History 33:4 (2002), 639–653. © New Literary History, University of Virginia. Reprinted with the permission of The Johns Hopkins University Press.

In his attempt to distinguish the specificity of cinema from language (and hence from the type of semiotic analysis derived from structural linguistics), Pasolini reminds us that film exists first and foremost on the basis of a system of "visual communication" (168). With a concept such as communication, he emphasizes the communal and social character of film, a character that cannot be simply assimilated to the Saussurean notion of "differences *without positive terms*,"[3] yet that is not primal nature either. This, I believe, is the juncture at which his definition of film may provide us with a viable notion of the everyday-in-representation. The recipient of film, Pasolini explains, is already accustomed to "reading" reality visually; such a reality, suffused with a vast collectivity of actions, gestures, movements, and habits, constitutes what he calls a "brute" speech, on which cinema then constructs its (secondary) level of signification. He gives elements of this brute speech the name "kinemes," whose presence he describes as infinite and obligatory, and untranslatable (201–2). Filmmaking, then, is a matter of organizing the kinemes into image-signs (or im-signs), without the kinemes ever completely disappearing. Because of this, the recipient of film is always simultaneously engaged with both of these levels of signification, in a manner that never quite lets go of the kinemes or the system of "visual communication" that exists prior to the im-signs of cinema. Rather, the continual presence of these elements of the brute speech will give the film audience an experience similar to memory and dreams. As Pasolini writes in his well-known essay "The 'Cinema of Poetry'":

> [T]he intended audience of the cinematographic product is also accustomed to "read" reality visually, that is, to have an instrumental conversation with the surrounding reality inasmuch as it is the environment of a collectivity, which also expresses itself with the pure and simple optical presence of its actions and habits. A solitary walk in the street, even with stopped up ears, is a continual conversation between us and an environment which expresses itself through the images that compose it: the faces of people who pass by, their gestures, their signs, their actions, their silences, their expressions, their arguments, their collective reactions (groups of people waiting at traffic lights, crowding around a traffic accident or around the fish-woman at Porta Capuana); and more — billboards, signposts, traffic circles, and, in short, objects and things that appear charged with multiple meanings and thus "speak" brutally with their very presence. (168)

I believe Pasolini's approach is germane to some outstanding examples of contemporary Chinese cinema insofar as the latter specializes in the sentimentalism of nostalgia, that is, a mode of filmmaking that often invokes specific eras of the past as its collective imaginary, and that consciously deploys everyday phenomena, including banal human relationships, familiar locations, and mundane objects, as its means of signifying. What Pasolini has offered is a way of thinking about the historically precedent — what is already seen prior to the film experience — without reducing it to a simply naturalistic reality. The brute speech in his account is another semiotic system whose integration into cinema does not completely strip it of this earlier identity. The question this leaves us, then, is the kind of value filmmakers and audiences alike invest in this brute history, and how this other plane of a prior communication is charged with present significance even as its "visually read" or previously experienced quality continues to be present. The interplay, in the medium of film (with its literal, obvious modes of signification, its ready visuality), between this empirical "always already" and its contemporary screen cathexes is where I'd locate the problematic of the everyday in contemporary Chinese cinema.

To be sure, the everyday in this context often becomes synonymous with a crude materialism, which is in turn identified with history, culture, specific time periods, and so forth, against which the present (of film watching) is positioned. And yet, in order to grasp the relationship between the cinematic and the quotidian, it is necessary to defer these more habitually accepted assumptions about the everyday (at times coming from directors themselves) and instead examine first the manners in which the everyday emerges in a network of filmic elements (visual, narrative, auditory). Only then would it be possible to speculate on the aesthetic and emotional effects produced by the film and on the larger ideological issues involved. If the everyday in and by itself is always already a semiotically coded set of phenomena, as Pasolini's writing suggests, any cinematic rendering of the everyday would suggest compounded levels of coding, whereby signs of different orders are superimposed upon and interact with one another in a hybrid — often temporally synergized — fashion.

In Zhang Yimou's and Wong Kar-wai's recent works, *The Road Home* (Chinese title: *Wo de fu qin mu qin,* or "My father and mother," 2000) and *In the Mood for Love* (Chinese title: *Hua yang nianhua,* or "When flowers were in full bloom," 2000), it is possible to identify a number of resonant elements, which in their transcultural contexts confirm once again the predominantly sentimental drift in contemporary Chinese cinema since the mid-1980s.[4] As my title suggests, both films can be seen as a return journey, one that takes us to a temporal and/or locational past. Zhang tells the story of a son's (Luo Yusheng) visit home after his father died. This visit becomes the occasion for a cinematic replay of how his mother and father's relationship began in the 1950s, when the father (Luo Changyu) was sent as a teacher to the village in which the mother (Zhao Di) lived. This trip to the past reveals in particular the mother's devotion to the father; it is she who now insists that his dead body be brought home on foot, in honor of the traditional belief that a body returned this way will never forget the road home. The narrative return to the past is hence concluded with an actual physical trip by the father's many former students who carry his body back to the village, where the new school he had begun building will, we are told, be completed in memory of his life's achievements. Wong, on his part, takes us to the Hong Kong of the early 1960s, when Su Lizhen and Zhou Muyun, the lead characters, happen to rent rooms in adjacent apartments in a district inhabited by immigrants from Shanghai. The film is also a return journey in the sense of an exploration of a relationship that ended as elusively as it began, an affair whose meanings seem far from being exhausted and invite revisiting. To this extent, the titles of the two films may be seen as interchangeable: "in the mood for love" (or "the time when flowers were in full bloom") can be used to describe the colorful recollections of the two young people falling in love in the countryside in the People's Republic of China of the 1950s; "the road home" can be used to describe the cinematic return visit to the scene of Su and Zhou's involvement in the 1960s. If we take Wong Kar-wai's suggestion that the little boy in Su's apartment at the end of the film might be the offspring of her relationship with Zhou,[5] then Wong's film, too, may be called "my father and mother."

Apart from the comparable notions of a return journey in the two works, both directors draw on a memorable collection of daily phenomena, including objects, practices, life activities, and exchanges, to furnish the environments of their respective stories. Both make use of extraordinary visual and auditory effects to construct the ordinary. The everyday is given to us through some of the most sophisticated manipulations of the cinematic apparatus. What semiotic and affective implications do such manipulations entail? What do these films by two of the best-known contemporary Chinese filmmakers tell us about cinema and the everyday in general, and how?

The Road Home

As recalled by the son, Luo Yusheng, the father and the mother in *The Road Home* meet when the father was sent to teach at the village where the mother, then a girl of eighteen, and her blind mother live. As in Wong's film, we witness one of the most ordinary everyday happenings: a chance encounter between a male and a female that develops into a relationship. Unlike other everyday practices, a chance encounter is not an entirely passive or entirely active event; it typically occurs when one is engaged in something else and is thus, strictly speaking, an accidental by-product of some other activity. Such serendipity gives it the fatefulness of the unconscious, of the dream in which one runs into things or people in ways that cannot be planned in advance. Unlike even an activity such as walking, it is not entirely certain that there is a conscious subject in command of the activity whose body is engaged and whose mind serves as a receptor of outside impressions. Yet in Zhang's film, we soon see a conscious attempt to steer this chance encounter in a purposeful direction.

Interestingly, this attempt to take control comes from Zhao Di, the beautiful peasant girl, who has so far remained unpersuaded by proposals for an arranged marriage. As she catches sight of Luo Changyu, however, she becomes interested in him and begins a series of efforts to have further contact. She waits, for instance, by the road where she knows he would pass with his students. She brings water up from the well facing the school where he teaches, so she can see him. She walks by the school in order to listen to him reading texts to his students even though, being illiterate, she does not understand the words. She cooks special dishes and puts them in a large bowl with indigo patterns (a *qinghua wan*), in the hope that he will select the right bowl and taste her cooking amid all the lunch items prepared by other village girls for the men working in the village. When he comes to her house for a meal, she takes special care to prepare the dishes, pointing out to him the significance of the bowl. When he is recalled to the city for interrogation, she waits for his return in the midst of a snowstorm, almost losing her life in a fever afterward.[6] We are told that, eventually, when her beloved returns to the village and they are able to get married, he will never again leave her until his death. Finally, it is she, now an old woman, who insists on having his body carried home, and who donates the family's savings to the village in order to have the school completed.

Zhao Di recalls the series of determined female characters in Zhang's other films — Jiuer in *Red Sorghum*, Judou in *Judou*, Yan'er in *Raise the Red Lantern*, Qiuju in *The Story of Qiuju*, Wei Minzhi, the girl teacher in *Not One Less*, and the blind girl in *Happy Time* — who would risk their lives in order to remain faithful to a personal goal or collective cause, and who typically refuse to compromise on their commitment until they have completed the task they have set themselves. This characteristically feminine determination places the woman not merely in the role of the cinematic fetish but also of the fetishist — she is the one who actively finds ways of catching a glimpse of her object of interest — who fetishizes his voice as he reads texts to school children, for instance. Contrary to convention, the male here becomes the object of love, with little subjectivity of his own.[7] This conscious will, placed with the woman, means that what begins as a chance encounter quickly loses its unpredictability — its randomness, as it were — and turns into a deliberate *production* of meaning and value. Narratively speaking, there is thus a clear telos organizing the unfolding of the events, not only sexually (a happy marriage, which leads to the birth of a son) but also in the larger, social unit of the village. The determination of the woman results in her union with the man of her choice and procures for the village a pedagogical father figure and, over the long term, a revered site of learning. By the end of the film, therefore, the recollections and the present time blend into each other, the son helping to complete his mother's and his father's wishes.

Visually speaking, this production of meaning and value is most evident in Zhang's manner of capturing plain daily objects. Unlike Wong's film, in which the crowded conditions of urban living are reflected in households filled with disposable commodified belongings, Zhang's picture shows a rural environment in which material culture is scarce. Instead of the glamour of things, Zhang focuses on the *activity* of the people involved: Zhao Di chopping vegetables, steaming dumplings, or frying pancakes; Zhao Di putting on the red padded jacket that Changyu likes; Zhao Di putting on the hairpin given to her by Changyu as a gift; Zhao Di sitting at the loom weaving; Zhao Di running on the road numerous times to catch a glimpse of Changyu, or to greet him returning; and so forth. When the bowl with the indigo patterns that Zhao Di uses to hold the food breaks as she falls in her run to catch up with him, her mother has it repaired by a traveling craftsman, whose meticulous handiwork is captured in detail on the screen, reminding us of a primitive kind of technology — possessed and performed by the peasant classes, from generation to generation — that is fast becoming extinct.

Be it in the form of rustic utensils, activities, or behaviors, then, the everyday is cinematically offered with the connotations of human *labor* — its persistence and endurance, and its redemptive power. To return to the notion of a "brute" speech as mentioned by Pasolini, the everyday is here invoked precisely as a remembered, already-experienced collective purpose, a form of life that is able to survive the hardships of a politically repressive climate and the physical death of individuals. This collectivity, which Zhang attaches to the countryside, can arguably be seen as that "pre-grammatical history" in all its intensity, the kinemes drawn from this history, in the form of all the recognizable rural objects, habitats, gestures, movements, and exchanges, being configured into the cinematic story (with its many im-signs) before us. (Importantly, the story of the mother and father as young lovers is retold in color, whereas the present, the time of the narration, is shot in black and white.) In this manner, the everyday takes on the import of an allegorical, indeed symbolic, correspondence between human activity and the natural environment. The latter, shown alternately in stunning, picturesque autumnal hues and in the prohibitive severity of wintry grays and blues, becomes simply a background from which human beings courageously carve out their social destinies. It is tempting to conclude that cinematic allure in this instance is still part of the logic of a socialist ideal, with the belief in bringing people together, in forging a bond and coherence between human action and the universe.[8]

The road home, then, is the road to the father and the mother, the return to a time inhabited by the others/elders. At the same time, it is the road to the utopian possibility of determination, happiness, and communal purpose — constituents of another, older kind of sociality.

When Flowers Were in Full Bloom

Whereas the chance encounter structurally gives way to sexual intent and social direction in *The Road Home*, in Wong Kar-wai's hands it never transcends the casual, arbitrary, and unexpected aura of "it so happens ..." that characterizes most of his film narratives to date. *In the Mood for Love* begins with a series of unremarkable coincidences. In Hong Kong in 1962, both Su Lizhen and Zhou Muyun happen to be looking for a room to rent in a district inhabited by Shanghai immigrants.[9] They find their rooms in adjacent apartments, and move in on the same day. Their chance encounter now takes the form of casual chatting as the movers keep misplacing their belongings in each other's unit. After settling in, they keep brushing past each other in the company of their spouses and neighbors, at the mah-jong table, and on the stairway leading up to their apartments. One day, over coffee at a restaurant, they confirm each other's suspicions that their spouses may be having an affair. At this point, the two, perhaps from despondency, actively turn what has so far been a series of chance events into a conscious exploration: asking themselves how their spouses might have begun their affair, they start seeing each other on a regular basis, enacting by turns imagined scenes of seduction, confrontation, and breaking-up as though they were rehearsing performances on a stage set.

Su and Zhou's relationship is, strictly speaking, a double one. As Wong describes it, they must simultaneously be themselves and the other couple, jointly engaged in a conspiracy of keeping a secret they have discovered together.[10] In contrast to Zhao Di and Luo Changyu, who transform their chance encounter into a meaningful relationship by overcoming various obstacles, Su and Zhou perpetuate the chance element of their encounter by improvising other people's lives, assuming identities that are at once their own and not their own. In this process of playacting, Zhou eventually notices that he has fallen in love with Su. This discovery of his own emotions — and of the fact that he is, after all, not so different from the adulterous others that he is trying vicariously to understand — prompts him to leave for Singapore and put an end to their relationship. Su looks for him by arriving in Singapore herself, but strangely, as she succeeds in locating him by phone at his workplace and is on the verge of reuniting with him, she hangs up. Back in Hong Kong in 1966, Su has rented (or bought) her old apartment where she now lives with her child and a servant, and Zhou shows up next-door one day to visit his old landlord, who has moved. Although they are within a few steps of each other, Su and Zhou narrowly miss each other. The "encounter" of the "chance encounter" fails to happen this time and fails to become anything more substantial. Zhou is next shown visiting the Angkor Wat in Cambodia, confessing his secret in a hole on a wall, around the time of Cambodia's independence from France.

Like Zhang, Wong inserts numerous daily objects in his picture, but whereas the objects in *The Road Home* are imbued with a primitive, rural, and timeless quality, Wong's objects are much more specific to the chronological referent he depicts. From the coiffures, the make-up style, *qipaos*, and shoes worn by Su; to household items such as the electric rice cooker, the thermos for carrying hot noodles, the radio set (broadcasting song request programs), newspapers; public spaces such as offices and restaurants with their old-fashioned décor; deserted street corners with peeling wall advertisements; and the darkish, upholstered interiors of taxicabs at night, Wong offers glimpses of a Hong Kong that no longer exists. Reportedly, he was so intent on recreating the ambience of the 1960s that he "hired a chef to cook Shanghai dishes for the cast and crew"; "engaged retired Hong Kong radio announcers, now in their seventies, to record radio programs for the soundtrack featuring bits of Mandarin pop and Chinese opera"; and used quotations from a popular newspaper columnist and novelist to frame his story.[11] Are not these objective reminders of a bygone era again a compelling instance of that "brute" speech alluded to by Pasolini? Especially for audiences acquainted with the Hong Kong of the 1960s, these ethnographic details arguably constitute a kind of already-read text, one that evokes, in the midst of the contemporary filmic rendering, the sense of a community that has been but no longer is.

Remarkably, however, even as these everyday details, like the melodic refrains of the popular songs that punctuate them, are repeated, their repetition functions for a purpose rather distinct from their empirical objective presence: they are deployed, as it were, in order to conjure a subjective, yet pervasive, mood of melancholy. To see this, it would be instructive to compare a few details in Wong's film with similar ones in Zhang's:

Body movement. In Zhang's film, the many shots of Zhao Di moving — walking slowly or briskly, running, tripping and falling, and getting up again — are examples of a capacity for and an aspiration toward a certain goal, the young girl's goal of seeing and being with her beloved male. Body movements in their everyday simplicity become expressive actions toward that goal, and mere treading on earth is never an aimless peregrination. In Wong's film, body movements, even when they pertain to two people meeting (such as when Su and Zhou meet on the stairway leading up to their apartments, or when they brush past each other at the mah-jong table), are a means rather of dramatizing the ephemerality of the encounter (as in the Chinese expression, *cha shen er guo*). The technique of the slow motion, used by Zhang to pictorialize and externalize the young girl's subjectivity (her delight at the prospect of seeing the young man), becomes in Wong's hands a way of extending the duration and thus of magnifying the granularity of an otherwise automatized, because transitory, set of motions. Whereas Zhang uses movements to unify body and mind, Wong, like some of the French New Wave directors of the 1960s whose techniques he often borrows, turns such movements into occasions for an alternative experience, that of defamiliarizing the nature of (repetitive, habitual) motion through a manipulation of its cinematic texture and of viewing time.

Eating. In Zhang's film, the various aspects of eating, including the preparation and consumption of meals, are shown with a straightforward gusto. Food is the communal service provided by one group of workers to another group in the village, as well as the means of bonding between the girl and the young man. In Wong's film, food, or rather the routine of meals, is rather a sign of ennui and forlornness (Su repeatedly turns down her landlady's invitation to dinner and insists on getting noodles by herself.) Alternatively, it is the occasion for exploring the nuances of an extramarital relationship (think of the scenes of Su and Zhou munching their Hong Kong-style Western food at the restaurant and sharing noodles from a thermos when they are stuck in his room, of them rehearsing Su's confrontation of her husband over a meal, or of Su making sesame porridge for everyone but really in order to please Zhou, who has fallen sick). Food consumption is linked to the minutiae of labor in one case and to those of languor in the other.

Clothes. In Zhang's film, Zhao Di has only a couple of padded jackets, but she makes a point of always putting on the bright red one that Changyu likes. Again, the simple act of dressing is filled with a purpose — that of pleasure giving — that is redirected into the story, as part of the motivation that propels the plot. In Wong's film, in contrast, one of the unforgettable things is the large number of expert-tailored, splendid-looking *qipaos* worn by Su, whose pristine figure remains unperturbed even in pouring rain. The gorgeous colors, patterns, and shapes as embodied by Su are not exactly necessary to the action of the story. In their invariable perfection, in their almost mechanical (because impeccable) appearances, they are rather directed at some other gaze, for which the figure of Su stands like an uncanny, doll-like fetish (in the Freudian sense) for some unexpressed or inarticulate emotion — one, moreover, that belongs not to any individual character within the story but to a force outside the diegesis, structuring it.

Despite the historically and geographically concrete setting, therefore, the audience does not learn a realistic account about the 1960s in Hong Kong. Instead, it is a Hong Kong remembered in oneiric images — households are shown at partial angles (through windows, doorways, and corridors); streets are dimly lit with restricted views; routes of taxi rides are shadowy and unidentifiable; food stalls are signified simply by trails of steam from cooking; a hotel counter is glimpsed only through its framed reflection in a mirror. At once objective (that is, available for all to see) and subjective (that is, mediated by a particular consciousness), these visual details raise questions about the exact relationship between the everyday as such and its historical referent. Whereas in Zhang, that relationship can be traced to a residual socialist sentimentalism with its faith in the import of human action, in Wong the everyday points rather to something clichéd: the fundamentally unfulfilled — and unfulfillable — nature of human desire, to which history itself becomes subject and subordinate.

The concreteness of the many everyday details of the 1960s notwithstanding, what gives Wong's film its unique imprint of a nostalgic sentimentalism, as is often the case in his works, is rather the elusiveness of communication and missed communication between human beings. If Su and Zhou begin communicating because of a series of coincidences (both begin by renting a room; both are married to partners who seem often absent; both discover that their partners may be having an affair with each other; both are plunged into a condition of anxiety and disillusionment), the fateful symmetry of their situations does not exactly guarantee fulfillment or permanence of their relationship. The symmetry simply leads, almost matter-of-factly, to the improvisations that become the basis of their entanglement. But improvisations are a matter of hits and misses, so to speak: as in Wong's famous method of directing,[12] an improvised plot does not know where it is going until it has run its course. Even though the improvised version may be the only version there is — and it may be a remarkable one at that — the volatile relationships it projects and the aura of loss that surrounds them are strong indications of a kind of longing, one that can be detected in different manners in Wong's other works, despite their generic variations.[13] Ultimately, his work seems to say, human relationships, even the most unforgettable ones, are only a matter of fortuitous playacting — and perhaps not so much by human beings as by chance or fate itself.

The sentimentalism of Wong's film, in other words, is to be identified not merely at the level of the old objects and interiors from the 1960s but more palpably in the theme of the impermanence of human togetherness to which he repeatedly returns. To this extent, the spectacular, indeed visually stunning, images stand as a paradox: the more colorful and beautiful they are — and the more locally concrete they seem to be — the more they become an index to the capricious nature of the human universe that revolves around them. The material fullness of the sounds and images becomes in this manner a screen for a fundamental lack, for what might be called an unhappy consciousness. *Cinematic allure, existential angst*: this disjuncture, or synergy, between sensuous plenitude and spiritual longing stands as the hallmark of a trans-social, trans-cultural human drama, for which the everyday functions as artifice, as stage props.

Wong's film ends with scenes from the ancient ruins of the Angkor Wat in Cambodia, which the camera captures in a steady pace against the somber music of Umebayashi Shigeru (originally part of his score for Suzuki Seiji's film *Yumeji*). These ruins remind one of the scenes of the magnificent Iguazu Falls in Argentina in Wong's previous film *Happy Together*, suggesting a persistence and endurance that transcends the human world. Whereas for Zhang, it is the persistence and endurance of the human will which triumphs over impediments imposed by nature (be they snowstorms, a harsh landscape, or sheer physical distance), for Wong the ruins of an exotic land, ravaged for ages by the elements yet standing still erect in the midst of political turmoil, offer the final solace.

Sentimentalism: The Symptom of a Collective Critical Impasse?

If these two films are any indication, the everyday is for certain a popular convention adopted by contemporary Chinese filmmakers. Although this by itself is not a novel revelation and perhaps not peculiar to cinema, it is of interest as to why the everyday — in the form of casual happenings such as chance encounters, or in the form of the inorganic, the mundane trivia that make up living environments — has emerged at this moment as a viable and compelling way of telling stories on the screen. Is the everyday simply a stand-in for history and reality?

In Pasolini's approach to the everyday in cinema, what remains thought-provoking is not simply the equation of the "pre-grammatical" history of brute objects with reality; rather, it is Pasolini's insistence that such bruteness has the ability to alter — indeed, to adulterate — the metaphorical nature of cinematic signification itself by constraining the latter's flight toward pure abstraction, by directing such tendency toward abstraction back toward a conventional objectivity. As he writes (in the passage cited in the epigraph to the present essay), cinema "will not be able to 'reproduce' (write) a tree: it will reproduce a pear tree, an apple tree, an elder tree, a cactus — but not a tree." In "The 'Cinema of Poetry'" he puts it this way:

> [The filmmaker] chooses a series of objects, or things, or landscapes, or persons as syntagmas (signs of a symbolic language) which, *while they have a grammatical history invented in that moment* — as in a sort of happening dominated by the idea of selection and montage — *do, however, have an already lengthy and intense pregrammatical history.* (171; emphases in the original)

> [C]inema, lacking a conceptual, abstract vocabulary, is powerfully metaphoric; as a matter of fact, *a fortiori* it operates immediately on the metaphoric level. Particular, deliberately generated metaphors, however, always have some quality that is inevitably crude and conventional. Think of the frenzied or joyous flights of doves which are meant to express metaphorically the state of anxiety or joy in the mind of the character. In short, the nuanced, barely perceptible metaphor, the poetic halo one millimeter thick ... would not seem possible in cinema. Whatever part of the poetically metaphoric which is sensationalistically possible in film, it is always in close osmosis with its other nature, the strictly communicative one of prose. (174)

An outcome of cinema's twin bases in the thorough permeation by technology and the residual empiricism of material life, this paradox of *a propensity toward the metaphoric and the literal at once* leads Pasolini to speak of cinema as having a "double nature": "it is both extremely subjective and extremely objective (to such an extent that it reaches an unsurpassable and awkward naturalistic fate). The two moments of the above-mentioned nature are closely intertwined and are not separable even in the laboratory" (173).

This double nature may well be the reason cinema lends itself so appropriately to the sentimentalism of nostalgia as it centers on the everyday. In the two films under discussion, for instance, the everyday objects we encounter in their immediacy constitute a uniquely and subjectively composed visual representation, one that is unavoidably metaphorical in that it is bound to be read as pointing to something beyond the objects themselves (such as the nature of human interactions, or a general ambience of purposefulness or disappointment). Yet this visual representation is simultaneously what renders these objects historical, communal, already-looked-at-by-others — what, precisely because of the objects' recognizability, recalls that pre-grammatical intensity, that obligatory social life of the everyday we perceive with our senses before it is organized (by a particular *auteur*) into a particular audiovisual filmic composition. The lyrical or allegorical styling of these everyday relationships, practices, and objects notwithstanding, this other, literal aspect of cinematic visuality suggestively casts such objects in the light of an empirical place and time, evoking a multitude, a collective way of living that "once existed." When mapped narratively onto the passing of time (the 1950s and 1960s in the two films), this double nature of filmic signification easily produces the effect of retrospection and hence — since the past is made to appear so beautiful and elusive — of nostalgia and its attendant sentimentalism.

As most of us watch movies increasingly in the form of globally portable technologies such as VCDs and DVDs, the sentimentalism generated by these filmic accounts of the past has also taken on a life of rapid circulation. It is such circulation, such movement, as it were, that gives sentimentalism its contemporary groundedness. Rather than being opposed, the affective tenacity of sentimentalism and the technological changeability of its representations together form a kind of capital-in-flux in the global circuit, turning the most locally specific everyday elements simultaneously into the most fabulous, because infinitely transmissible, phantasmagorias. In this sense, the "brute speech" and "pre-grammatical history" Pasolini theorizes, too, may ultimately become, as in Zhang's and Wong's films, parts of what Fredric Jameson argues as a postmodern reification of ethnic culture,[14] a reification whose typicality is most evident, ironically, when directors make their most unique attempts to revive, indeed to arrest, a historical time and place with all its "cultural particulars." [In other words, precisely as directors try to communicate "literally" by invoking concrete objects, in a globalized cinematic context in which audiences scan spectacles without necessarily knowing anything about the historical specifics behind them, the "metaphorical" side of film tends to take over, translating or reducing even the most local details into generalizable events. Instead of the pear tree, apple tree, elder tree, or cactus, they will, most likely, simply understand "tree." Instead of Chinese history, they will, most likely, simply understand universal human drama, romance, etc. Contrary to Pasolini, therefore, it is increasingly the abstract — in the form of the reified spectacle — which allows for transmissibility and enables "communication" at the transcultural level, while the literal, being concrete yet parochial, easily ends up posing a limit to such communication.]

To that end, the polarity between Zhang's and Wong's aesthetic and political approaches — and the difference between their respective sentimentalisms — may simply be symptomatic of the *range* of a larger ideological impasse that confronts all those engaged in one way or another with the study of transnational culture at the turn of the twenty-first century. Prasenjit Duara describes this impasse succinctly from the perspective of critical historiography:

> Critical historiography which had found its inspiration in Marxist and other radical social theory encounters a world in which the possibilities of non-capitalist emancipation have receded and one where the revolutionary states have been discredited. At the same time, capitalist globalisation continues to widen the gap between the powerful and the powerless while the erosion of a national society itself unleashes a reaction which results in still more violent and exclusive reifications of nation, race or culture.[15]

Insofar as Zhang remains committed to the vestiges of a socialist humanism, his recent works, such as *Not One Less* and *Happy Time* as well as *The Road Home*, are marked by a distinctive nationalist quality. Chineseness in Zhang is a residual structure of feeling that results from the specifics of a country's political history. However aesthetically controlled, a film such as *The Road Home* would not have made sense without the messiness of that history and the burden of hope it tries to salvage therein. This attempt at redemption, incidentally, is quite different from Zhang's early works, in which the criticism of history is much more bleak and violent, and the everyday, such as is associated with wedding rituals, household customs, and various folk practices and objects, tends to be a matter of fabrication.[16] For Wong, ethnicity is at once more local and more fluid. Rather than being concerned with the Chinese nation as such, his interest is focused on the Shanghai community in the Hong Kong of the 1960s; this attachment to a group already in diaspora prefigures his film's much more casual, tenuous relation to

Chineseness as a geopolitical or national issue. Instead, the film stages an essentially human drama. This other humanism, bound not to the fraught legacy of the nation's (failed) political aspirations the way Zhang's is but rather to an image-proliferating nostalgia in which history tends always already to have transmuted into pastiche and simulacra, travels with great felicity (and efficiency) the world over, its structure of feeling appealing to diverse audiences in Moscow, New York, Paris, and Beijing alike. Precisely because Wong's film does not consciously re-collect itself as "Chinese" even as it uses a small Chinese migrant enclave as its site, it achieves a relevance that is arguably universal. Chineseness, now dis-placed and dispersed in such ways as never again to form any cohesive continuum, has become an anonymous, hence globally interchangeable, part object, whose defining character is no longer history but image, artifice, and commodity.

Between the aestheticized spectacle of a socialist humanism that has become politically bankrupt and the aestheticized spectacle of a metaphysics of human desire that has acquired global currency, these sentimental returns in contemporary Chinese cinema present us with new problems in critical practice. Should we hold on to the utopic, however untimely, as part of an aesthetics of redemption — of what was or could have been? Should we merge with the global flow of chance potentialities in the spirit of a seasoned and resigned "human understanding"— of the way things are and will always be? The everyday, considered in this light, may yet be the paradigmatic case of the theoretical predicament we face in our time, and its representation will always demand some hard rethinking.

Notes

Chapter 1

1. We would like to thank the Chiang Ching-kuo Foundation, the Social Sciences and Humanities Research Council of Canada, and the University of Lethbridge for funding assistance.
2. Robert J. C. Young's *Postcolonialism: An Historical Introduction,* for example, defends the coherence of "postcolonialism" as a "national internationalism," a coherent body of thought emerging during the twentieth century, "a revolutionary Black, Asian and Hispanic globalization, with its own dynamic counter-modernity" (2).
3. Shohat is one among many who have raised concern about the "ahistorical and universalizing" use of the term: she also usefully elaborates upon tensions between historical and epistemological uses of the postcolonial (101).
4. See, for instance, Holden's own discussion of the recent popularity of the term diaspora in "Questioning Diaspora ..."
5. See, for instance, Chatterjee's insistence that "the journey that might take us beyond the nation must first pass through the currently disturbed zones within the nation-state" through a consideration of conflicts within national political societies (57).
6. Unless specified, all quotations refer to the 1994 essay "On Not Speaking Chinese," not the book.
7. As a result of more Chinese from Hong Kong and Taiwan, the cityscape of Vancouver also begins to resemble Hong Kong and Taipei in certain aspects, featuring high-rise apartments, regional cuisines, specialty grocery stores, and fashion boutiques that cater to East Asian clientele.

8. If anything, cities such as Vancouver reach out to these potential consumers. For example, ATM outlets in Vancouver and the suburbs provide Chinese language service.

9. Ang in *On Not Speaking Chinese* (2001). Ng's experience in Canadian prairie towns indicates that rural Alberta is not at all Asianized.

10. The last scene in *Brokeback Mountain* is a close-up of a closet that contains mementoes of the love affair between the two main characters.

Chapter 2

1. For example, *Qiaoxiang Ties*.

2. For example, Ong and Nonini, eds., and comments by Madeline Hsu in *Dreaming of Gold, Dreaming of Home,* p. 8.

3. McKeown, 1999, pp. 73–110.

4. An exception is Ngai.

5. For example, *Qiaoxiang Ties*; Douw and Post, eds.; and Kuah.

6. Zhuang, p. 174.

7. Pu, "Dangdai," pp. 179–85; Purcell, 1965, pp. 494–5; Zhuang, p. 173, n 11; See, 1981, p. 230; Shi Zhenmin [Chinben See], 1976, p. 157. In an official Republic of China publication, the figure for 1954 is given as 250,000. *Huaqiao Jingji,* 1958, pp. 36ff.

8. Field research in Gulangyu, 1994; Cook, Chapter 3 and illustrations of houses; Zhuang, pp. 171–81; Dai, pp. 159–68; Pu, "Dangdai," pp. 187ff.

9. Wickberg, 1965/2000, Chapter 1; Weightman, pp. 315–23. On *intsik*, see Tan, pp. 191–2.

10. Wickberg, 1997, pp. 166–7; Peck, pp. 128–43.

11. Cook, pp. 408ff; Dai, pp. 159–68; Carino, 1998, pp. 20ff; Blaker, pp. 130–1, 142.

12. Shi Zhenmin, 1976, p. 159; Zhuang, pp. 176ff; See, 1981, p. 230.

13. Shi Zhenmin, 1976, pp. 126–7; Oguma, 112; Wickberg, 1997, p. 163.

14. *Quanzhou-shi Huaqiao Zhi,* Chapter 4, especially pp. 175, 185, 193–200, 217, 241, 253–99; Pu, "Dangdai," p. 189.

15. Manila interviews, 1966; Wickberg, 1997, p. 169; Carino, 1998, pp. 24, 42–6, 62–4; Carino, 2001, pp. 99–102; Shi Zhenmin, 1976, p. 173.

16. Shi Zhenmin, 1976, p. 173; Carino, 1998, pp. 42–3; Blaker, pp. 206ff. On the purposes of the Grand Family Association, the federation of all major surname associations, compare Shi Zhenmin, 1976, p. 173, and Amyot, p. 123.

17. Blaker, pp. 207ff, 243ff., 252; Carino, 1998, pp. 44, 63; Wickberg, 1997, p. 169; Liu Chi Tien, pp. 785–806; Tan, pp. 189–90.

18. Manila interviews, 1990, 1992; Amyot (p. 63) observed in the 1950s that Taiwan-sponsored education stressed the nation and de-emphasized "territory."

19. Chinben See, personal communication, 1983; Shi Zhenmin, 1976,

pp. 186–9; Chen, pp. 172–87. Some surname association ancestral tablets were brought to the Philippines from Taiwan. Amyot, p. 109.

20. Tan, p. 187.
21. Guldin, p. 162.
22. Manila interviews, 1990.
23. Wu, pp. 114–18; *Quanzhou-shi Huaqiao Zhi*, Tables 4-2 and 4-6, pp. 176, 178.
24. *Quanzhou-shi Huaqiao Zhi,* pp. 176, 178, 185–299; Wu, pp. 114–8.
25. Tan, pp. 177–203; Ang See, pp. 38–46.
26. Cebu interviews, 1991.
27. Shi Zhenmin, 1976, pp. 180–1, 204; See, 1981, pp. 230–1.
28. Guldin *passim*. Note the writings of Elizabeth Sinn and Hong Liu on home district associations as bases for, among other things, remittance facilitation.
29. Shi Zhenmin, 1976, pp. 174ff.
30. Shi Zhenmin, 1976, pp. 167, 170; See, 1981, p. 240; Amyot, Chapter 7.
31. Amyot, p. 117.
32. Manilla interviews, 1966.
33. At the same time, some Filipino journalists began to criticize the excessive influence of Taiwan, and especially the KMT, on local Chinese society. Tan, pp. 188–9.
34. See, 1988, pp. 327–31 and note 22; Wickberg, 1997, p. 171, note 52.
35. Manila interviews and personal experience, 1966.
36. See reports of statements by Ralph Nubla [Gao Zuru] in *Huaqiao Shangbao* [*Chinese Commercial News*], issues of late 1960s and early 1970s.
37. Interview with Ambassador Hang Liwu, Manila, Summer 1966.
38. Shi Zhenmin, 1976, pp. 160, 162, note 2.
39. Carino, 1998, pp. 77–9.
40. Carino, 1998, pp. 61–4; See, 1988, pp. 327–31 and note 22.
41. Tan, pp. 189–90; See, 1985, pp. 37–8; Wickberg, 1990, p. 26; Cheong, pp. 105–9.
42. Wickberg, 1990, p. 26; See, 1985, p. 40.
43. Wickberg, 1990, p. 27.
44. *Quanzhou-shi Huaqiao Zhi.* pp. 178–9.
45. Field research, Jinjiang and Shishi, 1994; Song, pp. 198–201, especially p. 201.
46. Xiamen interviews, 1994; Zhuang, p. 175; Shi Zhenmin, 1976, p. 157; Pu, "Lun Fujian," pp. 25–30; Pu, "Dangdai," pp. 179–85.
47. Wickberg, 1990, p. 28; Wickberg, 1997, p. 171; Tan, pp. 194ff; See, 1985, pp. 38–40; Manila interviews, 1990.
48. For many examples, see issues of the center's publication, *Edukasyong Tsino* (*Huawen Jiaoyu*).
49. For example, Zhuang, p. 174 and Hong Liu, 1999, pp. 101–3. But compare Douw, 1996, pp. 43–5 and Douw, 1999, p. 35.
50. Zhuang, p. 174; Douw, 1999, p. 35. Douw does note the role of Taiwan in the Philippine case.

51. McKeown, 2001, Chapter 8.
52. See, 1981, p. 240.
53. Amyot, p. 165. He related it to their university education.
54. Amyot, p. 154; Ang See, pp. 40-42.
55. Wickberg, 1997, pp. 163–6.
56. McBeath, *passim*; Tilman, *passim*; see also Tan, pp. 187–93.
57. Note Amyot's implicit version: not an absence of Chinese culture but an absence of village cultural contact combined with a presence of university education. Amyot, p. 165.
58. Ishida, 1991, Chapters 16–20.
59. Cf. McKeown, 2001, p. 283.

Chapter 3

1. Although Patricia Roy has argued that Chinese railway workers were not technically coolies because they came to work voluntarily, most historians agree that the conditions of their labour were almost identical to that of indenture. Roy writes that "the Chinese ... were not technically [coolies] having come to Canada as free labourers or under voluntary term contracts: the true coolie was usually a captive who had no choice about where he went or what he did" (18). However, Chinese railway workers had very little choice about where they went, and the conditions of their arrival produced an informal indenture system. Chinese labourers usually had their head tax and transportation fees paid for first by a contractor or subcontractor, and they would be expected to eventually work off those debts, producing a system of indentured labour that was never formally named as such in Canada. The elaborate system of subcontracting made it particularly easy for the Canadian government to declare that it was not employing indentured labour. See Lee, p. 47; Li, pp. 20–3; and Wickberg, pp. 20–4.
2. See also Spivak's "Diasporas old and new" and Mishra's "The diasporic imaginary."
3. See Anderson, pp. 22–36.
4. In the opening paragraph of "Dissemination," Bhabha names the subjects of this essay as those who have lived in "the scattering of the people that in other times and other places, in the nations of others, becomes a time of gathering" (139). And in that gathering he includes "the gathering of people in the diaspora: indentured, migrant, interned" (139).
5. In "The diasporic imaginary," Mishra differentiates between "the older diasporas of classic capitalism and the mid- to late-twentieth-century diasporas of advanced capital to the metropolitan centres of Empire, the New World and the former settler colonies" (421). Similarly, Spivak uses the term *old diasporas* as "the results of religious oppression and war, of slavery and indenturing, trade and conquest,

and intra-European economic migration which, since the nineteenth century, took the form of migration and immigration into the United States" (245).

6. Chinese workers were often abandoned wherever the contracts for work on the railway line ended, and unemployment in these areas produced drifting communities. In some of the worst cases, starving workers resorted to petty theft and eating garbage from the streets. See Morton, pp. 106–7.

7. See Ashcroft, Griffith, and Tiffin's *The Empire Writes Back*, and Ania Loomba's chapter, "Colonialism and Literature" in *Colonialism/Postcolonialism*.

8. Although the Provincial Archives of Alberta does not have a date for the New Dayton menu, I have dated the menu to the 1920s. In conversation with archivists at the Gault Museum in Lethbridge, Alberta, we have agreed that this is a reasonable approximation of the time of this menu. According to a publication of the New Dayton Historical Society, Hoy Fat Leong came to New Dayton in 1917 with his son Charlie Chew Leong. They bought land from Jim Reid and then operated the first café in New Dayton. In 1923, the café was destroyed by fire. Charlie Chew rebuilt the café with four tables, stools, a glass counter, and modern gas lamps (a big improvement on the old kerosene ones). The menu we now have, which includes items such as pastries that could be displayed at a glass counter and ice cream sodas, would have been part of the menu of the rebuilt New Dayton Café. Also, the menu names "C. L. Chew" as the proprietor and not Charlie's father, Hoy Fat Leong.

9. See my "Re-reading Head Tax Racism."

10. Please see in particular "How Newness Enters the World" in *The Location of Culture* for a discussion of Bhabha's concept of time lag.

Chapter 4

1. Josey's transcription of Lee's words has several inconsistencies with the original tape, and I have modified the transcript accordingly. See Josey, pp. 285–6.

2. See also James Minchin's commentary on the incident and on Bloodworth's and Josey's reactions (155).

3. Wallerstein's elaboration of the concept of a world-system has consumed much of his intellectual career over the last quarter century. Originating in Western Europe in the sixteenth century, the modern world system, Wallerstein notes, has extended its reach century by century, until it presently encompasses the whole globe. Core regions of the world, such as Europe and North America, are thus part of a globally structured economy that keeps a peripheral area materially disadvantaged. Singapore's position as an entrepôt places it at an intriguing — and, perhaps, ambiguous — position in such a world-system. As Tommy Koh has noted, Singapore is the most trade-dependent country in the world, international trade amounting to ninety-three percent of its GDP (181).

4. Appadurai, however, may well be too optimistic in celebrating a transnationalism in which Wallerstein's distinction between centre and periphery has vanished.

5. For a larger contextualization of this process, which he terms "national culturalism," see Wee's article, "Capitalism and Ethnicity: Creating 'Local' Culture in Singapore."

6. For a more extended discussion of New Labour's policy debts to Lee, see Holden's "Paper Tiger, Paper Lion ..."

7. Dawn Thompson makes an interesting parallel point in an article in discussing Canadian multiculturalism, noting that through technologies such as "immigration policies, census questions, financial support for ethnic associations" (56) and so on, the state incites a belief in its ability to promote equality in a free labor market of individualized subjects (57).

8. The most extended documentation of Lee's views on race is Michael D. Barr's chapter on "Culture, Race and Genes" in his *Lee Kuan Yew: The Beliefs Behind the Man* (185–210).

9. The transformation in the ruling party's ideology has been noted by many commentators. Vasil terms it "asianising," Chua observes that the weakening of the hegemony of pragmatism as a governing ideology led to the development of a communitarian ideology in the 1990s (*Communitarian Ideology* 20–37), while Wee sees the change as being from an "'ethnically neutral' policy underpinned by a rational commitment to cultural modernization, to the international appearance of the 'Asian values' discourse and the 1980's re-ethnicization of Singaporeans into hyphenated identities" (129).

10. See Holden, "Postcolonialism as Genealogy ..." (289–90) for a more extended discussion of the community centre as a site of self-fashioning for national subjects.

11. My translation. Renan's 1882 Sorbonne Lecture "Qu'est-ce qu'une nation?" is a much-quoted statement of the principles behind nineteenth-century European nationalism.

12. The problematics of Mandarinization are reflected in the character's name. *Kiasu* is a Hokkien word that literally means "afraid of losing" and is used to describe one aspect of the compulsive competitiveness of Singaporeans. It is a word used by all Singaporeans, and the same Chinese characters, spoken in Mandarin, *pa shu*, have no resonance.

Chapter 6

1. This short autobiographical piece is published in *Making Face, Making Soul/ Haciendo Caras*.

2. For a discussion of hunger in Chinese fiction see, for example, "Three Hungry Women" by David Der-wei Wang, in which he focuses on texts by Lu Ling, Eileen Chang, and Chen Yingzhen.

3. Sau-ling Wong identifies two major sets of alimentary motifs in Asian American literature: "big eating," typically associated with the immigrant generation, and "food prostitution": " 'selling' oneself for treats in the case of the American-born" (55). "Food pornography" is a third survival strategy: making a living by exploiting the "exotic" aspects of one's culture. To gain a foothold in mainstream society, the "food pornographers" exaggerate their otherness.

4. *Pancit* is a traditional Filipino noodle-based dish with pork, chicken, and various vegetables.

5. Just as much as Keiko functions as Elena's "racial shadow," Steve in "Below the Line" can be read as May's "racial shadow" onto whom she projects her alienation. The story emphasizes the similarities between the two lovers. Steve has a relationship equally as close to his sister April as does May to Gary. All four arrived in the United States when they were children. Like May, Steve feels "orphaned" because he is "neither American nor immigrant" (137), but unlike Gary, he and May "hadn't grown up to chase big bucks" (137). May inflicts physical pain on the part of her "racial shadow's" body, i.e., the ear, through which emotional pain and abuse are inflicted on her.

6. The other writer of Japanese descent publishing in German is Hisako Matsubara. Her historical and semi-autobiographical novels focus on life in Japan.

7. Yoko Tawada was born in Tokyo in 1960 and has been living in Hamburg since 1982. Narrative texts that originally appeared in German are: *Wo Europa anfängt* [*Where Europe Begins*] (1991), *Ein Gast* [*A Guest*] (1993), and *Opium für Ovid* [*Opium for Ovid*] (2000). "The Bath" was originally published in Japanese.

8. As this piece has not (yet) been translated into English, the translation of the title is my own.

Chapter 7

1. This chapter was greatly improved by the insightful comments of two of my colleagues at Lawrence University: Birgit Tautz, Department of German [now at Bowdoin College], and Lifongo Vetinde, Department of French. I would also like to thank Professor Maria Ng, Associate Professor, Department of English, The University of Lethbridge, for her hard work as conference organizer of the International Conference on Chinese Transnationalism in the Age of Migration and Immigration, October 12–14, 2001, in Edmonton, Alberta, Canada, at which a draft of this chapter was presented. I would also like to thank the anonymous reviewer of the chapter for suggestions for revision and expansion.

2. See, for example, Jeanne R. Smith, "Cross-cultural Play: Maxine Hong Kingston's *Tripmaster Monkey*" in Laura E. Skandera-Trombley, *Critical Essays on Maxine Hong Kingston* (New York: G.K. Hall & Co., 1998), p. 334, who states that "Mikhail Bakhtin's conception of the multivocal, dialogic novel

and his recognition of various points of view within and outside of a language or culture make him useful to critics of ethnic literature." Lee Quinby speaks of the "I" in Kingston's texts as "in the Bakhtinian sense, overtly dialogical." See "The Subject of Memoirs: *The Woman Warrior*'s Technology of Ideographic Selfhood," in *Critical Essays on Maxine Hong Kingston*, p. 126. Malini Johar Schueller in "Questioning Race and Gender Definitions: Dialogic Subversions in *The Woman Warrior*," *Criticism* 31 (1989), p. 424, asserts that Kingston uses a "language in which opposed and diverse voices constantly coexist." Amy Ling in "Maxine Hong Kingston and the Dialogic Dilemma of Asian American writers" reads Kingston's first book, *The Woman Warrior*, as "an extended exploration of the internal dialogism of three words: *Chinese, American* and *female*." See *Critical Essays on Maxine Hong Kingston*, p. 172.

3. M. M. Bakhtin, *The Dialogic Imagination: Four Essays* (Austin, TX: University of Texas Press, 1981), p. 427.

4. M. M. Bakhtin, *The Dialogic Imagination*, p. 76. See also Graham Allen, *Intertextuality*, p. 165: "Dialogism does not necessarily means a 'conversation' between subjects equally empowered within the language game; it refers, more specifically, to a clash between languages and utterances which can foreground not only social division but a radically divided space of discursive formations within an individual subject."

5. M. M. Bakhtin, *The Dialogic Imagination*, p. 324.

6. M. M. Bakhtin, *The Dialogic Imagination*, p. 304.

7. M. M. Bakhtin, *The Dialogic Imagination*, p. 324.

8. M. M. Bakhtin, *The Dialogic Imagination*, p. 12.

9. Azade Seyhan, *Writing Outside the Nation*, p. 10.

10. Robert Scholes, *Semiotics and Interpretation*, p. 16. In *The Pursuit of Signs*, Jonathan Culler echoes Scholes's words: "Literary works are to be considered not as autonomous entities, 'organic wholes,' but as intertextual constructs: sequences which have meaning in relation to other texts which they take up, cite, parody, refute, or generally transform [38]."

11. See Andrew H. Plaks's succinct summation of the narrative tradition of the text, "The Journey to the West" in Barbara S. Miller, ed., *Masterworks of Asian Literature in Comparative Perspective: A Guide to Teaching* [Armonk, NY: M.E. Sharpe, 1994], pp. 272–84. The multivolume translation *The Journey to the West* by Anthony C. Yu [Chicago: University of Chicago Press, 1977–83] is a complete translation with scholarly introduction, but a more accessible and lively rendition is the 1943 abridged translation by Arthur Waley, *Monkey*, reprinted by Grove Press in 1958.

12. Kingston parodies Monkey's religious name when Wittman is fired from his job as department store clerk: "Fired. Aware of Emptiness now. Ha ha." [67]

13. Maxine Hong Kingston, *Tripmaster Monkey: His Fake Book* (New York: Vintage, 1990), p. 327.

14. Kingston, *Tripmaster Monkey*, p. 44.
15. Kingston, *Tripmaster Monkey*, p. 3.
16. See, for example, Isabella Furth, "Bee-e-een! Nation, Transformation, and the Hyphen of Ethnicity in Kingston's *Tripmaster Monkey*," in *Critical Essays*, p. 309; Jeanne R. Smith, *Critical Essays*, p. 341; and Jennie Wang, "Tripmaster Monkey: Kingston's Postmodern Representation of a New 'China Man,'" *MELUS* 20:1 (Spring, 1995), p. 118; and E. D. Huntley, *Maxine Hong Kingston: A Critical Companion* (Westport, CT: Greenwood Press, 2001), p. 158.
17. *Tripmaster Monkey*, p. 8.
18. *Tripmaster Monkey*, p. 251.
19. *Tripmaster Monkey*, p. 34. Malini Johar Schueller says of this chapter ending: "Kingston's appropriation of *Moby Dick,* the classic American epic, is an act of empowerment through which the Chinese Other can have a voice in America." See Schueller, "Theorizing Ethnicity and Subjectivity: Maxine Hong Kingston's *Tripmaster Monkey* and Amy Tan's *The Joy Luck Club*," *Genders* 15 [Winter, 1992], p. 74. Schueller does not, however, connect the opening episode with *Moby Dick*.
20. *Tripmaster Monkey*, p. 9.
21. *Tripmaster Monkey*, p. 9.
22 *Tripmaster Monkey*, p. 306. A later scene in Chapter Six, "A Song for Occupations," echoes this early scene as a reader when Wittman meditates on the cultural differences between individualistic Americans and other cultures who had their own "reader of the tribe" to pass along shared communal myths, history and values. "O Right Livelihood" he muses, reverting to Whitmanesque exaggeration. *Tripmaster Monkey*, pp. 246–7.
23. Bhabha, *The Location of Culture* (London: Routledge, 1994), p. 2.
24. *The Location of Culture*, p. 2.
25. *The Location of Culture*, p. 13.
26. *The Location of Culture*, p. 157.
27. *Tripmaster Monkey*, p. 5.
28. *Tripmaster Monkey*, p. 44.
29. *Tripmaster Monkey*, pp. 46–7.
30. *The Location of Culture*, p. 172.
31. *The Location of Culture*, p. 155.
32. *Tripmaster Monkey*, pp. 60–1.
33. *Tripmaster Monkey*, p. 83.
34. *Tripmaster Monkey*, p. 85.
35. *The Dialogic Imagination*, p. 12.
36. *Tripmaster Monkey*, p. 85.
37. Mikhail Bakhtin, *Problems of Dostoevsky's Poetics* (Ann Arbor, MI: Ardis, 1973), p. 157.
38. *Problems of Dostoevsky's Poetics*, p. 160.
39. *Tripmaster Monkey*, p. 13.

40. *Tripmaster Monkey*, pp. 290–3.
41. *Tripmaster Monkey*, p. 34.
42. *Tripmaster Monkey*, p. 73.

Chapter 8

1. Bai Xianyong's fiction was first introduced to China in 1979. See "Yongyuan de Yin Xueyan," *Shouhuo* [Harvest], 1(1979). Yu Lihua's first novel to appear in China was *Youjian Zonglu, Youjian Zonglu* [Seeing the Palm Trees Again]. (Fuzhou: Fujian chubanshe, 1980).
2. In the spring of 1979, my teacher, Professor Ye Jiaying of the University of British Columbia, while lecturing in Beijing, contacted me on behalf of the People's Literature Press and asked me to compile and edit the materials for these three anthologies. I was told later in a letter of apology by the publisher that, according to the general practice of the time in China, the name of the compiler/editor was not mentioned in these three anthologies.
3. See Rao Pengzi, "Shiji zhi jiao: haiwai huawen wenxue de huigu yu zhanwang" [Reviews and Prospects of Overseas Chinese Literature at the Turn of the Century], *Ji'nan xuebao:shezhe ban* (Ji'nan University Journal, Social Sciences and Philosophy Edition), 4(2002), pp. 1–3; and Gu Yuanqing, "Zhongguo 15 nian lai shijie huawen wenxue yanjiu de zouxiang" [Research Trends of Global Chinese-Language Literature in the Past 15 Years in China], *Nanfang wentan* (The Literary Field of Southern China), 6(1999), pp. 52–6.
4. Ibid. Rao and Gu.
5. For instance, see Chen Xuanbo, "Cong Lin Yutang dao Tang Tingting: zhongxin yu bianyuan de wenhua xushi" [From Lin Yutang to Maxine Hong Kingston: the Narrative of the Center and the Periphery], *Waiguo wenxue pinglun* [Foreign Literature Criticism], 4(1995), pp. 92–9; Wang Yuqiu, "Jin ershi nian lai Meiguo huayi wenxue de jueqi" [The Emergence of Chinese American Literature in the Past Twenty Years], *Waiguo wenxue yanjiu* (Foreign Literature Studies), 1(2000), pp. 114–20.
6. Laifong Leung, "Dapo bainian chenmo: Jianada huayi Yingwen xiaoshuo chutan" [Breaking the Silence of a Hundred Years: A Preliminary Study of Fiction in English by Chinese Canadian Writers], *Shijie Wenxue* [World Literature], 2(1998), pp. 278–90.
7. Email message from Zhao Xifang of the Chinese Academy of Social Sciences, November 22, 2002. However, he added that this view seemed controversial to him.
8. For instance, Rao Pengzi, "Haiwai huaren wenxue de Zhongguo yishi" [The Chinese Consciousness in Overseas Chinese Literature], *Ji'nan xuebao:shezhe ban* (Ji'nan University Journal: Social Sciences and Philosophy Edition), 1(1997), pp. 81–9.

9. For instance, Fan Shouyi, "Yi bu wang hua: Beimei huayi xiaoshuojia diyiren Shuixianhua de xinlu licheng" [Not Forgetting China: The Psychological Journey of Sui Sin Fa, the First North American Chinese Fiction Writer], *Waiguo wenxue* [Foreign Literature], 3(1998), pp. 67–82.

10. Tang Junyi (1909–76), "Zhonghua minzu zhi huaguo piaoling" ["The Scattering of Chinese People Like Petals and Fruits"], collected in *Zhonghua renwen yu dangjin shijie* [The Chinese Humanities and the Contemporary World], vol. 7, *Tang Junyi wenji* [The Complete Collection of Tang Junyi], Taipei: Xuesheng shuju, 1984, pp. 11–37.

11. There are exceptions. See Susie Lan Cassel, "To Inscribe the Self Daily: The Discovery of the Ah Quin Diary," in Susie Lan Cassel, ed., *The Chinese in America* (Walnut Creek, CA: Altamira Press, 2002), pp. 54–74.

12. First published in 1966 by the Huangguan chubanshe in Taipei; in 1980 by Fujian chubanshe in Fuzhou; in 1984 by Youyi chubanshe in Beijing.

13. Mark Lai Him, *Cong Huaqiao dao huaren: ershi shiji Meiguo huaren shehui fazhanshi* [From Overseas Chinese to Chinese: History of the Social Development of the Chinese Community in the United States] (Hong Kong: Joint Publishing Company, 1990), p. 512.

14. Wang Ling-chi, "Roots and the Changing Identity of the Chinese in the United States," in Tu Weiming, ed. *The Living Tree: The Changing Meaning of Being Chinese Today* (Stanford, CA: Stanford University Press, 1994), p. 205.

15. Qian Ning, *Liuxue Meiguo* [Studying in the United States] (Nanjing: Jiangsu wenyi chubanshe, 1996), p. 81.

16. Ibid. p. 102.

17. Zhou Li, *Manhedun de Zhongguo nuren* [A Chinese Woman in Manhattan] (Beijing: Beijing chubanshe, 1992).

18. Cao Guilin, *Beijingren zai Niuyue* [A Beijinger in New York] (Beijing: Zhongguo wenlian chuban gongsi, 1991).

19. Shao Jun has published many books based on his works on the Internet, such as *Xin yimin: wanglu xinqing gushi* [New Immigrants: Stories on the Net] (Taipei: Shimao chubanshe, 2000). Also see Guo Huanhuan ed., *Yuedu Shao Jun* [Reading Shao Jun] (Beijing: Qunzhong chubanshe, 2002).

20. Chen Juntao, ed., *Zhongguo liuxueshengwenxue daxi* [A Collection of Foreign Student Literature], 6 vols., Shanghai: Shanghai wenyi chubanshe, 2000.

21. For instance, a multi-volume collection is under preparation in Shandong University.

22. For a survey of Chinese American writing, see Sau-ling Cynthia Wong, "Chinese American," in King-kok Cheung's *An Interethnic Companion to Asian American Literature* (New York: Cambridge University Press, 1997), pp. 39–68.

23. See Amy Ling, *Between Worlds: Women Writers of Chinese Ancestry* (New York: Pergamon Press, 1990), pp. 21–55.

24. For example, a typical novel on Chinese living in America by Lin Yutang is

Chinatown Family: A Novel (Melbourne/London/Toronto: William Heinemann, 1949).

25. Maxine Hong Kingston, *The Woman Warrior: Memoirs of a Girlhood Among Ghosts* (New York: Alfred Knopf, 1976).

26. Amy Tan, *The Joy Luck Club* (New York: G.P. Putnam's Sons, 1989).

27. For a discussion of Chinese Canadian writing, see Lien Chao, *Beyond Silence: Chinese Canadian Literature in English* (Toronto, ON: Tzar Publications, 1997).

28. Evelyn Lau, *Runaway: Diary of a Street Kid* (Toronto, ON: HarperCollins, 1989).

29. Sky Lee, *Disappearing Moon Café* (Vancouver, BC: Douglas and McIntyre, 1990). Winner of the 1990 City of Vancouver Book Award, and nominee for the Governor General's Award.

30. Denise Chong, *The Concubine's Children* (Penguin, 1994). Nominated for the Governor General's Award.

31. Wayson Choy, *The Jade Peony* (Vancouver, BC: Douglas and McIntyre, 1995). Winner of the Trillium Book Award and the City of Vancouver Book Award.

32. Paul Yee, *Ghost Train* (Toronto, ON: Groundwood Books, 1996). Winner of the 1996 Governor General's Award.

33. Ken Ling, Miriam London, and Ta-ling Lee, *The Revenge of Heaven: Journal of a Young Chinese* (New York: Putnam, 1972).

34. Liang Heng and Judith Shapiro, *Son of the Revolution* (New York: Alfred A. Knopf, 1983).

35. Nien Cheng, *Life and Death in Shanghai* (London: Grafton Books, 1986).

36. Rae Yang, *Spider Eaters* (San Francisco, CA: University of California Press, 1997).

37. Jung Chang, *Wild Swans: Three Daughters of China* (New York: Simon & Schuster, 1991).

38. Li Yan, *Daughters of the Red Land* (Toronto, ON: Sister Vision Press, 1995).

39. Ye Xingting, *A Leaf in the Bitter Wind* (Toronto, ON: Doubleday Canada Limited, 1997).

40. Lulu Wang, *The Lily Theater*, trans. by Hester Velmans (New York: Nan A. Talese/Doubleday, 2000).

41. Ying Chen, *Ingratitude* (Toronto, ON: Douglas and McIntyre, 1998).

42. Dai Sijie, *Balzac and the Little Chinese Seamstress* (New York: Alfred A. Knopf, 2001).

43. Ha Jin, *Waiting* (New York: Pantheon, 1999); *The Crazed* (New York: Pantheon, 2002).

44. The film *Red Sorghum* was directed by Chen Kaige; *Judou* and *Raise the Red Lantern* by Zhang Yimou.

45. For Wang Anyi, see *Love in a Small Town*, trans. by Eva Hung (Hong Kong: Chinese University Press, 1988), *Love on a Barren Mountain*, trans. by Eva Hung (Hong Kong: Chinese University Press, 1991), *Brocade Valley*, trans. by Bonnie S. McDougall and Chen Maiping (New York: New Directions Publishing

Corporations, 1992), and *Baotown*, trans. by Martha Avery (New York: W.W. Norton, 1989); for Zhang Xianliang, see *Half of a Man is Woman,* trans by Martha Avery (London: Viking 1988), and *Getting Used to Dying*, trans. by Martha Avery (New York: Harper Collins, 1991); for Wang Meng, see *Butterfly and Other Stories* (Beijing: Panda Books, 1983), and *The Stubborn Porridge and Other Stories* (New York: George Braziller, 1994).

46. S. A. M. Adshead, *China in World History* (London: Macmillan, 1988), p. 103.

Chapter 9

1. By March 2001, *Crouching Tiger Hidden Dragon* had become the highest grossing foreign-language film in American history. Out of ten Oscar® nominations, the most ever for a foreign language film, it won in four categories: Art Direction, Cinematography, Original Score, and Foreign Picture. The film also received Golden Globe Awards for Best Director and Best Foreign Film. At Cannes, it took home four of top prizes; in England, the awards included Best Director. The Best Director's award eluded Ang Lee in Taiwan, but in the Hong Kong awards, occurring a month after the Oscars®, his film won eight awards, including Best Director and Best Picture.

2. For recent views of globalization, see Chow (2001) and Li (2000). Rey Chow criticizes Derrida for "recycled clichés" that run counter to the "euphoria of inclusionist, boundary-crossing thinking in current talk about globalization" (Chow 2001, 70). Because there is a disparity between material reality and the rhetoric of globalization, Victor Li wants to "forget globalization" as a global concept (Li 2000, 3).

3. *Wedding Banquet* won the Golden Bear Award, Best Picture in the Berlin International Film Festival, and shared the Palme d'Or at Cannes. *Eat Drink Man Woman* won the Best Picture award at the Asia-Pacific Film Festival and was nominated for Best Foreign Film at the Oscars®. Ang Lee's other films are *Sense and Sensibility* (1995), *Ice Storm* (1997), and *Ride with the Devil* (1999).

4. In May 2001, an associate professor of music in Guangzhou launched a plagiarism suit against Tan Dun for what he believed to be unauthorized use of the musical score played during the desert fighting scenes with Zhang Ziyi and Chang Chen. Tan Dun's response to the media is that the Shanghai Orchestra had paid for the rights to use the score.

5. Wang Dulu was an elementary school teacher who wrote serialized novels to supplement his income. Author of twenty novels, he is known as one of the four representatives of the northern school of *wuxia* novels (Hong 1994; Liang 1990; Pei 1991).

6. Ang Lee has planned a prequel to *Crouching Tiger Hidden Dragon* to showcase the young Mu Bai and Shu Lien. The filming is scheduled to take place in Yunnan Province, southwest China.

Chapter 10

1. I am especially indebted to Teresa Zackodnik for reading drafts of this chapter and for her gracious support, encouragement, and insightful comments. I am grateful, too, to Maria Ng for her valuable advice and for her confidence in this work.

2. The first part of my title is an allusion to the trilogy of Lee's self-styled "Father Knows Best" films: *Pushing Hands* (1992), *The Wedding Banquet* (1993), and *Eat Drink Man Woman* (1994). Produced with a budget of US$750,000, *The Wedding Banquet* was shot on location in New York City in five weeks.

3. Gina Marchetti has cogently remarked that *The Wedding Banquet* is a movie about "defining the closet, constructing the closet, legitimizing the closet, coming out of the closet, staying in the closet, and exposing the closet" (282–3).

4. *Porcelain* is part of Yew's Whitelands trilogy that includes *A Language of Their Own* and *Wonderland* (Román 364 n15). *Wonderland* (1999) is one of the four plays in *The Hyphenated American* (2002).

5. Lauren Berlant and Michael Warner have usefully defined heteronormativity as follows: "Community is imagined through scenes of intimacy, coupling, and kinship; a historical relation to futurity is restricted to generational narrative and reproduction. A whole field of social relations becomes intelligible as heterosexuality, and this privatized sexual culture bestows on its sexual practices a tacit sense of rightness and normalcy. This sense of rightness — embedded in things and not just in sex — is what we call heteronormativity" (554).

6. Nonini and Ong have productively defined the concept of diaspora as follows: "[A] pattern that marks a common condition of communities, persons, and groups separated by space, an arrangement, moreover, that these persons see themselves as sharing ("we Chinese ... "). This pattern is continually reconstituted throughout the regions of dispersion, and it is characterized by multiplex and varied connections of family ties, kinship, commerce, sentiments and values about native place in China, shared memberships in transnational organizations, and so on" (18). It is in this spirit that I suggest the closet is of utmost importance to the Chinese family in performing the codes of Chineseness and maintaining communal ties and survival within the diaspora.

7. Critics have discussed what Rey Chow calls the "habitual obsession with 'Chineseness,' " "a kind of cultural essentialism" in which "what begins as resistance to the discriminatory practices of the older Western hegemony becomes ethnicist aggression" ("Introduction" 5). For further articulations of Chineseness, see Ien Ang's "Can One Say No to Chineseness? Pushing the Limits of the Diasporic Paradigm" and Arif Dirlik's "Asians on the Rim: Transnational Capital and Local Community in the Making of Contemporary Asian America."

8. I understand the vexed question of using the term "Third World," a reference

that generalizes and homogenizes women in developing countries. Nevertheless, I use "Third World" self-consciously and only for lack of a better term, with the recognition that this entity is contested both within and outside political and academic discourses.

9. For a discussion of migration of mainland Chinese women to Taiwan and Hong Kong, see Shu-mei Shih, "Gender and a Geopolitics of Desire: The Seduction of Mainland Women in Taiwan and Hong Kong Media."

10. As well, the film shows moments in which both Wai Tung and the father are inside and emerging from the bathroom respectively, gesturing toward their closetedness. To conceal his relationship with Simon, Wai Tung skulks in the bathroom and talks to Simon on his cellular phone. To show the father's secret knowledge of his son's sexual identity, the father comes out of the bathroom just as Wai Tung sleepily opens the door, slightly shocked by the sight of his father.

11. Simon must keep secret the father's awareness of Wai Tung's deception. As Mr Gao says in Chinese, "If I didn't let everyone lie to me, I'd never have gotten my grandchild!"

12. Toward the penultimate paragraph of their discussion of *The Wedding Banquet,* Dariotis and Fung pose these questions with regard to the subject of homosexuality: "What of the sign of 'surrender' when the father raises his hands in the final moment of the film? Is it one of acceptance or one of emasculation?" (206).

13. Mr Gao's rank is significant because it evokes the father and president of Taiwan (1950–75), Chiang Kai-shek, who was a Chinese general and Kuomintang statesman prior to his retreat from China after World War II.

14. For a detailed discussion of the closet and its different configuration in the diaspora and the film's elision of the "representations of the Taiwanese diaspora in the United States," see Chiang (391).

15. Henning Bech's argument connecting "erotics" and "feelings of unity and being together" bears significance for the link between the father and Old Chen, which is "very much about presence," rather than "the physical-orgasmic act" (69).

16. Lee has been only too keen to point out that the film "is more a family drama than a gay movie. It's about relationships and ambiguities" (Bruni 1).

17. I mobilize the inscription proposed by David Parker through which the Chinese people in Britain are identified (211). In Britain, "Asian" is a signifier for South Asian (people who originally come from India, Pakistan, and Bangladesh), a term that excludes Chinese and other East Asians (214).

18. I am following Yew's spelling of "*Madame*" (*Porcelain* 72, 78).

19. *Madama Butterfly* is derived from a one-act play by David Belasco produced in the US in 1900 and published in 1917. See David Mesher, "Metamorphosis of a Butterfly." Yew also deploys the final scene of Bizet's *Carmen* to bring the play to a climax.

20. Richard Knowles introduces the possibility of thinking about perversion in relation to "disrupt[ing] the complacent and voyeuristic satisfactions and containments provided by dramatic catharsis" (226). Thanks to Rob Appleford for this article.

21. In "Perils of the Body and Mind," Gary Y. Okihiro argues that aspects of the model minority stereotype are interimplicated in elements of the yellow peril (142). For more on the concept of "model minority," see Robert Chang's "Why We Need a Critical Asian American Legal Studies"; and "Success Story of One Minority Group in U.S."

22. For a discussion of the use of violence to claim an American identity, see Viet Thanh Nguyen's "The Remasculinization of Chinese America: Race, Violence, and the Novel."

23. The shooting scene can be unsettling to the reader, and this is a legitimate concern. What does one do with the image of a young Asian man shooting a white man? It challenges the reader because it is perverse and over-the-top. In her analysis of *M. Butterfly,* Dorinne Kondo writes: "Must one reinscribe stereotypes in order to subvert them? And in so doing, doesn't one inevitably reinscribe other stereotypes — in this case, sneaky Oriental? Though the issue is vexed, I have argued elsewhere (1990) that there can be no pristine space of resistance, and that subversion and contestation are never beyond discourse and power" (53). Following Kondo, I read the staged violence in *Porcelain* as a site for critical engagement and as a self-conscious dramatization of the contradictions and histories of social alienation and racial disempowerment. Yew's reflection on his earlier plays is telling in this regard: "*Porcelain* was about how I fit into straight White America ... . I am always embarrassed to revisit an old play. It's like seeing myself again at 18, embarrassed by the childish obsessions, needs, and desires of that age" (Román, "Los Angeles" 246). In response to Yew's acknowledgement of the identifications and vulnerabilities of Asian queer desires, I want to argue for a more complex understanding of the question of representations of Asian men and women in literature and film. Here, I am informed by Jun Xing's astute observation that the "positive image" is "both a reductionist idea and a misleading strategy" ("Media Empowerment" 20).

24. A bystander uses a cinematic reference, *Prick up Your Ears* (1987), to explain sex in public lavatories (*Porcelain* 14). *Prick up Your Ears,* a tragic love story between Joe Orton and Kenneth Halliwell, was the first commercial production depicting sex scenes between adults in public restrooms (*Celluloid Closet* 271). *Porcelain* takes sex in public space further by depicting an underage boy and an adult engaging in sexual activities, defying the state's regulation of sexuality and age of consent.

25. For discussion of Britain's age of consent law, see, for example, Stephen Jeffrey-Poulter, *Peers, Queers, and Commons: The Struggle for Gay Law Reform from 1950 to the Present* (London: Routledge, 1991); "Legislating Fairly for Consenting

Homosexuals," *The Lancet* Jan. 22, 1994: 185–6; "Chain Male: Gay Sex," *The Economist* Jan. 29, 1994: 60–1; "A Question of Conscience," *New Statesman & Society* Feb. 25, 1994: 4; Peter Tatchell, "Sweet Fourteen," *New Statesman & Society* June 23, 1995: 25; "Fair's Fair: Gay Law Reform," *The Economist* July 12, 1997: 50. The last decade of the twentieth century has witnessed public debate over same-sex marriage and sexual citizenship. Under the *Civil Partnership Act* (2004), same-sex partners will be given equal tax rights as heterosexual married couples beginning December 5, 2005 ("Gay Couples Join Together on Tax").

26. By "father of the law," I allude to the law of patriarchy and a web of discourses that secure the regulatory regime of heterosexuality, and determine his subjects in cultural, social, and sexual terms.

27. A few person-on-the-street characters discuss the term "cottaging" in Scene 2 of the play. One of them gives an etymology of the term: "Cottaging. Why yes, I believe that the term came from the fact that public conveniences were once designed in the style of Swiss cottages. You know the little white brick cottages with black wooden frames. Very *Sound of Music*" (12).

28. d'Arch Smith traces Wilde's social interactions and literary network in order to understand the implicit allusions of *The Importance of Being Earnest*. I am grateful to Wilhelm Emilsson for bringing Oscar Wilde to my attention.

29. I am grateful to Philip Holden for reminding me of Lee Kuan Yew.

30. For an excellent discussion of masculinity in Singapore, see Philip Holden, "A Man and an Island: Gender and Nation in Lee Kuan Yew's *The Singapore Story*" and "The Significance of Uselessness: Resisting Colonial Masculinity in Philip Jeyaretnam's *Abraham's Promise*."

Chapter 11

1. As a slight amendment to this pronouncement, I would direct the reader to recent English-language academic work on Tsai and his films that has appeared since this article was first written: Kent Jones, "Here and There: The Films of Tsai Ming-liang" in *Movie Mutations: The Changing Face of World Cinephilia*, ed. Jonathan Rosenbaum and Adrian Martin (London: BFI, 2003): 44–51; Fran Martin, "Perverse Utopia: Reading *The River*" in *Situating Sexualities: Queer Representation in Taiwanese Fiction, Film and Public Culture* (Hong Kong: Hong Kong University Press, 2003): 163–84; Yvette Biro, "Perhaps the Flood: The Fiery Torrent of Tsai Ming-Liang's Films," *PAJ: Journal of Performance and Art* 3 (2004): 78–86; Giuliana Bruno, "Architects of Time: Reel Images from Warhol to Tsai Ming-Liang," *Log* 2 (Spring 2004): 81–94.

2. Léaud's cameo appearance as a world-weary choral figure in this Taiwanese film on the one hand seems to mirror the more substantial presence of both Léaud and Maggie Cheung in Olivier Assayas's *Irma Vep* (1996), another

filmmaker and film undertaking a reassessment of French cinema of the 1960s. But on the other hand it adds to a growing context of work engaging in meaningful ways with a Europe/East Asian axis of borrowing, referencing, and mutually inflected cross-cultural aesthetic desire, or at least in ways more meaningful than the flawed and romanticized dalliances of the European political Left with "the great Chinese experiment" some three decades earlier (cf. Godard's *La Chinoise* [1967]).

3. I address Tsai's most recent feature, *Goodbye Dragon Inn* (2003), in the postscript of this article; I note the film here only to call attention to its metacinematic features, and the degree to which they constitute the most pronounced exploration yet in Tsai's *oeuvre* of the "machine of the visible" that was itself the subject of Apparatus theory in the period following the break-up of the European new waves post-1968.

4. For an overview of this position, see Murray Smith's "Modernism and the avant-gardes" in *The Oxford Guide to Film Studies*, ed. John Hill and Pamela Church Gibson (Oxford: Oxford University Press, 1998): 395–412. An earlier important argument was articulated by Peter Wollen in his "The Two Avant-Gardes," *Edinburgh '76 Magazine,* no. 1 (Edinburgh Film Festival, 1976): 77–85.

5. I am indebted for this reading to Kien Ket Lim's paper "To Build a House," presented at the Crossroads in Cultural Studies 4th Annual Conference in Tampere, Finland, on July 2, 2002.

6. The reference becomes explicit, and in fact an indelible narrative strand, in *Goodbye Dragon Inn*, wherein Tien Miao appears as one of the patrons in a movie theater on its last night, and watches himself on screen as a man and actor almost forty years younger.

7. Fredric Jameson, "Third-World Literature in the Era of Multinational Capital," *Social Text* 15 (1986): 70. Aijaz Ahmad's critique is entitled "Jameson's Rhetoric of Otherness and the 'National Allegory,'" *Social Text* 17 (1987): 3–25. For Jameson's reading of Taiwanese history/culture/aesthetics through Yang's film, see his "Remapping Taipei" in *The Geopolitical Aesthetic: Cinema and Space in the World System* (Bloomington, IN: Indiana University Press, 1995). 114–57.

8. I address this issue in my forthcoming book *Remapping European Art Cinema*.

9. Two interesting pieces have appeared recently as well in the online journal *Senses of Cinema*: Fran Martin's "The European Undead: Tsai Ming-liang's Temporal Dysphoria" (June 2003) and Brian Hu's "Goodbye City, Goodbye Cinema: Nostalgia in Tsai Ming-liang's *The Skywalk is Gone*" (October 2003).

Chapter 12

1. Rey Chow, "Sentimental Returns: On the Uses of the Everyday in the Recent Films of Zhang Yimou and Wong Kar-wai," *New Literary History* 33.4 (2002): 639–54. ©*New Literary History*, University of Virginia. Reprinted with the permission of The Johns Hopkins University Press.

2. Pier Paolo Pasolini, "Appendix: Quips on the Cinema," *Heretical Empiricism*, ed. Louise K. Barnett, trans. Ben Lawton and Louise K. Barnett (Bloomington and Indianapolis, IN: Indiana University Press, 1988), pp. 231–2. Hereafter, references to this book are included in parentheses in the text.

3. Ferdinand de Saussure, *Course in General Linguistics*, intro. Jonathan Culler, ed. Charles Bally and Albert Sechehaye in collaboration with Albert Reidlinger, trans. Wade Baskin (Glasgow: Collins, 1974), p. 120; emphasis in the original.

4. I have hitherto considered this sentimental drift in relation to nostalgia. See, for instance, my arguments in the following publications: "A Souvenir of Love," in *Ethics after Idealism: Theory — Culture — Ethnicity — Reading* (Bloomington and Indianapolis, IN: Indiana University Press, 1998), pp. 133–48 (originally published in *Modern Chinese Literature* 7.2 [Fall 1993]: 59–78); "Seductions of Homecoming: Place, Authenticity, and Chen Kaige's *Temptress Moon*," *Narrative* 6.1 (January 1998): 3–17; "Nostalgia of the New Wave: Structure and Wong Kar-wai's *Happy Together*," *camera obscura* 42 (1999): 31–48. For related discussions pertaining to Hong Kong cinema, see also Leung Ping-kwan, "Urban Cinema and the Cultural Identity of Hong Kong" and Natalia Chan Sui Hung, "Rewriting History: Hong Kong Nostalgia Cinema and Its Social Practice," both in *The Cinema of Hong Kong: History, Arts, Identity*, ed. Poshek Fu and David Desser (Cambridge: Cambridge University Press, 2000), pp. 227–51; 252–72. Chan's essay offers an extended examination of the history, features, and critical analyses of nostalgia film. In the present essay, my interest is less in making the argument about nostalgia over again than in exploring the place of the everyday in the general sentimentalism affined with nostalgia, and the theoretical implications this has for the study of mediatized culture.

5. In an interview conducted in New York, Wong is reported to have said: "The child we see with Maggie Cheung may be Tong Leung's, or may be not." *Ming Pao Daily News* (North American edition), October 4, 2000, A3; my translation from the Chinese.

6. In a film review, Zhao Di is described in the following manner: "This is a woman who, on recognizing her destiny, will let nothing stand in the way of her seizing it." Stephen Holden, "Two Lives in China, With Mao Lurking," *New York Times*, May 25, 2001, B14.

7. I am grateful to Christopher Lee for this important point.

8. Tao Jie attributes this to Zhang's reaching middle age. By this, he means that Zhang's film demonstrates a worldview that can be summarized as "what is lost can finally be found"— in other words, a worldview that stresses harmony,

unity, and togetherness. See Tao Jie, "Da tuanyuan de Zhang Yimou," *Ming Pao Daily News* (North American edition), January 8, 2001, B18.

9. Su Lizhen is also the name of one of the two young female characters in Wong's *Days of Being Wild*, which is set in 1960. *In the Mood for Love* may hence be seen as a kind of sequel to the earlier film.

10. Wong said in an interview: "From the very beginning I knew I didn't want to make a film about an affair. That would be too boring, too predictable ... What interested me was the way people behave and relate to each other in the circumstances shown in this story, the way they keep secrets and share secrets ... [T]he central characters were going to enact what they thought their spouses were doing and saying. In other words, we were going to see both relationships — the adulterous affair and the repressed friendship — in the one couple." Tony Rayns, "In the Mood for Edinburgh: Wong Kar-Wai Talks about His Most Difficult Film-Making Experience with Tony Rayns," *Sight and Sound* 10.8 (August 2000): 14–9.

11. Leslie Camhi, "Setting His Tale of Love Found in a City Long Lost," *New York Times*, January 28, 2001, 11. The novelist in question is the well-known Liu Yichang, whose novel *Duidao* (first serialized in 1972 and then rewritten in 1981) gave Wong the inspiration for his film (in which some lines have been cited from Liu's work). See Liu, *Duidao* (Hong Kong: Holdery Publishing Enterprises, 2000). For a perceptive analysis of the conceptual connections between the two works, see Pan Guoling, "'Huayang nianhua' yü 'Duidao,'" *Ming Pao Daily News* (North American edition), October 28, 2000, 22.

12. Actress Maggie Cheung's description gives a good idea of Wong's improvisatory method: "At the beginning, we were given a four-page short story by a Japanese writer from the 1960s, about an affair between two neighbors," Ms Cheung said. "There was not a lot of detail. Then, during every hair and makeup session, we would receive a still-warm fax with some lines of dialogue to be shot later that day, and which Kar-wai had clearly written that morning." "Sometimes we would shoot the same scenes with the dialogues between myself and Tony reversed," she said. "Or we would film the same dialogues but on a different set." Leslie Camhi, "Setting His Tale of Love Found In a City Long Lost," p. 26.

13. I am thinking in particular of Wong's *Ashes of Time* (1994), a film which generically resembles a martial arts legend but which foregrounds the theme of unfulfilled longing (and dislocated or mismatched identities) that underlies all his stories.

14. See, for instance, Fredric Jameson, *Postmodernism, or, the Cultural Logic of Late Capitalism* (Durham, NC: Duke University Press, 1991).

15. Prasenjit Duara, "Leftist Criticism and the Political Impasse: Response to Arif Dirlik's 'How the Grinch Hijacked Radicalism: Further Thoughts on the Postcolonial,'" *Postcolonial Studies* 4.1 (2001): 81–8. The quoted passage is on p. 87.

16. I am thinking, for instance, of the rituals of wine making, of transporting the bride in a wedding, of raising lanterns in a rich household, and so forth. See a more extended discussion of such "ethnographic details" in Zhang's early works in Part II, Chapter 4 of my book *Primitive Passions: Visuality, Sexuality, Ethnography, and Contemporary Chinese Cinema* (New York: Columbia University Press, 1995).

Works Cited

Chapter 1

Ang, Ien. "On Not Speaking Chinese." *New Formations* 24 (Winter 1994): 1–18.
———. *On Not Speaking Chinese: Living Between Asia and the West*. London: Routledge, 2001.
Appadurai, Arjun. "Disjuncture and Difference in the Global Cultural Economy." *Theory, Culture & Society* 7 (1990): 295–310.
Bhabha, Homi K. *The Location of Culture*. London: Routledge, 1994.
Chatterjee, Partha. "Beyond the Nation? Or Within?" *Social Text* 56, 16.3 (Fall 1998): 57–69.
"Chinatown's Virus Fears." *BBC News*. Accessed October 4, 2003. <http://newsvote.bbc.co.uk/mpapps/ pagetools/print/ news.bbc.co.uk/1/hi/health/2924399.stm>.
"Chinese Guests Barred from Film Festival." *BBC News*. Accessed October 4, 2003. <http://newsvote.bbc.co.uk/mpapps/pagetools/print/news.bbc.co.uk/1/hi/entertain-ment/film>.
Freeze, Colin. "Mistry Suffers 'Visions of Guantanamo'." *Globe and Mail*. Accessed May 5, 2003. <http://www.globeandmail.com/servlet/ArticlenNews/front/RTGAM/20021103/wxmist1102/Fron>
Habermas, Jürgen. *The Philosophical Discourse of Modernity: Twelve Lectures*. Trans. Frederick G. Lawrence. Cambridge, MA: MIT Press, 1990.
Holden, Philip. "Questioning Diaspora: Wang Gungwu's *Pulse*" *ARIEL* 33.3–4 (2002): 105–32.
"Kew Dock Yip." *Globe and Mail* July 27, 2001: R5.
Kuo Pao Kun. "Knowledge Structure and Play — A Side View of Civil Society

in Singapore." *State-Society Relations in Singapore*. Eds. Gillian Koh and Ooi Giok Ling. Singapore: Oxford University Press, 2000. 210–8.

Mitchell, Katharyn. "In Whose Interest? Transnational Capital and the Production of Multiculturalism in Canada." *Global/Local: Cultural Production and the Transnational Imaginary*. Eds. Rob Wilson and Wimal Dissanayaki. Durham, NC: Duke University Press, 1996. 219–51.

Ng Wing Chung. *The Chinese in Vancouver 1945–80*. Vancouver, BC: University of British Columbia Press, 1999.

Ong, Aihwa. *Flexible Citizenship: The Cultural Logics of Transnationality*. Durham, NC: Duke University Press, 1999.

Ong, Aihwa and Donald Nonini, eds. *Ungrounded Empires: The Cultural Politics of Modern Chinese Transnationalism*. New York: Routledge, 1997.

Shohat, Ella. "Notes on the 'Post-Colonial'." *Social Text* 31–32 (Spring 1992): 99–113.

Ward, Doug. "Dramatic Shift in Languages across the Lower Mainland." *The Vancouver Sun* December 11, 2002: A1 and A5.

Wilson, Rob and Wimal Dissanayaki, eds. *Global/Local: Cultural Production and the Transnational Imaginary*. Durham, NC: Duke University Press, 1996.

Young, Robert. *Postcolonialism: An Historical Introduction*. London: Blackwell, 2002.

Chapter 2

Amyot, Jacques. *The Chinese Community of Manila: A Study of Adaptation of Chinese Familism to the Philippine Environment*. Chicago, IL: University of Chicago Department of Anthropology, 1960.

Ang See, Teresita. "Immigration and Identity: Social Changes in the post World War II Philippine Chinese Community." *Asian Culture/Yazhou Wenhua* 14 (September 1990): 38–46.

Blaker, James. *The Chinese in the Philippines. A Study of Power and Change*. Ph.D. Dissertation, Ohio State University, 1970. UMI #70-26,252.

Carino, Theresa 1998. *Chinese Big Business in the Philippines: Political Leadership and Change*. Singapore: Times Academic Press, 1998.

Carino, Theresa 2001. "Chinese Chambers of Commerce in the Philippines: Communal, National and International Influence." *Chinese Populations in Contemporary Southeast Asian Societies*. Eds. M. Jocelyn Armstrong, R. Warwick Armstrong, and Kent Mulliner. Richmond, Surrey: Curzon, 2001. 97–122.

Chen Yande. *Xiandai-Zhong de Quantong: Feilubin Huaren Shehui Yanjiu* [Tradition in the Contemporary Era: Studies in Philippine Chinese Society]. Xiamen: Xiamen Daxue Chubanshe, 1998.

Cheong, Caroline Mar Wai Jong. *The Chinese-Cantonese Family in Manila. A Study in Culture and Education*. Manila: Centro Escolar University, 1983.

Cook, James A. *Bridges to Modernity: Xiamen, Overseas Chinese and Southeast Coastal*

Modernization, 1843–1937. Ph.D. Dissertation, University of California, San Diego, 1998.

Dai, Yifeng. "Overseas Migration and the Economic Modernization of Xiamen City during the Twentieth Century," *South China: State, Culture and Social Change During the 20th Century.* Eds. L.M. Douw and P. Post. Amsterdam: North-Holland; New York/Tokyo: Oxford, 1996. 159–68.

Douw, Leo 1996. "South China: The Fragmentation of the Transnational Middle Class." *South China: State, Culture and Social Change during the 20th Century.* Eds. Douw and Post, 1990. 37–47.

Douw, Leo 1999. "The Chinese Sojourner Discourse." *Qiaoxiang Ties: Interdisciplinary Approaches to Cultural Capitalism in South China.* Eds. Leo Douw, Cen Huang, and Michael Godley. London/New York: Kegan Paul International, 1999. 22–44.

Douw, Leo and Peter Post, eds. *South China: State, Culture and Social Change during the 20th Century.* Amsterdam: North-Holland; New York/Tokyo: Oxford, 1996.

Edukasyong Tsino [Huawen Jiaoyu]. Manila: Feilubin Huawen Jiaoyu Yanjiu Zhongxin, 1991–.

Guldin, Gregory E. *Overseas At Home: The Fujianese of Hong Kong.* Ph.D. Dissertation, University of Wisconsin, 1977. UMI#77-25,822.

Hsu, Madeline Y. *Dreaming of Gold, Dreaming of Home.* Stanford, CA: Stanford University Press, 2000.

Huaqiao Jingji Nianjian. [Annual Chronicle of Overseas Chinese Economic Life]. Taibei: Overseas Chinese Affairs Commission, 1957–.

Huaqiao Shangbao. [Overseas Chinese Commercial News] Manila: Chinese Commercial News. 1921–72; and (as *Shangbao [Siongbo]*) 1986–. Issues of 1947–72 are available on microfilm.

Ishida Hiroshi. *Chugoku Noson no Rekishi to Keizai* [History and Economy of Rural China]. Osaka: Kansai Daigaku Shuppanbu, 1991.

Kuah, Khun Eng. *Rebuilding the Ancestral Village: Singaporeans in China.* Aldershot: Ashgate, 2000.

Liu Chi Tien. *Zhong-Fei Guanxi Shi* [History of China-Philippine Relations] Taibei: Zhengzhong Shuzhu, 1964.

Liu, Hong 1998. "Old Linkages, New Networks: The Globalization of Overseas Chinese Voluntary Associations and its Implications." *China Quarterly* 155 (September 1998): 582–609.

Liu, Hong 1999. "Bridges Across the Sea: Chinese Social Organizations in Southeast Asia and the Links with Qiaoxiang, 1900–49." *Qiaoxiang Ties:* 87–112.

Manila Interviews, 1966, 1990, 1992.

McBeath, Gerald. *Political Integration of the Philippine Chinese.* Berkeley, CA: Center for South and Southeast Asian Studies, University of California, 1975.

McKeown, Adam. "Transnational Chinese Families and Chinese Exclusion, 1875–1943." *Journal of American Ethnic History* 18.2 (Winter 1999): 73–110.

McKeown, Adam. *Chinese Migrant Networks and Cultural Change: Peru, Chicago, Hawaii, 1900–1936*. Chicago: University of Chicago Press, 2001.

Ngai, Mae M. "Legacies of Exclusion: Illegal Chinese Immigration during the Cold War Years." *Journal of American Ethnic History* 18.1 (Fall 1998): 3–35.

Oguma Makoto. "Fuirippin Kakyo to Kokyo", [Philippine Overseas Chinese and their Home Districts]. *Shimposhiumu Kanan: Kakyo to Kokyo* [Symposium on South China: Overseas Chinese and Home Districts]. Ed. Kani Hiroaki. Tokyo: Keio University Center for Area Studies, 1992. 111–21.

Ong, Aihwa and Nonini, Donald, eds. *Ungrounded Empires: The Cultural Politics of Chinese Transnationalism*. New York: Routledge, 1997.

Peck, Cornelius J. "'Nationalism,' 'Race' and Development in the Philippine Law of Citizenship." *Journal of Asian and African Studies* 2 (January–April 1967): 128–43.

Pu Yonghao. "Dangdai Fujian Guoqi Yimin Guocheng de Xiaoying jiqi Pingjie" [Effects and Evaluations of International Immigration Processes in Contemporary Fujian]. *Zhongguo Shehui Kexue* [Social Science in China] 1988.4 (April 1988): 179–97.

Pu Yonghao. "Lun Fujian Qiaoxiang Renkou Guoqi Qianyi de Shehui, Jingji, Wenhua Yishi Xiaoying" [The Significant Social, Economic, and Cultural Effects of International Population Movements from Fujian's Overseas Chinese Home Districts]. *Renkou Yanjiu* [Population Studies] 1988.5 (May 1988): 25–30.

Purcell, Victor. *The Chinese in Southeast Asia*. 2nd ed. London: Oxford, 1965.

Qiaoxiang Ties: Interdisciplinary Approaches to Cultural Capitalism in South China. Eds. Leo Douw, Cen Huang, and Michael R. Godley. London/New York: Kegan Paul International, 1999.

Quanzhou-shi Huaqiao Zhi [Gazetteer of Overseas Chinese of Quanzhou Administrative City]. Beijing: Zhongguo Shehui Chubanshe, 1996.

See, Chinben. "Chinese Clanship in the Philippine Setting." *Journal of Southeast Asian Studies* 12.1 (March 1981): 224–47.

See, Chinben. "Chinese Education and Ethnic Identity." *Chinese in the Philippines*. Ed. Theresa Carino. Manila: DelaSalle University, 1985. 32–42.

See, Chinben. "Chinese Organizations and Ethnic Identity in the Philippines." *Changing Identities of the Southeast Asian Chinese Since World War II*. Eds. Jennifer Cushman and Wang Gungwu. Hong Kong: Hong Kong University Press, 1988. 319–34.

Shi Zhenmin [Chinben See]. "Feilubin Huaren Wenhua de Zhixu: Zhongqin yu Tongxiang Zuzhi zai Haiwai de Yanbian" ["Persistence and Preservation of Chinese Culture in the Philippines"]. *Zhongyang Yanjiu Yuan Minzuxue Yanjiusuo Jikan* [Bulletin of the Institute of Ethnology, Academia Sinica, Taiwan] 42 (1976): 119–206.

Sinn, Elizabeth. "Xin Xi Guxiang: A Study of Regional Associations as a Bridging

Mechanism in the Chinese Diaspora: The Hong Kong Experience." *Modern Asian Studies* 31.2 (1997): 375–97.

Song, Ping. "An Analysis of Models: How Schools are run by Overseas Chinese in South Fujian." Eds. Douw and Post. 197–204.

Tan, Antonio S. "The Changing Identity of the Philippine Chinese." *Changing Identities of the Southeast Asian Chinese since World War II*. Eds. Cushman and Wang: 177–203.

Tilman, Robert O. "Philippine Chinese Youth: Who Are They?" *Solidarity* 7 (10 October 1972): 25–33.

Weightman, George H. "The Philippine Chinese Image of the Filipinos." *Pacific Affairs* 40.3 (Fall–Winter 1968): 315–23.

Wickberg, Edgar. *The Chinese in Philippine Life, 1850–1898*. New Haven, CT: Yale University Press, 1965; Manila: Ateneo de Manila Press, 2000.

———. "Some Comparative Perspectives on Contemporary Chinese Ethnicity in the Philippines." *Asian Culture/Yazhou Wenhua* 14 (April 1990): 23–37.

———. "Anti-Sinicism and Chinese Identity Options in the Philippines." *Essential Outsiders: Chinese and Jews in the Modern Transformation of Southeast Asia and Central Europe*. Eds. Daniel Chirot and Anthony Reid. Seattle, WA: University of Washington Press, 1997. 153–83.

Wu, Chun-hsi. *Dollars, Dependents, and Dogma: Overseas Chinese Remittances to Communist China*. Stanford, CA: Hoover Institution, 1967.

Zhuang, Guotu. "The Social Impact on their Home Town of Jinjiang Emigrants' Activities During the 1930s." Eds. Douw and Post. 169–81.

Chapter 3

Anderson, Benedict. *Imagined Communities: Reflections on the Origin and Spread of Nationalism*, 2nd ed. London and New York: Verso, 1991.

Ang, Ien. "Can One Say No to Chineseness? Pushing the Limits of the Diasporic Paradigm." *boundary 2* 25.3 (1998) 223–42.

Ashcroft, Bill, Gareth Griffiths, and Helen Tiffin. *The Empire Writes Back: Theory and Practice in Post-Colonial Literatures*. London and New York: Routledge, 1989.

Barthes, Roland. *Mythologies*. Trans. Annette Lavers. New York: Hill and Wang, 1972.

Bhabha, Homi. *The Location of Culture*. London and New York: Routledge, 1994.

Benjamin, Walter. "The Work of Art in the Age of Mechanical Reproduction." *Illuminations*, 1968. Ed. Hannah Arendt. Trans. Harry Zohn. New York: Schocken Books, 1969.

Chakrabarty, Dipesh. *Provincializing Europe: Postcolonial Thought and Historical Difference*. Princeton and Oxford: Princeton University Press, 2000.

Cho, Lily. "Re-reading Head Tax Racism: Redress, Stereotype and Anti-Racist Critical Practice." *Essays on Canadian Writing* 75 (Winter 2002): 62–84.

Chow, Rey. *Writing Diaspora: Tactics of Intervention in Contemporary Cultural Studies.* Bloomington and Indiana, IN: Indiana University Press, 1993.

Gandhi, Leela. *Postcolonial Theory: A Critical Introduction.* New York: Columbia University Press, 1998.

Gilroy, Paul. *Against Race: Imagining Political Culture beyond the Color Line.* Cambridge, MA: Harvard University Press, 2000.

———. *The Black Atlantic: Modernity and Double Consciousness.* Cambridge, MA: Harvard University Press, 1993.

Hennessy, Rosemary. *Materialist Feminism and the Politics of Discourse.* New York and London: 1993.

Koselleck, Reinhart. "Modernity and the Planes of History." *Futures Past: On the Semantics of Historical Time.* Trans. Keith Tribe. Cambridge, MA and London: MIT Press, 1985. 3–20.

Lee, David. "Chinese Construction Workers on the Canadian Pacific." *Railroad History* 148 (1983): 43–57.

Li, Peter. *The Chinese in Canada,* 2nd ed. Toronto and Oxford: Oxford University Press, 1998.

Loomba, Ania. *Colonialism/Postcolonialism.* London and New York: Routledge, 1998.

Mishra, Vijay. "The Diasporic Imaginary: Theorizing the Indian Diaspora." *Textual Practice* 10.3 (1996): 421–47.

Morton, James. *In the Sea of Sterile Mountains: The Chinese in British Columbia.* Vancouver, BC: J.J. Douglas, 1974.

New Dayton Historical Society. *Memories: New Dayton and District 1900–1978.* Lethbridge, AB: Robins Southern Printing Ltd, 1978.

Ong, Aihwa. *Flexible Citizenship: The Cultural Logics of Transnationality.* Durham and London: Duke University Press, 1999.

Reiter, Ester. *Making Fast Food: From the Frying Pan into the Fryer,* 2nd ed. Montreal and Kingston: McGill-Queen's Press, 1996.

Roy, Patricia. "A Choice Between Evils: The Chinese and the Construction of the Canadian Pacific Railway in British Columbia." *The CPR West.* Ed. Hugh A. Dempsey. Vancouver and Toronto: Douglas and McIntyre, 1984.

Spivak, Gayatri. "Diasporas Old and New: Women in the Transnational world." *Textual Practice* 10.2 (1996): 245–69.

Sprang, Rebecca. *The Invention of the Restaurant: Paris and Modern Gastronomic Culture.* Cambridge and London: Harvard University Press, 2000.

Wah, Fred. *Diamond Grill.* Edmonton, AB: NeWest Press, 1996.

Wickberg, Edgar. *From China to Canada: A History of the Chinese Communities in Canada.* Toronto, ON: McClelland and Stewart, 1982.

Chapter 4

Appadurai, Arjun. *Modernity at Large: Cultural Dimensions of Globalization.* Minneapolis, MN: University of Minnesota Press, 1996.

Barr, Michael D. *Lee Kuan Yew: The Beliefs Behind the Man.* Richmond: Curzon, 2000.

Bloodworth, Dennis. *Chinese Looking Glass.* London: Secker and Warburg, 1967.

Chua Beng Huat. "'Asian-Values' Discourse and the Resurrection of the Social." *Positions* 7 (1999): 573–92.

———. *Communitarian Ideology and Democracy in Singapore.* London: Routledge, 1995.

Cumming-Bruce, Nick and Michael White. "Blair Unveils Economic 'Big Idea.' " *Guardian* Jan 8, 1996: Home Page 1.

Foucault, Michel. "Technologies of the Self." *Technologies of the Self: A Seminar with Michel Foucault.* Eds. Luther H. Martin et al. Amherst, MA: University of Massachusetts Press, 1988. 16–49.

Furnivall, J.S. *Colonial Policy and Practice: A Comparative Study of Burma and Netherlands India.* New York: New York University Press, 1956.

Giddens, Anthony. "Jürgen Habermas." *The Return of Grand Theory in the Human Sciences.* Ed. Quentin Skinner. Cambridge: Cambridge University Press, 1990. 121–39.

Holden, Philip. "Paper Tiger, Paper Lion: British Responses to the Asian Currency Crisis." *Trends* 91 (March 28–29 1998): 13.

———."Postcolonialism as Genealogy: Questioning Culture and Modernity in Singapore." *Compr(om)ising Post/Colonialism(s): Challenging Narratives and Practices.* Eds. Greg Ratcliffe and Gerry Turcotte. Sydney: Dangaroo, 2000. 283–95.

Josey, Alex. *Lee Kuan Yew.* Revised ed. Singapore: Donald Moore Press, 1971.

Koh, Tommy. "Size is Not Destiny." *Singapore: Re-engineering Success.* Eds. Arun Mahizhnan and Lee Tsao Yuan. Singapore: Oxford University Press, 1998. 172–87.

Lee Kuan Yew. Address at the Singapore Union of Journalists Lunch, August 16, 1959. *Prime Minister's Speeches, Press Conferences, Interviews, Statements, etc.* Vol. 1, 1959–61. Republic of Singapore: Prime Minister's Office, 1962.

———. Speech at a Dinner given at the University of Malaya Society, July 25, 1959. *Prime Minister's Speeches, Press Conferences, Interviews, Statements, etc.* Vol. 1, 1959–61. Republic of Singapore: Prime Minister's Office, 1962.

———. *The Singapore Story: Memoirs of Lee Kuan Yew.* Singapore: Singapore Press Holdings, 1998.

———. Talk to the Nanyang University Political Science Society, March 29, 1960. *Prime Minister's Speeches, Press Conferences, Interviews, Statements, etc.* Vol. 1, 1959–61. Republic of Singapore: Prime Minister's Office, 1962.

————. "The Vigilante Corps Recruitment Campaign at Tanjong Pagar Community Centre, 10 December, 1966." *Excerpts of Speeches by Lee Kuan Yew on Singapore, 1959–1973.* Ed. Douglas Koh. Unpublished collection, National University of Singapore Library, 1976.

Minchin, James. *No Man Is an Island: A Study of Singapore's Lee Kuan Yew.* Sydney: Allen and Unwin, 1986.

"The Modernising Nationalism." *The Mirror: A Weekly Almanac of Current Affairs* 6.16 (April 20, 1970): 1.

Renan, Ernest. *Qu'est-ce qu'une nation?* Accessed October 26, 2001. <http://www.bmlisieux.com/archives/nation01.htm>

Siah Kang Li, Cindy. *History of the Chinese Development Assistance Council, an Ethnic Based Self-Help Group.* Honours Academic Exercise, Dept. of History, National University of Singapore, 2000.

Thompson, Dawn. "Technologies of Ethnicity." *Essays on Canadian Writing* 57 (Winter 1995): 51–69.

Vasil, Raj. *Asianising Singapore; the PAP's Management of Ethnicity.* Singapore: Heinemann Asia, 1995.

Wee, C. J. W.-L. "Capitalism and Ethnicity: Creating 'Local' Culture in Singapore." *Inter-Asia Cultural Studies* 1 (2000): 129–43.

"Will a Singapore Tribe Emerge?" *Straits Times* 5 June 1999: 28–9.

Chapter 5

Foucault, Michel. *Discipline and Punish; the Birth of the Prison.* Trans. Alan Sheridan. New York: Vintage/Random House, 1995.

Hong, Ying. *Summer of Betrayal.* Trans. Martha Avery. New York: Grove Press, 1997.

Levy, Primo. "The Memory of Offense." *Bitburg in Moral and Political Perspective.* Ed. Geoffrey Hartman. Bloomington, IN: Indiana University Press: 1986. 130–7.

McGee, Patrick. "Theory in Pain." *Genre* 20.1 (1987): 67–84.

Okuizumi, Hikaru. *The Stones Cry Out.* Trans. James Westerhoven. New York: Harvest/Harcourt, 1993.

Scarry, Elaine. *The Body in Pain; the Making and Unmaking of the World.* Oxford: Oxford University Press, 1985.

Yi Mun-yol. *The Poet.* Trans. Chong-wha Chung and Brother Anthony of Taizé. London: The Harvill Press, 2001.

Chapter 6

Anzaldúa, Gloria. "Haciendo caras, una entrada." *Making Face, Making Soul/Haciendo Caras: Creative and Critical Perspectives by Feminists of Color.* Ed. Gloria Anzaldúa. San Francisco, CA: Aunt Lute, 1990. xv–xxviii.

Barthes, Roland. *Empire of Signs.* Trans. Richard Howard. New York: Hill and Wang, 1983.

Boelhower, William. *Through a Glass Darkly: Ethnic Semiosis in American Literature.* New York: Oxford University Press, 1987.

Campomanes, Oscar V. and N.V.M Gonzalez. "Filipino American Literature." *An Interethnic Companion to Asian American Literature.* Ed. King-Kok Cheung. New York: Cambridge University Press, 1997.

Cheung, King-Kok. *Articulate Silences: Hisaye Yamamoto, Maxine Hong Kingston, Joy Kogawa.* Ithaca, NY: Cornell University Press, 1993.

Chin, Sara. *Below the Line.* San Francisco, CA: City Lights, 1997.

Creef, Elena Tajima. "Notes from a Fragmented Daughter." *Making Face, Making Soul/Haciendo Caras: Creative and Critical Perspectives by Feminists of Color.* Ed. Gloria Anzaldúa. San Francisco, CA: Aunt Lute, 1990. 82–4.

Espiritu, Yen Le. *Asian American Panethnicity: Bridging Institutions and Identities.* Philadelphia, PA: Temple University Press, 1992.

Galang, Evelina. *Her Wild American Self.* Minneapolis, MN: Coffee House Press, 1996.

Hogan, Ron. Interview with Christina Chiu. The Beatrice Interview: 2002. Accessed May 13, 2004 <http://www.beatrice.com/interviews/chiu/>.

Kingston, Maxine Hong. *The Woman Warrior: Memoirs of a Girlhood among Ghosts.* New York: Alfred A. Knopf, 1977.

Ng, Fae Myenne. *Bone.* New York: Harper Perennial, 1994.

Tawada, Yoko. "The Bath." *Where Europe Begins.* Trans. Susan Bernofsky and Yumi Selden. New York: New Directions, 2002. 3–55.

Wang, David Der Wei. "Three Hungry Women." *Modern Chinese Literary and Cultural Studies in the Age of Theory.* Ed. Rey Chow. Durham, NC: Duke University Press, 2000. 48–77.

Wong, Sau-ling Cynthia. *Reading Asian American Literature: From Necessity to Extravagance.* Princeton, NJ: Princeton University Press, 1993.

Chapter 7

Allen, Graham. *Intertextuality.* London: Routledge, 2000.

Bakhtin, Mikhail. *Problems of Dostoevsky's Poetics.* Ann Arbor, MI: Ardis, 1973.

———. *The Dialogic Imagination: Four Essays.* Austin, TX: University of Texas Press, 1981.

Culler, Jonathan. *The Pursuit of Signs — Semiotics, Literature, Deconstruction*. Ithaca, NY: Cornell University Press, 1981.

Furth, Isabella. "Bee-e-een! Nation, Transformation, and the Hyphen of Ethnicity in Kingston's Tripmaster Monkey." *Critical Essays on Maxine Hong Kingston*. Ed. Laura E. Skandera-Trombley. New York: G.K. Hall & Co., 1998. 304–17.

Huntley, E.D. *Maxine Hong Kingston: A Critical Companion*. Westport, CT: Greenwood Press, 2001.

Kingston, Maxine Hong. *Tripmaster Monkey: His Fake Book*. New York: Vintage, 1990.

Lin, Patricia. "Clashing Constructs of Reality: Reading Maxine Hong Kingston's *Tripmaster Monkey: His Fake Book* as Indigenous Ethnography." *Critical Essays on Maxine Hong Kingston*. Ed. Laura E. Skandera-Trombley. New York: G. K. Hall & Co., 1998. 291–303.

Ling, Amy. "Maxine Hong Kingston and the Dialogic Dilemma of Asian American writers." *Critical Essays on Maxine Hong Kingston*. Ed. Laura E. Skandera-Trombley. New York: G.K. Hall & Co., 1998. 168–81.

Lu, James. "Enacting Asian American Transformations: An Inter-ethnic Perspective." *MELUS* 23:4 [Winter, 1998]: 85–100.

Melville, Herman. *Moby Dick*. New York: W. W. Norton, 1967.

Miller, Barbara Stoler, ed. *Masterworks of Asian Literature in Comparative Perspective — A Guide to Teaching*. Armonk, NY: M. E. Sharpe, 1994.

Quinby, Lee. "The Subject of Memoirs: *The Woman Warrior*'s Technology of Ideographic Selfhood." *Critical Essays on Maxine Hong Kingston*. Ed. Laura E. Skandera-Trombley. New York: G. K. Hall & Co., 1998. 125–45.

Scholes, Robert. *Semiotics and Interpretation*. New Haven, CT: Yale University Press, 1982.

Schueller, Malini Johar. "Questioning Race and Gender Definitions: Dialogic Subversions in *The Woman Warrior*." *Criticism* 31 (1989): 421–37.

———. "Theorizing Ethnicity and Subjectivity: Maxine Hong Kingston's *Tripmaster Monkey* and Amy Tan's *The Joy Luck Club*." *Genders* 15 (Winter, 1992): 72–85.

Seyhan, Azade. *Writing Outside the Nation*. Princeton, NJ: Princeton University Press, 2001.

Simmons, Diane. *Maxine Hong Kingston*. New York: Twayne, 1999.

Smith, Jeanne R. "Cross-cultural Play: Maxine Hong Kingston's *Tripmaster Monkey*." *Critical Essays on Maxine Hong Kingston*. Ed. Laura E. Skandera-Trombley. New York: G. K. Hall & Co., 1998. 334–48.

Yu, Anthony C. *The Journey to the West*. Chicago, IL: The University of Chicago Press, 1977–83. 4 volumes.

Waley, Arthur. *Monkey*. London: 1943; rpt., New York: Grove Press, 1958.

Wang, Jennie. "Tripmaster Monkey: Kingston's Postmodern Representation of a New 'China Man.'" *MELUS* 20:1 (Spring, 1995): 101–15.

Chapter 8

Adshead, S.A.M. *China in World History*. London: Macmillan, 1988.

Cao, Guilin. *Beijingren zai Niuyue* [A Beijinger in New York]. Beijing: Zhongguo wenlian chuban gongsi, 1991.

Cassel, Susie Lan. "To Inscribe the Self Daily: The Discovery of the Ah Quin Diary." *The Chinese in America*. Ed. Susie Lan Cassel. Walnut Creek, CA: Altamira, 2002. 54–74.

Chang, Jung. *Wild Swans: Three Daughters of China*. New York: Simon & Schuster, 1991.

Chao, Lien. *Beyond Silence: Chinese Canadian Literature in English*. Toronto, ON: Tsar, 1997.

Chen, Juntao, ed. *Zhongguo liuxuesheng wenxue daxi* [A Collection of Foreign Student Literature]. 6 vols. Shanghai: Shanghai wenyi chubanshe, 2000.

Chen, Xuanbo. "Cong Lin Yutang dao Tang Tingting: zhongxin yu bianyuan de wenhua xushi" [From Lin Yutang to Maxine Hong Kingston: the Narrative of the Center and the Periphery]. *Waiguo wenxue pinglun* [Foreign Literature Criticism] 4(1995): 92–9.

Chen, Ying. *Ingratitude*. Toronto, ON: Douglas and McIntyre, 1998.

Cheng, Nien. *Life and Death in Shanghai*. London: Grafton, 1986.

Chong, Denise. *The Concubine's Children*. Toronto, ON: Penguin, 1994.

Choy, Wayson. *The Jade Peony*. Vancouver, BC: Douglas and McIntyre, 1995.

Dai, Sijie. *Balzac and the Little Chinese Seamstress*. New York: Alfred A. Knopf, 2001.

Fan, Shouyi. "Yi bu wang hua: Beimei huayi xiaoshuojia diyiren Shuixianhua de xinlu licheng" [Not Forgetting China: The Psychological Journey of Sui Sin Fa, the First North American Chinese Fiction Writer]. *Waiguo wenxue* [Foreign Literature] 3(1998): 67–82.

Gu, Yuanqing. "Zhongguo 15 nian lai shijie huawen wenxue yanjiu de zouxiang" [Research Trends of Global Chinese-Language Literature in the Past 15 Years in China]. *Nanfang wentan* [The Literary Field of Southern China] 6(1999): 52–6.

Guo, Huanhuan, ed. *Yuedu Shao Jun* [Reading Shao Jun]. Beijing: Qunzhong chubanshe, 2002.

Ha, Jin. *Waiting*. New York: Pantheon, 1999.

Kingston, Maxine Hong. *The Woman Warrior: Memoirs of a Girlhood among Ghosts*. New York: Alfred Knopf, 1976.

Lau, Evelyn. *Runaway: Diary of a Street Kid*. Toronto, ON: HarperCollins, 1989.

Li, Yan. *Daughters of the Red Land*. Toronto, ON: Sister Vision Press, 1995.

Lee, Sky. *Disappearing Moon Café*. Vancouver: Douglas & McIntyre, 1990.

Leung, Laifong. "Dapo bainian chenmo: Jianada huayi Yingwen xiaoshuo chutan." [Breaking the Silence of a Hundred Years: A Preliminary Study of Fiction in English by Chinese Canadian Writers.] *Shijie Wenxue* [World Literature] 2(1998): 278–90.

Liang, Heng and Judith Shapiro. *Son of the Revolution*. New York: Alfred A. Knopf, 1983.

Ling, Amy. *Between Worlds: Women Writers of Chinese Ancestry*. New York: Pergamon Press, 1990.

Lin, Yutang. *Chinatown Family, A Novel*. Melbourne/London/Toronto: William Heinemann, 1949.

Ling, Ken, London, Miriam and Lee Ta-ling. *The Revenge of Heaven: Journal of a Young Chinese*. New York: Putnam, 1972.

Mark, Lai Him. *Cong Huaqiao dao huaren: ershi shiji Meiguo huaren shehui fazhanshi* [From Overseas Chinese to Chinese: History of the Social Development of the Chinese Community in the United States]. Hong Kong: Joint Publishing Company, 1990.

Qian, Ning. *Liuxue Meiguo* [Studying in the United States]. Nanjing: Jiangsu wenyi chubanshe, 1996.

Rao, Pengzi. "Haiwai huaren wenxue de Zhongguo yishi" [The Chinese Consciousness in Overseas Chinese Literature]. *Ji'nan xuebao: shezhe ban* [Ji'nan University Journal: Social Sciences and Philosophy Edition] 1(1997): 81–9.

———. "Shiji zhi jiao: haiwai huawen wenxue de huigu yu zhanwang" [Reviews and Prospects of Overseas Chinese Literature at the Turn of the Century]. *Ji'nan xuebao: shezhe ban* [Ji'nan University Journal, Social Sciences and Philosophy Edition] 4(2002): 1–3.

Shao, Jun. *Xin yimin: wanglu xinqing gushi* [New Immigrants: Stories on the Internet]. Taipei: Shimao chubanshe, 2000.

Tan, Amy. *The Joy Luck Club*. New York: G.P. Putnam's Sons, 1989.

Tang, Junyi. "Zhonghua minzu zhi huaguo piaoling" [The Scattering of Chinese People Like Petals and Fruits]. *Zhonghua renwen yu dangjin shijie* [The Chinese Humanities and the Contemporary World] vol.7 *Tang Junyi wenji* [The Complete Collection of Tang Junyi]. Taipei: Xuesheng shuju, 1984: 11–37.

Wang, Anyi. *Love in a Small Town*. Trans. Eva Hung. Hong Kong: Chinese University Press, 1988.

———. *Love on a Barren Mountain*. Trans. Eva Hung. Hong Kong: Chinese University Press, 1991.

———. *Brocade Valley*. Trans. Bonnie S. McDougall and Chen Maiping. New York: New Directions, 1992.

———. *Baotown*. Trans. Martha Avery. New York: W.W. Norton, 1989.

Wang, Ling-chi. "Roots and the Changing Identity of the Chinese in the United States." *The Living Tree: The Changing Meaning of Being Chinese Today*. Ed. Tu Weiming. Stanford, CA: Stanford University Press, 1994. 185–212.

Wang, Lulu. *The Lily Theater*. Trans. Hester Velmans. New York: Nan A. Talese/ Doubleday, 2000.

Wang, Meng. *Butterfly and Other Stories*. Beijing: Panda, 1983.

———. *The Stubborn Porridge and Other Stories*. New York: George Braziller, 1994.

Wong, Sau-ling Cynthia. "Chinese American." *An Interethnic Companion to Asian American Literature*. Ed. Cheung King-kok. New York: Cambridge University Press, 1997. 39–68.

Wang, Yuqiu. "Jin ershi nian lai Meiguo huayi wenxue de jueqi" [The Emergence of Chinese American Literature in the Past Twenty Years]. *Waiguo wenxue yanjiu*. [Foreign Literature Studies]. 1(2000): 114–20.

Yang, Rae. *Spider Eaters*. San Francisco, CA: University of California Press, 1997.

Ye, Xingting. *A Leaf in the Bitter Wind*. Toronto, ON: Doubleday, 1997.

Yee, Paul. *Ghost Train*. Toronto, ON: Groundwood, 1996.

Yu, Lihua. *Seeing the Palm Trees Again* [Youjian zonglu, youjian zonglu]. Beijing: Youyi chubanshe, 1984.

Zhang, Xianliang. *Half of a Man Is Woman*. Trans. Martha Avery. London: Viking 1988.

———. *Getting Used to Dying*. Trans. Martha Avery. New York: HarperCollins, 1991.

Zhou, Li. *Manhedun de Zhongguo nüren* [A Chinese Woman in Manhattan]. Beijing: Beijing chubanshe, 1992.

Chapter 9

Aragon, Caroline. 2001. "Tigre et Dragon: Decoupage du film plan a plan." *L'Avant-Scene cinema* 502. *Tigre et Dragon*.

CNN.com. 2001. "Chinese-Americans, Studio Praise Ang Lee." March 26, 2001. <http://www.cnn.com/2001/WORLD/asiapcf/east/03/26/china.oscar.miss/index.html>

Cai, Lan. 2001. "Ping Wohu canglong." *Yizhou kan*. March 8, 2001: 178–9.

Chow, Rey. 2001. "How (the) Inscrutable Chinese Led to Globalized Theory." *PMLA* 116.1: 69–74.

———. 1995. *Primitive Passions: Visually, Sexuality, Ethnography, and Contemporary Chinese Cinema*. New York: Columbia University Press.

Chung, Pei-Chi. 2000. "Asian Filmmakers Moving into Hollywood: Genre Regulation and Auteur Aesthetics." *Asian Cinema* 11.1: 33–50.

Chute, David. 2000. "East Meets West in Ang Lee's Latest." *National Post*. December 4, 2000: D1.

Corliss, Richard. 1999. "Back to China." *AsiaTime*. November 29, 1999: 154. 21.

———. 2000a. "Martial Masterpiece." *Asia Time*. July 10, 2000: 156.1.

———. 2000b. "Year of the Tiger." *Time*. December 4, 2000: 124–6.

Dai Jinhua. 1995. "Invisible Women: Contemporary Chinese Cinema and Women's Film." *Positions* 3.1: 254–80.

Dariotis, Wei Ming and Eileen Fung. 1997. "Breaking the Soy Sauce Jar: Diaspora and Displacement in the Films of Ang Lee." Lu 1997a: 187–220.

Guardian/NFT. 2000. "Inteview with Ang Lee and James Schamus." November 7, 2000.

Hu Qingyang. 2001. "Li An: Zhongyu neng wei guopian zhuo dianshi [Ang Lee can finally do something for national cinema.] Udnnews.com 2001.01.23. Accessed March 26, 2001. <http://www.udnnews.ocm/NEWS/ENTERTAINMENT/CHRISTMAS/138753.shtml>

Jian, Zhengzhen. 2000. "Wohucanglong: shixiang di yunlü [Crouching Tiger Hidden Dragon: Rhythm in cinematography."] *Lianhe xinwenwang* March 8, 2001.

Johnson, Brian D. 2000. "In the Mood for Asia." *Macleans*. February 26, 2001: 60–1.

Kaufman, Anthony. 2000. "Ang-tastic!" *Cinema Scope*. Summer 2000: 4.

———. 2001. "Interviews with Ang Lee, James Schamus, Michelle Yeoh." IndieWire, April 6–12, 2001. Accessed April 5, 2001. <http://www.indiewire.com/film/interviews/int_Crouching>

Kirkland, Bruce. 2000. "Ang Lee's a Dragon in Hiding." *Toronto Sun*. December 3, 2000.

Klein, Joshua. 2000. "Interview with James Schamus." *Onion*.

Ko, Dorothy. 1997. "The Body as Attire: The Shifting Meanings of Footbinding in Seventeenth-Century China." *Journal of Women's History* 8.4: 8–27.

Lee, Ang. 1992. *Pushing Hands*.

———. 1993. *Wedding Banquet*.

———. 1994. *Eat Drink Man Woman*.

———. 1995. *Sense and Sensibility*.

———. 1997. *Ice Storm*.

———. 1999. *Ride with the Devil*.

———. 2000. *Crouching Tiger Hidden Dragon*. Sony Pictures.

Li, Victor. 2000. "What's in a Name? Questioning "Globalization." *Cultural Critique* 45: 1–39.

Liang Shouzhong. 1990. *Wuxia xiaoshuo hua gujin* [Martial chivalry novels in the past and present.] Hong Kong: Zhonghua shuju.

Liu Shijie. 2001. "Hangxiao celue zouxiao de "Qiu" guijian" [Marketing strategies key to obtaining the Golden Globe.] Udnnews.com 2001.01.23. Accessed March 26, 2001. <http://www.udnnews.ocm/NEWS/ENTERTAINMENT/CHRISTMAS/138753.shtml>

Lu, Sheldon Hsiao-peng. 1997a. *Transnational Chinese Cinemas: Identity, Nationhood, Gender*. Honolulu, HI: University of Hawaii Press.

———. 1997b. "Historical Introduction." In Lu 1997a: 1–31.

Ma, Sheng-mei. *1998. Immigrant Subjectivities in Asian American and Asian Diaspora Literatures*. Albany, NY: State University of New York Press.

Major, Wade. 2000. "Tiger Time." Box Office Online. Accessed April 30, 2001. <http://www.boxoff.com/issues/dec00/crouching.html>

Mitchell, Elvis. 2000. "Ang Lee Cooks Up Heady, Delirious Brew." *The New York Times*: December 22, 2000.

Morris, Gary. 2001. "Beautiful Beast. Ang Lee's Crouching Tiger, Hidden Dragon." *Bright Lights Film Journal*. Accessed April 26, 2001. <http://search.netscape.com /cgi-bin/search?search=crouching+tiger&x=188y=>

Pei, Xiaoxiong. 1991. "Wang Dulu" Ma Liangchun and Li Futian, eds. *Zhongguo wenxue da cidian* [Dictionary of Chinese literature.] Tianjin: Tianjin renmin chuban she.

Schaefer, Stephen. 2001. "Mr. Showbiz Interview with Ang Lee." Accessed April 5, 2001. <http://mrshowbiz.go.com/interviews/572_1.html>

Shih Shu-mei. 2000. "Globalisation and Minoritisation: Ang Lee and the Politics of Flexibility." *New Formations* 40: 86–101.

Sony Picture Classics. 2000. Official Website for Crouching Tiger, Hidden Dragon. Accessed May 10, 2001. <http://www.crouchingtiger.com" http://www. crouchingtiger.com>

Wang Dulu. 2000. *Wohu canglong* [Crouching tiger hidden dragon.] Hong Kong: Tiandi tushu youxian gongsi. Originally serialized in 1941 in Qingdao daxin minbao.

———. 1985. *Tieqi Yinping* [The Iron horseman and silver vase.] Taibei: Lianjing.

Wang Huiping. 2001. "Li An qule ge 'Biyan huli'" [Ang Lee married a Jade Fox]. "Li An jin 'Qiu' bishang 'ma' rongyi" [It's easier for Ang Lee to get a Golden Globe than a Golden Horse]. Udnnews.com 2001.01.23. Accessed March 26, 2001. <http://www.udnnews.ocm/NEWS/ENTERTAINMENT/ CHRISTMAS/138753.shtml>

Wang Jianyu. 2001. "Li An+Lin Huijia=lixin yu ganxing" [Ang Lee+Jasmine Lin=sense and sensibility]. Telephone Interview from Taibei to New York. Udnnews.com 2001.01.23. Accessed March 26, 2001. <http://www.udnnews. ocm/NEWS/ENTERTAINMENT/CHRISTMAS/138753.shtml>

Yang + Yin: Gender in Chinese Cinema. 1996. London: Connoisseur Video.

Chapter 10

"A Question of Conscience: Vote for Lowering the Age of Consent for Homosexuals in U.K." Editorial. *New Statesman & Society* Feb. 25, 1994: 4.

Althusser, Louis. "Ideology and Ideological State Apparatuses." *Contemporary Critical Theory*. Ed. Dan Latimer. San Diego, CA: Harcourt, Brace, Jovanovich, 1989. 61–102.

Ang, Ien. "Can One Say No to Chineseness? Pushing the Limits of the Diasporic Paradigm." *Modern Chinese Literary and Cultural Studies in the Age of Theory: Reimagining a Field*. Ed. Rey Chow. Durham, NC: Duke University Press, 2000. 281–300.

Bech, Henning. *When Men Meet: Homosexuality and Modernity.* Trans. Teresa Mesquit and Tim Davis. Chicago, IL: The University of Chicago Press, 1997.

Berlant, Lauren, and Michael Warner. "Sex in Public." *Critical Inquiry* 24 (1998): 547–66.

Bruni, Frank. "Taiwanese Filmmaker Ang Lee Breaks the Stereotypes." *Knight-Ridder/Tribune News Service* Aug. 26, 1993. *InfoTrac.* University of Alberta Library. October 2, 2001.

"Chain Male: Gay Sex." *The Economist* Jan. 29, 1994: 60–1.

Chang, Robert. "Why We Need a Critical Asian American Legal Studies." Wu and Song, *Asian American Studies: A Reader.* 363–78.

Chiang, Mark. "Coming Out into the Global System: Postmodern Patriarchies and Transnational Sexualities in *The Wedding Banquet.*" Eng and Hom, *Q & A* 374–95.

Chow, Rey. "Introduction: On Chineseness as a Theoretical Problem." *Modern Chinese Literary and Cultural Studies in the Age of Theory: Reimagining a Field.* Durham, NC: Duke University Press, 2000. 1–25.

d' Arch Smith, Timothy. *Love in Earnest: Some Notes on the Lives and Writings of English 'Uranian' Poets from 1889 to 1930.* London: Routledge & Kegan Paul, 1970.

Dariotis, Wei Ming and Eileen Fung. "Breaking the Soy Sauce Jar: Diaspora and Displacement in the Films of Ang Lee." *Transnational Chinese Cinemas: Identity, Nationhood, Gender.* Ed. Sheldon Hsiao-peng Lu. Honolulu, HI: University of Hawai'i Press, 1997. 187–220.

Davis, Tim. "The Diversity of Queer Politics and The Redefinition of Sexual Identity and Community in Urban Spaces." *Mapping Desire: Geographies of Sexualities.* Ed. David Bell and Gill Valentine. London: Routledge, 1995. 284–303.

Dirlik, Arif. "Asians on the Rim: Transnational Capital and Local Community in the Making of Contemporary Asian America." *Across the Pacific: Asian Americans and Globalization.* Ed. Evelyn Hu-DeHart. Philadelphia, PA: Temple University Press, 1999. 29–60.

Drake, David. "Fusion." *Lambda Book Report* 7.4 (1998): 3 pp. *EBSCOhost* University of Alberta Library. Sept. 2, 2001.

Eng, David L. "Out Here and Over There: Queerness and Diaspora in Asian American Studies." *Social Text* 52/53 (1997): 33–52.

Eng, David L. and Alice Y. Hom, eds. *Q & A: Queer in Asian America.* Philadelphia, PA: Temple University Press, 1998.

"Fair's Fair: Gay Law Reform." *The Economist* July 12, 1997: 50.

Foucault, Michel. *Discipline and Punish: The Birth of the Prison.* Tran. Alan Sheridan. New York: Vintage Books, 1995.

———. *The History of Sexuality: Volume 1. An Introduction.* Trans. Robert Hurley. New York: Vintage Books, 1990.

———. "Intellectuals and Power." Lotringer, *Foucault Live* 74–82.

————. "Talk Show." Lotringer, *Foucault Live* 133–145.

Fung, Richard. "Looking for My Penis: The Eroticized Asian in Gay Video Porn." *Q & A: Queer in Asian America.* Ed. David L. Eng and Alice Y. Hom. Philadelphia, PA: Temple University Press, 1998. 115–34.

"Gay Couples Join Together on Tax." *BBC News Online* Mar. 16, 2005. Accessed Apr 28, 2005. <http://news.bbc.co.uk/1/hi/business/4354855.stm>

Groen, Rick. "In Person: Films Reveal Ang Lee's Sense and Sensibilities." *Globe and Mail* Sept. 13, 1999. *InfoTrac* University of Alberta Library. December 1, 2001.

Heng, Geraldine and Janadas Devan. "State Fatherhood: The Politics of Nationalism, Sexuality, and Race in Singapore." *The Gender/Sexuality Reader: Culture, History, Political Economy.* New York: Routledge, 1997. 107–21.

Holden, Philip. "The Significance of Uselessness: Resisting Colonial Masculinity in Philip Jeyaretnam's *Abraham's Promise." Jouvert* 2.1 (1998). Nov. 8, 1998. <http://social.chass.ncsu.edu/jouvert/i1v2/Holden.htm.>

————. "A Man and an Island: Gender and Nation in Lee Kuan Yew's *The Singapore Story. Biography* 24.2 (2001): 401–24.

Irigaray, Luce. *This Sex Which Is Not One.* Trans. Catherine Porter with Carolyn Burke. Ithaca, NY: Cornell University Press, 1985.

Jeffrey-Poulter, Stephen. *Peers, Queers & Commons: The Struggle for Gay Law Reform From 1950 to the Present.* London: Routledge, 1991.

Knowles, Richard Paul. "The Dramaturgy of the Perverse." *Theatre Research International* 17.3 (1992): 226–35.

Kondo, Dorinne. *About Face: Performing Race in Fashion and Theater.* New York: Routledge, 1997.

Lane, Christopher. "'Living Well is the Best Revenge': Outing, Privacy, and Psychoanalysis." Leap, *Public Sex/Gay Space,* 247–85.

Leap, William L., ed. *Public Sex/Gay Space.* New York: Columbia University Press, 1999.

"Legislating Fairly for Consenting Homosexuals." Editorial. *The Lancet* Jan. 22, 1994: 185–6.

Lotringer, Sylvère, ed. *Foucault Live (Interviews, 1961–1984).* Trans. Lysa Hochroth and John Johnston. New York: Semiotext(e), 1996.

Marchetti, Gina. "*The Wedding Banquet:* Global Chinese Cinema and the Asian American Experience." *Countervisions: Asian American Film Criticism.* Ed. Darrell Y. Hamamoto and Sandra Liu. Philadelphia, PA: Temple University Press, 2000. 275–97.

Mesher, David. "Metamorphosis of a Butterfly." *San José Studies* 17.3 (1991): 4–21.

Nguyen, Viet Thanh. "The Remasculinization of Chinese America: Race, Violence, and the Novel." *American Literary History* 12.1 & 2 (2000): 130–57.

Nonini, Donald M. and Aihwa Ong, eds. "Chinese Transnationalism as an

Alternative Modernity." *Ungrounded Empires: The Cultural Politics of Modern Chinese Transnationalism.* New York: Routledge, 1997. 3–33.

Okihiro, Gary. "Perils of the Body and Mind." *Margins and Mainstreams: Asians in American History and Culture.* Seattle, WA: University of Washington Press, 1994. 118–47.

Parker, David. *Through Different Eyes: The Cultural Identities of Young Chinese People in Britain.* Aldershot: Avebury, 1995.

Prick Up Your Ears. Dir. Stephen Frears. Perf. Gary Oldman and Alfred Molina. Santa Monica, CA: Metro Goldwyn Mayer, 1987.

Roetz, Heiner. *Confucian Ethics of the Axial Age: A Reconstruction under the Aspect of the Breakthrough toward Postconventional Thinking.* Albany, NY: State University of New York, 1993.

Román, David. "Los Angeles Intersections: Chay Yew." *The Color of Theater: Race, Culture, and Contemporary Performance.* Ed. Roberta Uno with Lucy Mae San Pablo Burns. New York: Continuum, 2002. 237–52.

———. "Visa Denied." *Queer Frontiers: Millennial Geographies, Genders, and Generations.* Ed. Joseph A. Boone, et al. Madison, WI: The University of Wisconsin Press, 2000. 350–64.

Russo, Vito, ed. *The Celluloid Closet: Homosexuality in the Movies.* Rev. ed. New York: HarperPerennial, 1987.

Sedgwick, Eve Kosofsky. *Epistemology of the Closet.* Berkeley, CA: University of California Press, 1990.

Shih, Shu-mei. "Gender and a Geopolitics of Desire: The Seduction of Mainland Women in Taiwan and Hong Kong Media." *Spaces of Their Own: Women's Public Sphere in Transnational China.* Ed. Mayfair Mei-hui Yang. Minneapolis, MN: University of Minnesota Press, 1999. 278–307.

"'Success Story of Minority Group in U. S.' *U. S. News and World Report* 26 Dec 1966." Wu and Song, *Asian American Studies: A Reader* 158–63.

Tatchell, Peter. *Europe in the Pink: Lesbian & Gay Equality in the New Europe.* London: Gay Men Press, 1992.

———. "Sweet Fourteen." *New Statesman & Society* 23 June 1995: 25.

The Wedding Banquet. Dir. Ang Lee. Perf. Winston Chao, Mitchell Lichtenstein, and May Chin. Alliance Releasing Home Video, 1994.

Wilde, Oscar. *The Importance of Being Earnest and Related Writings.* Ed. Joseph Brislow. London: Routledge, 1992.

Wu, Jean Yu-wen Shen and Min Song, eds. *Asian American Studies: A Reader.* New Brunswick, NJ: Rutgers University Press, 2000.

Xing, Jun. "Media Empowerment, Smashing Stereotypes, and Developing Empathy." *Reversing the Lens: Ethnicity, Race, Gender, and Sexuality Through Film.* Ed. Jun Xing and Lane Ryo Hirabayashi. Boulder, CO: University Press of Colorado, 2003. 11–25.

Yao, Xinzhong. *An Introduction to Confucianism.* Cambridge: Cambridge University Press, 2000.

Yew, Chay. *Porcelain and A Language of Their Own*. New York: Grove Press, 1997. 5–116.

———. *The Hyphenated American*. Four Plays. New York: Grove Press. 2002.

Chapter 11

Ahmad, Aijaz. "Jameson's Rhetoric of Otherness and the 'National Allegory.'" *Social Text* 17 (1987): 3–25.

Berry, Chris. "Happy Alone? Sad Young Men in East Asian Gay Cinema." *Journal of Homosexuality* 39, no. 3/4 (2000): 187–200.

———. "These Nations Which Are Not One: History, Identity and Postcoloniality in Recent Hong Kong and Taiwan Cinema." *Span (South Pacific Association for Commonwealth Literature and Language Studies)* 34/35 (Oct 1, 1992): 37–49.

Biro, Yvette. "Perhaps the Flood: The Fiery Torrent of Tsai Ming-Liang's Films." *PAJ: Journal of Performance and Art* 3 (2004): 78–86.

Bruno, Giuliana. "Architects of Time: Reel Images from Warhol to Tsai Ming-Liang." *Log* 2 (Spring 2004): 81–94.

Chong, Woei Lien. "Alienation in the Modern Metropolis: The Visual Idiom of Taiwanese Film Director Tsai Ming-Liang." *China Information* (Leiden) 9, no. 4 (Spring 1995): 81–95.

Dussell. Enrique. "Beyond Eurocentrism: The World-System and the Limits of Modernity." Trans. Eduardo Mendieta. *The Cultures of Globalization*. Eds. Fredric Jameson and Masao Miyoshi. Durham, NC: Duke University Press, 1998. 3–31.

Horton, Andrew, ed. *The Last Modernist: The Films of Theo Angelopoulos*. Westport, CT: Praeger, 1997.

Hu, Brian. "Goodbye City, Goodbye Cinema: Nostalgia in Tsai Ming-liang's *The Skywalk is Gone*." *Senses of Cinema* (October 2003). <http://www.sensesofcinema.com/contents/03/29/skywalk_is_gone.html>

Jameson, Fredric. "Remapping Taipei." *The Geopolitical Aesthetic: Cinema and Space in the World System*. Bloomington, IN: Indiana University Press, 1995. 114–57.

———. "Third World Literature in the Era of Multinational Capitalism." *Social Text* 15 (Fall 1986): 65–88.

Jones, Kent. "Here and There: The Films of Tsai Ming-liang." *Movie Mutations: The Changing Face of World Cinephilia*. Eds. Jonathan Rosenbaum and Adrian Martin. London: BFI, 2003. 44–51.

Leong, Toh Hai. "Aspects of Chinese Cinema Today." *Kinema* 7 (Spring 1997): 47–56.

"Love, Life and Lies: The films of Tsai Ming-Liang in the context of the new Taiwanese Cinema." *Toto: Cinema Matters*. <http://www.cse.unsw.edu.au/~peteg/toto/tsai.htm>

Lu, Tonglin. *Confronting Modernity in the Cinema of Taiwan and Mainland China.* Cambridge: Cambridge University Press, 2001.

Lutze, Peter C. *Alexander Kluge: The Last Modernist.* Detroit, MI: Wayne State University Press, 1998.

Martin, Fran. "The European Undead: Tsai Ming-liang's Temporal Dysphoria." *Senses of Cinema* (June 2003). <http://www.sensesofcinema.com/contents/03/27/tsai_european_undead.html>

————. "Perverse Utopia: Reading *The River.*" *Situating Sexualities: Queer Representation in Taiwanese Fiction, Film and Public Culture.* Hong Kong: Hong Kong University Press, 2003. 163–84.

Rayns, Tony. "Chaos And Anger." *Sight and Sound* 4, no. 10 (1994): 12–5.

————. "Confrontations: Sex and isolation drive the films of Tsai Ming-Liang, a major new talent." *Sight and Sound* 7, no. 3 (1997): 14–8.

Smith, Murray. "Modernism and the avant-gardes." *The Oxford Guide to Film Studies.* Eds. John Hill and Pamela Church Gibson. Oxford: Oxford University Press, 1998. 395–412.

Stephens, Chuck. "Intersection: Tsai Ming-liang's yearning bike boys and heartsick heroines." *Film Comment* 32, no. 5 (Sept.–Oct. 1996): 20–3.

Viella, Fiona A. "Notes on Tsai Ming-Liang's *The River.*" *Senses of Cinema* (January 2001). <http://www.sensesofcinema.com/contents/01/12/river.html>

Wollen, Peter. "The Two Avant-Gardes." *Edinburgh '76 Magazine*, no. 1. Edinburgh Film Festival, 1976. 77–85.

Works Consulted

Bordwell, David. "Transcultural Spaces: Toward a Poetics of Chinese Film." *Post Script* 20.2/3 (Winter/Spring/Summer 2001): 924.

Chiao, Hsiung-Ping. "The Distinct Taiwanese and Hong Kong Cinemas." *Perspectives on Chinese Cinema.* Ed. Chris Berry. London: BFI, 1991.

Chow, Rey. *Primitive Passions: Visuality, Sexuality, Ethnography, and Contemporary Chinese Cinema.* New York: Columbia University Press, 1995.

Lu, Sheldon Hsiao-peng, ed. *Transnational Chinese Cinemas Identity, Nationhood, Gender.* Honolulu, HI: University of Hawaii Press, 1997.

Rapfogel, Jared. "Tsai Ming-Liang: Cinematic Painter." *Senses of Cinema* (May 2002). <http://www.sensesofcinema.com/contents/02/20/tsai_painter.html>

Zhang, Xudong. *Chinese Modernism in the Era of Reforms.* Durham, NC: Duke University Press, 1997.

Index